"I want to share with you the
adventures of my life. Maybe they
will offer you hope. Maybe they will
comfort you. Maybe they will give
you the courage to face tomorrow without
fear. Maybe—and I'm really counting
on this—they will make you laugh. One thing
I know: if I can make it, if I can
survive a lifetime of troubles and live
to tell about them, so can you."

—Virginia Graham

IF I MADE IT, SO CAN YOU

BY VIRGINIA GRAHAM

BANTAM BOOKS · TORONTO · NEW YORK · LONDON

IF I MADE IT, SO CAN YOU
A Bantam Book / November 1978

ISBN 0-553-11576-6

Published simultaneously in the United States and Canada

PRINTED IN THE UNITED STATES OF AMERICA

I dedicate this book to
my darling grandchildren—Jan
and Stephen, young mountain
climbers. May they know
the joy of reaching the peaks
of self-achievement.

ACKNOWLEDGMENT

Writing is a very lonely task.
In writing this book I was not lonely,
because I had the listening ear of
a wonderful editor and friend,
Murray McCain. His experience, his
patience, and his understanding
made writing this book a joy.

CONTENTS

IF I MADE IT, SO CAN YOU

Here She Comes Again

I've known the heights of joy and happiness, and the very depths of despair. I'll know them again.

Now, suddenly, it's fourteen years since I wrote my first book, *There Goes What's Her Name*. All those tomorrows I dreamed about are yesterdays, and past. When you think about how long a day can seem, if you've got pressure, and how short your whole life span is, you just have to say, "Well, let's get going, we've got a job to do."

Sometimes, I think that life is like a big waiting room in a doctor's office. All our worries are a rare disease, for which we pray a cure has been found. Suppose the doctor himself has called in sick. Can we live another twenty-four hours? I have to believe that we carry a medicine kit with us, that God has thoughtfully attached it somewhere on our bodies. Sometimes it may be an idea, an insight that enables us to make a new choice, a new decision. And sometimes it may be a simple (*simple?*) reflex action that enables us to steer the wheels of our car six inches to the left in order to keep from hitting the little boy on the skateboard, because of course he can't see us.

That's called survival—the will to live. I've got it. I'm a survivor. Nowadays, when people see me, they don't say, "There goes What's Her Name" unless they're still in diapers. Now they say, "Here she comes again. What *is* her name?"

Virginia. Virginia Graham. V-i-r-g-i-n-i-a G-r-a-h-a-m. How do you do? I'm very glad to meet you.

It's been said that Virginia is a state of mind. I don't think whoever said it meant me. I think he (or

1

she) was referring to a parcel of land atop the state of North Carolina. But the statement was truer than he or she knew. Because I, too, am a state of mind. The state of my mind is . . . is . . . well, you'll see. I'll show you. If I live to finish the book, that is. And I will, because I want to. I want to share with you once again the adventures of my life.

Maybe they will offer you hope. Maybe they will comfort you. Maybe they will give you the courage to face tomorrow without fear. Maybe—and I'm really counting on this—they will make you laugh. One thing I know: If I can make it, if I can survive a life-time of troubles and live to tell about them, so can you.

My last book took us to 1965. *Girl Talk* was a very successful show. For almost the first time in my life I was tasting success. I didn't have any problems. I guess problems are something that just happen to me; I don't know whether I ask for them, and become stronger in solving them. Everybody I've ever leaned on has been a pillar of Jell-O, and I've just never had anybody, you know, to turn to. I guess maybe that makes you strong.

But I'll tell you one thing I've learned. The weak absolutely destroy you. The Bible made a terrible misprint. It should say "The weak shall inherit the earth," not the meek. The meek go about their business and don't bother you, but the weak are living bloodsuckers. They sap your strength, they get you to do everything for them, they live to be a hundred. Hypochondriacs never die. I know people who would rather have two weeks at the Mayo Clinic than go to Europe. I have a cousin who would give anything to own a condominium in a hospital. When my dear mother was alive, she was voted Woman of the Year every twelve months by the AMA because she kept about a hundred doctors alive. She was very healthy, but she had to be reassured all the time, of her good health.

So here was the year of 1965, and I was about to try my first venture as a professional actress. A charm-ing man named Carl Stohn, Jr., was an avid viewer of

Girl Talk and felt that any woman who could talk to three women a day and not kill them on camera or show any sign of immediate aging had to be an actress.

He called me on the phone and said, "Miss Graham, how would you like to be an actress?" And I said, "I think that's what I've been doing all my life." As a matter of fact, I've often felt like a female impersonator because in school I took all the male leads. You see, my mother breast-fed me until I was five, I think, so I was big-boned and strong. I called most of the boys in my class navel men. They weren't sailors, that's where they came up to on me.

So Carl said, "I have a play for you called *Late Love* by Rosemary Casey. Arlene Francis did it on Broadway. We're at a dinner theater located in Pheasant Run, which is in St. Charles, Illinois, and it's a lovely play and would you like to do it?"

To me the salary at that time was very appealing, because I wasn't getting rich on *Girl Talk*, and I said yes. I was delighted.

I started to study my lines. My memory was quite good because I'd kept it working. When I'm in a play, none of my friends ever tell me how good I am, or what a wonderful interpretation I've built. They always say, "How did you memorize the lines?" That's the absolute charm for people, because they usually can't even remember their own phone numbers. I can't either; my best memory for phone numbers is in my fingers. I can dial, but if you were to ask me, in a million years I couldn't tell you half of the phone numbers. My brain must be partly in my fingers, because I remember what I feel. I also remember what I hear. I've tried to keep my mind alert, and I thank my producer Monty Morgan a lot for that because on *Girl Talk* I never had a note. Never. He made me memorize every name. I knew vaguely the subjects we were going to discuss, but I never, ever, had one cue card in all those years. And that was mental gymnastics. And that's where all of us should be. We rely too much on writing down what we should do. We attribute loss of memory to age. The only thing that's aging, I think, is our pencils.

To memorize my role, I hired a young actress to come in and read with me. Harry often volunteers for this job, but he becomes so engrossed in the stage business directions that our marriage would never survive such an ordeal. Waiting for a direct cue from Harry is like waiting for a train in a storm on the Long Island Railroad. I can't learn from reading. I never could. One reason I loved the Francis Parker School in Chicago so much as a child, and college later, was the way the teachers sounded. I am an audio person. I'm a hearer. Tell me something, I'll never forget it. Then I'll write it down, perhaps, but I have to hear it first to remember it.

Before I left New York I called Arlene Francis. She's a very charming woman. I said, "Arlene, can you give me any advice on this play?" And she said, "Virginia, we had the best cast in all the world, and we only lasted three months." She had Cliff Robertson, Elizabeth Montgomery, Lucile Watson, Neil Hamilton—oh, a fantastic cast. Just imagine my nerve attempting this play when this incredible woman had not been able to sell it to New York. But I have learned since that there's a different appetite in the dinner theater. Audiences are much more compassionate there. They don't demand the standards of a Broadway show. As a matter of fact, the critics sometimes review the food instead of the play.

Arlene said, "Be sure the actress who plays the mother in the play is a very solid citizen in the theater." I called Carl and told him what Arlene said, and he said, "We have a marvelous woman by the name of Virginia Gilman. She's a former actress and she's returning to the stage after fifty years." I said, "Fifty years?" Carl said, "She's charming. Her daughter Toni Gilman is a good friend and she assured me that her mother is perfect for the part."

Well, when I arrived to meet the group of young actors who're going to appear with me many times, I see they're all looking at me the way you might view a strange animal at the zoo. They're looking at this woman who has no theatrical background. There they are with all the years of training they've put into their craft, and this woman comes in as the lead. They're not only the supporting actors and actresses, they're going to have to be crutches, too. They're going to be required to hold me up. They must, in other words, be Hercules.

I am laughing and smiling. I've never been nervous, which I think is a malfunction of some part of the body and, oh, I'm delighted about the whole thing, thoroughly confident that Sarah Bernhardt is getting ready to ride again.

I meet the marvelous Virginia Gilman, and I looked into her beautiful blue eyes and it was love at first sight. When we started to do our reading, I found her not exactly knowing her lines. By that, I might say, she wasn't quite sure of the name of the play. After this went on and on for a while I said, "Why don't you come to my room at night and we'll study a little bit." And she said, "Oh, that would be wonderful."

Over and over again, we would read the lines. And it was like when you throw a stone across the top of a pond, it will skip the surface—there was no penetration whatsoever, and the eyes got vaguer and vaguer, almost calling out for help. So I would call up the producer and say: "I really like her, but I don't think we're getting it." He said, "I don't want you to worry." He said, "By opening night, they'll all know their lines." I said, "Well, I don't know theater. You do."

Comes the night of dress rehearsal and my beautiful Mrs. Gilman sits down and says, "I have an announcement to make." We brace ourselves to withstand what's coming. Everybody's tense because we've all gone through a rather difficult time. And Mrs. Gilman says, "I don't understand what this play is all about and I don't think I can make it."

We become statues, stone-still, human statues. At which point I sat down on the floor of the stage and went into hysterics of laughter. My debut. My whole family is coming. I should have figured something like this would happen.

Carl, who never loses his temper, looks at Toni, her daughter, who has recommended her mother—whose acting experience, I think, was rather limited. She was a very beautiful woman and I can imagine what a lovely-looking girl she was in her youth, a gift she gave to Toni. But I'm sure she did not have an extensive theatrical background. Her return to the theater was a form of group therapy.

There is dead silence. Toni gets up and says, "Everything is going to be all right. By tomorrow night my mother is going to be letter perfect." The rest of us proceed then as though nothing has happened. I found out later that Toni rushed over to the phone and called her husband, who had been an army captain, and said, "Bud, I want you to do something with Mother."

"What is it this time?" was his instant reply.

"You've got to help me," she said. "You used to work with walkie-talkies in the war. I want you to get in a helicopter and get over here right away with a walkie-talkie. I'm going to have to put one on me and one in Mother's bust. Get one that's small enough to fit in Mother's bust."

"That's easy," he said. "The hard part is to find one at all."

In the cast are another girl, Virginia Gilman and me, and I would say that our combined mammary area, commonly known as bust measurement, was—well, I would say there was two hundred pounds of breast on that stage, minimum. I have never seen anything as massive as the three of us. As a matter of fact, the young girl, when she came onstage and took her coat off one night, got a standing ovation from a convention of men that was there, so you can imagine what we all added up to.

For five weeks—the entire run of the play—Toni Gilman stood in the wings and broadcast the lines to her mother. Sometimes there was a ten-second lapse before her mother responded, and some of the audience, who could hear Toni coaching backstage, would yell, "Quiet!" and Mrs. Gilman would get this glazed look on her face. When poor atmospheric conditions prevailed, the walkie-talkie would go dead, but the nicest thing about this walkie-talkie was that it was on the same wavelength as the local airfield.

One night as I'm talking to her, I hear, coming through the antenna—which sprang into my face once, by the way, and hit me in the eye—and I hear: "Pull down your wheels, all clear on the runway, you're coming in for a landing." Mrs. Gilman is staring at me in sheer terror.

With all due credit to Mrs. Gilman, she was the most charming part of the show. She would come out in a garden dress and do a little dance, and the audience went wild over her.

Even on opening night I wasn't nervous. My manager came in, took a look at me, and said, "You're making me so nervous by not being nervous that I want a phenobarbital." All my cousins are in front. I need to explain to the world at large that sexual intercourse was practiced fervently in my family because I have a hundred and ten first cousins. My mother and father each were the eleventh child. In the long-ago days before television, people developed their own home sport.

Carl Stohn came to me at the beginning of the run and said, "I love you very much and want you to return, but if you do you must never tell your family." Because they would call up and tell the chef how they wanted their chicken fixed. Mary didn't like it with onions, Stella didn't like mushrooms, and Frank couldn't eat it fried. I think three chefs left during my run.

Like many of us, my leading man had more than a touch of vanity. He would sit and look at himself in the magnifying mirror. I had to kiss him in the play and I told the cast: "My mother's not going to take this well. This is pornography to my mother. I cannot tell you what she's going to do when she sees me kiss another man."

Late Love is about Graham Colby, a straightlaced

widower and successful writer who has been over-protected by his mother. (Graham was my destiny.) He has a daughter, Janet, who rebels against her grandmother's tight supervision and elopes with her father's male secretary, unbeknownst to her father. I am the visiting artist, who's come to paint Graham's portrait. We're all afraid that if he learns of his daughter's elopement, he'll have apoplexy, or have the marriage annulled.

During the third act, I send Graham's old family friend Billy (played by Bill Morey), also is a guest in the house, outdoors to cut the telephone wires. News of Janet's marriage has been published in the local paper, and we don't want Graham to receive calls from well-wishing friends. The way to keep the calls from coming in is to cut the outdoor telephone wires. I give Billy the shears to cut them with and he goes out. Then Janet and her new husband, the male secretary, have a little scene with me and then they leave. It is now time for Billy to return, mission completed.

Instead, on opening night, there occurs what is known as a pregnant pause. In fact, it was not only pregnant, it was overdue. On the stage, a minute of silence is like a decade, and there I am alone. We've all said our lines and Bill, who went out to cut the wires, still hasn't returned. I wait. Finally, I launch into a soliloquy meant to rival Hamlet's. But Shakespeare wrote Hamlet's, and I was on my own. "Imagine my sending him out to do such an important thing when his best friend's daughter's whole life and happiness absolutely depend on it. He's probably gone to a bar. I said to cut the wire and he probably thought I meant cut out of the house, and he probably hitchhiked to a bar. I wonder where he can be." Et cetera. Ad infinitum.

Now the stage manager, who was apparently also enjoying his first theatrical experience, begins to send people out on stage to cover up this inspired improvisation. The maid, who isn't due for some time, strolls by. A character who hasn't yet been introduced walks across the stage. The Colby living room is becoming a major urban thoroughfare.

At last, in sheer desperation, I decide to leave the stage altogether. "I'm going to find him," I inform the audience. "I'll be right back." Don't go away. So I rush off, leaving the stage without a human soul upon it, and whisper as softly as I can: "Where is he, for God's sake?" And the stage manager says, "We don't know. We're looking all over for him."

It could happen to any of us. Nature has called, and Bill is in the bathroom, safely ensconced in a cubicle, enjoying the raptures of relief, when he is dragged bodily from the throne and shoved onstage without having implemented his attire by that universal motion known as zipping up. When he finally returns, I say, "Where the hell have you been?"

Well, it was opening night, and we were all apprehensive about reviews. But thank heaven all was well. One critic wrote: "A triumph for Virginia Graham. She *is* Constance." I think dinner theater audiences, especially, enjoy such lapses. One night Mrs. Gilman simply turned to the audience and said, "I've forgotten my lines." I looked at her and said, "Now, Mrs. Gilman, darling, we're in a play called *Late Love* and you're my future mother-in-law . . ." And so forth. They loved it in St. Charles, Illinois.

And sure enough, when I have to kiss my leading man, on that first night, my mother jumps up and yells, "Harry!" In case you've forgotten, that's the name of my husband.

We had a marvelous season, and I will always treasure Virginia Gilman. Carl Stohn was the architect of my theatrical career, which at that time, it seemed to me, had a very shaky foundation. He introduced me to this kind of direct contact with people, and I will always be grateful to him for that.

Signs of Destiny

I never wanted to be an actress. I had never fantasized a theatrical life for myself, partly because it was too far removed from my environment. No one in our family had ever been drawn in that direction.

What I did want to be when I was a kid was a G-man. (A G-woman? A G-person.) I was always interested in finding out the truth, in locating where it was. That's one reason I eventually went into journalism.

After *Late Love*, I sat down to count the roles I'd been called upon to play in the course of my active life, and to this day I'm still counting. Would you believe that almost every week I discover myself playing a new role? Not all of them are major, mind you. I play a lot of walk-on roles, although usually I have at least a speaking part. I try to avoid the nonspeaking parts but . . . some roles we create for ourselves, and some roles are thrust upon us.

To begin with, I was cast in a Daughter role. At first, nearly everybody in the world plays either a Son role or a Daughter role. Later on, some confusion may develop over exactly which is which, but in the beginning the gender, the sex, of each newborn babe will usually be, in the now immortal words, perfectly clear.

Since becoming a Daughter (and simultaneously a Sister), and sticking to major roles only, I've played Friend (a number of times, I'm happy to say), Wife, Mother, Grandmother (these have been the basic female stock roles for some time; they are now being disputed by Women's Lib), Red Cross Volunteer, Writer, Hostess of a Talk Show (this involves many

10

roles, including Straightwoman and Comedienne) and finally, in Pheasant Run, Illinois, professional Actress. And in the role of Actress, I thought, was another whole new career opening up for Virginia Graham, another God-sent opportunity to get in touch with people and affect them. I was absolutely delighted, I couldn't help it, but I wasn't all that surprised, because I got off to the most tremendous start. Here's what happened:

I was born a firecracker! A genuine, honest-to-God, George M. Cohan, Yankee Doodle Dandy firecracker, born on the Fourth of July. It's true. I was red, Papa was white, and Mama was black and blue, because I was so impatient. I gave her a terrible time. After that fierce, forty-eight-hour struggle in a Chicago hospital, I came out slugging, a heavyweight already, weighing in at either ten pounds or twelve, depending on whether you believed Mama, who said ten (for the rest of her life she tried to take weight off me), or Aunt Celia, my mother's sister, who said twelve (Aunt Celia was the world's leading authority on everything and rarely, if ever, correct; you'll hear more about her later.) Take your pick. I'm comfortable with ten.

Color me patriotic.

Don't think it's easy being a firecracker. Exciting, yes, but easy? No, indeed. Fortunately, my only sibling, my beloved brother Juddy (Justin) had preceded me by some twenty-one months. So for Mama and Papa the initial drama, the trauma, of parenthood was over by the time I arrived. Thank God. I shudder for all concerned had I been a first or only child.

Juddy and I became very close. After all, we were almost the same age. Our whole enormous family was close-knit, with aunts, uncles, and cousins by the dozen. Whoever else I am, I warn you, whatever other roles I play, I'm a Family Girl, loyal to a fault. My family will be wandering in and out of these pages, as they do in the course of my days, in the years of my life, right up to the end.

But from the very first I was closest to Papa. Papa always made me feel special. I don't think Mama or Juddy ever fully understood the bond between Papa and me. They must have been puzzled and hurt often by the attention we lavished on each other. Children don't understand these things. It's only later, when we grow up and leave the family unit, that we can begin to understand our childhood years.

Papa, David Stanley Komiss, was born in Königsburg, Prussia. He came to New York as a teenager with capital assets of thirteen dollars, and then went west to Chicago by way of Kansas City, where he worked for his uncle. On the way, he learned to speak English. He also went to night school and continued to educate himself in every possible way for as long as he lived. To Papa, the highest form of human life was the life of the mind, the intellect. When he and Mama were married, Papa owned a successful women's specialty store.

Mama was Bessie Feiges when she married Papa, and a native of Chicago. She was one of the most beautiful, most elegant women in the world. Mama once wore a pink nightgown to the opera. She just pinned a rose to it. The society editor for the *Chicago Tribune* wrote it up.

I went to the Francis Parker School in Chicago, in a beautiful old building. It was a very strict school, a wonderful school. You walked in and there was a big glass cabinet that stood against the wall. In it was a stuffed owl that never blinked an eye. And you always knew that, if you were late, that owl had a direct line to the principal.

Recently, I returned to Francis Parker to speak at Morning Exercise. All the things I remembered were still present, the desk with the little bell on it, the smell of the wood, the fresh young faces of the pupils, all made more poignant by the power of memory. Memory reaches all our senses, and affects them. What a wonderful storehouse for all the infinitely rich experiences of life.

Colonel Francis Parker believed in small classes, with a maximum of individual attention. He believed in encouraging children to question, to disagree. He thought that only in pitting two minds against each other, two points of view, could learning reach its highest potential. We learned courage, we learned independence. That is the way we grew. A teacher was a god to me. When I saw a teacher walking down the street, I was filled with reverence and humility.

And, like Papa, I learned to respect the life of the mind, the power of the intellect. A good mind is beyond price, and it will serve you till the day you die.

I remember how I used to envy a girl at Francis Parker, a classmate. She was blonde and thin and aloof. She never felt she had to make people laugh or say outrageous things to make them like her. She only had to enter a room and people flocked to her. I never had that quality, and how I envied it in others.

It was at Francis Parker that I fell in love with the English language. I've had many love affairs and I confess here and now that my love of words was one of my best. If you should ever have reason to doubt that statement, just think of the trillions of words I've spoken already—thousands of them, some people will attest, nonstop. Not to mention the words I've written. And I'll tell you something. If you're lucky enough to fall in love with language, you need never fear rejection. Never, in all your life, will words forsake you. They will return your love a millionfold.

When Miss Sarah Greenabaum, our eighth-grade English teacher, took ill, they let me teach her class for the two weeks she was gone. Now what other school would let a twelve-year-old child do that? Then I was pushed ahead two years because I was always mature for my age. And besides, I think they wanted me out of the way. Get her out fast.

I remember one teacher who sent me out of the room to scrub my face because she said I had makeup on, but I didn't. I was a healthy child with flushed cheeks, and I'll never forget my tears and how mortified I was because she had shamed me in front of the class. I've never outgrown my childhood sensitivity.

There was a German teacher who would share with us her holiday cakes from Germany. She would come in with paper napkins, and divide each little cake into six pieces. She loved to share. Once a relative in Vermont sent her a flower called trailing arbutus. It was in a little cardboard box with holes, as though a lizard or a chameleon might be inside, on a bank of wet moss, and it had this wonderful, heavenly smell. She passed it around the room so we all could smell it.

And then there was my favorite teacher of all, Mr. Arthur Detmers, this gaunt, gaunt man who taught social studies. He might have been Plato or Socrates. He seemed to be one of those men who had lived forever. He might have been a medieval scholar or a Chinese philosopher. Because as you probably know by this time, I believe in many lives. I firmly believe in the evolution of the soul and of the personality. I believe that we have lived many times before and that, maybe, we will live again. I don't know if I have the strength for another life, but I know, I definitely know in my heart, that I have lived before.

And I believe that Mr. Detmers, too, had lived before. He was the teacher who said to me, "You may lose friends, Virginia. You may move away, and your family may die, and you may be left alone, but if you make words your friends, they will be with you forever."

Mr. Detmers is long dead, but the words he spoke to me, the reverence for language and understanding he instilled in my heart, will be with me forever.

I grew into young womanhood while going to Francis Parker. And although I was a good student, I kept myself occupied in other activities too. One day, attending a movie at the State and Lake Theater in Chicago, I was given a circular announcing the Paramount Search for Beauty contest.

Bravado made me enter, as though it was a dare. You had to submit a picture and a short bio on yourself. Well, I did, and they called me and I was absolutely stunned. I had never even thought about being a movie star, and here I was already a candidate for future stardom.

My friends, the only people to whom I confided my

secret, were impressed. I went through a couple of elimination stages where they made our group smaller and smaller to go to the finals. The big thrill was going to come when eight beauties were lined up onstage for the finals.

No talent at all, no brains. It was going to be my triumph, my surprise for Papa. He already thought I had brains. When he opened the newspaper to see the ad for his store the day after the winner was chosen, he'd read all about my stunning success as a beauty.

A Mr. Lipstone, who was the manager of all the Paramount theaters in Chicago, was called in to choose the winner from the final roster. Going over the names, Mr. Lipstone saw "Virginia Komiss." He asked the local theater manager if by any chance I might be David Komiss' daughter, because my father was a State Street merchant and Mr. Lipstone knew him very well.

"Yes, I think she is," the pleased local manager was delighted to inform him.

Knowing my background, highly amused at his friend's daughter entering the contest, Mr. Lipstone called my father. "David," he said, "would you like to come over for the finals and see whether Virginia wins or not?"

If Papa was surprised, he was also adamant. "I don't know who's going to be the winner," he said, "but I can tell you one girl who isn't."

When he found me, Papa said, "Virginia, this isn't for you." I was speechless with disappointment. "This would be a taste of something I don't think you want to pursue," Papa continued. "If you lost, you're so sensitive I think you'd be crushed. And if you won, I question whether it would be advisable for you to go on. I wish you had talked to me about it sooner."

I was really heartbroken, because I had spent $35 for a bathing suit. In those days, $35 was a fortune to spend for a bathing suit, but I think this one had the first built-in brassiere. I was always ample, not sample. I probably had a bra in my layette. And this was the first innovative supporter of women's abundance in a swimsuit and worth every penny to me.

But when I saw that withdrawing meant so much to Papa, I didn't even argue. I'm not sure he was right. I'm not sure that it wouldn't have been very good for me to have gone on and lost, or to have made the decision in any case. But in those days, if my father said something, there was no further question.

Years later, I became a Palmolive bride with "the skin you love to touch." And when I told Papa the agency had called me for the job, he furnished the bridal outfit for nothing. It was his way of trying to make up for my disappointment in the Search for Beauty contest.

Because I graduated early from Francis Parker and was therefore thought too young to enter the University of Chicago, Mama and Papa had me enroll in National Park Seminary in Forest Glen, Maryland. I was very much in love with this boy in Chicago then, but the idea of giving up dates with him that whole year didn't bother me too much because I was going to National Park with one of my dearest friends whose name, as it happened, was June Friend. She was too young to get into Vassar, which was also where I really wanted to go.

I don't think many seminaries exist anymore. But in Forest Glen, where Walter Reed Hospital now stands, National Park tried to instruct its girls in the arts and skills of young ladyhood, with the accent on the lady. Cigarettes were not allowed in our rooms. Boys were permitted to approach us only on weekends, and we were heavily chaperoned from the moment they arrived until the doors were securely locked behind them. Today, such customs seem quaint.

We all wore those Peter Thompson uniforms—middy blouses with pleated skirts, looking very similar, if not exactly alike, from the chin down. At night we would get dressed up in marvelous ball gowns with bodices up to the neck. Anything below the neck was cleavage. A mole that was in the center of your chest was exposure, and if it showed you were put in a room by yourself to repent. We'd get up in these splendid evening clothes and dance with each other, long gloves gracing our hands and arms. They would put something in the gravy at dinner that made us like dancing with each other. It was named after one of the saints. I think the soldiers used it during the war. Yes, old salty peter was there. If dancing was on the agenda, the shout would go up at dinner: "There's something in the gravy!" Rumor was that some daring girl had sent it out to be chemically analyzed.

We were summoned hither and yon by gongs. When you had a caller a hostess would sit in the room with you, and if you got to talking on a subject she felt was unladylike she rang a tiny bell. Well, I want you to know that I kept her little hands busy. On the evenings when I had callers, she played "The Bells of St. Mary's," tinkling away. We were absolutely convinced that two of our hostesses were men with wigs. One of them was definitely a drag, because the wig slipped one night when my date and I were discussing birth control. It hung there, on the side of her head, somewhat like a beret. They had to rub her wrists for two hours after my boy friend left.

Another of the things they used to do that was divine was teach you never to put a piece of bread directly into your mouth. You were supposed to bring it up from the plate with your fingers until it was close enough to be thrown ever so daintily into your open gullet. Waft it in gracefully, so to speak, like tossing a basketball. Crumbs were all over the place.

I edited the first school newspaper—the *Glen Tatler,* which died a natural death upon my graduation.

I never, never broke a rule. I wanted to do ladylike things: to set the table properly, to arrange flowers in an artful way, to shake hands with just the proper degree of aplomb, to remember the names of people I met. (And isn't it funny, when nobody remembers mine?) Little did I dream how useful that skill was to be to me in the years to come. Signs of destiny are everywhere!

But eventually, of course, true to my independent nature, I got rebellious. And the way I decided to express my rebellion was very typical of Virginia Graham, still known at home and abroad to one and all as Virginia Komiss, though it was little enough to prepare my parents for the many delights to come.

Presenting Lorelei Komiss

Anita Loos had introduced the world to a dazzling *femme fatale* named Lorelei Lee. Lorelei, doing little more than standing still, had compelled the entire male population to kneel at her feet. How could she do it, you ask? Easy. You see, gentlemen prefer blondes, and Lorelei just happened to be a blonde.

Now a natural blonde I would never be. My hair was a constant, recalcitrant brown. But maybe, I speculated, swept along by the sheer magnitude of Lorelei's conquests, maybe I could improve on nature. Quickly matching the action to the thought— something I was already famous for—I proceeded to put my plan in motion. The very next Monday in Washington with my friend June, I set out to rectify nature's perfectly understandable error.

"June," I said, "I'm going to become a blonde."

She thought I was crazy.

Next door to the Mayflower Hotel, I entered an establishment called Pierre's. There, hidden from the outside world, barricaded by an arsenal of lotions and ointments in the hands of those tireless soldiers in the war against the commonplace, I underwent my metamorphosis. Seven hours later I emerged, my hair a dazzling, breathtaking snow white. (I salute hairdressers everywhere. They are the plastic surgeons of the scalp.)

June was horrified. I was dizzy with excitement. In those days, tinted hair (most people said "dyed") was the mark of a wicked woman, if not a fallen one. The school, of course, was scandalized. The dean, Miss Mumford, called me into her office and sat there looking at me. She was the most marvelous

19

woman. She looked something like Laura Hope
Crews, but more austere. I adored her.

"What happened to you?" she said, her pompadour
securely pinned. It may or may not have been stuffed
with cotton batting.

"I'm sick and tired of being a brunette," I said. "I
don't like my type." But my vanity cut no ice with
Miss Mumford. I was confined to the campus for
two months.

My battle with my appearance, however, had only
just begun. For the next twenty-one days, three entire weeks, I proceeded to eat only one ball of ice
cream a day. Twenty-one balls of chocolate ice cream.
I lost seventeen pounds. I based this diet on a fast
I went on as a child using rye bread. Every single
day I would take a piece of rye bread and sit in the
living room and pretend I was on a desert island and
this was all the food I had until tomorrow. Psychiatry
would have had a field day with my motives.

Not one single student reported me, and I managed
to lose seventeen pounds. The campusing itself didn't
bother me too much, because visits with other seminaries were usually quite boring. If you've seen one
seminary for young ladies, you've seen them all. But
meanwhile, nature's ever-ready paintbrush was beginning to discolor the roots of my hair.

I wasted no time. The second my campusing was
over, I was on my way to Pierre's for a touch-up.

This time Miss Mumford wrote to Papa: "Virginia went out, unbeknownst to us, and had her hair
dyed blonde." Papa had no sooner received the letter than he called me.

"How are you, darling? How do you look?"

I told him that I looked all right. "Good, Papa," I
said. "I look pretty good." I thought I looked divine,
and I must have reassured him, because Papa put up
no objections. The school, recognizing a lost cause
when they saw one, gave up.

Color me incorrigible.

If I hadn't been such a good student, I don't know
what further punishment Miss Mumford would have
found to impose, because it was a very strict school.

When your parents came to visit, you had to wait upstairs until they were "announced." Waiting for anything is an ordeal if you're sixteen and in a girls' school, and waiting for visitors was torture, especially when you could hear the whistle of the train they were coming in on sound in the distance.

We used to listen to the trains coming and going, in the long-ago years when trains were in their heyday. Nothing was sadder than the mournful whistle that hinted of faraway arrivals and departures, in an outside world from which we were excluded. Was there anything more melancholy than a rainy autumn Sunday in the glen when the leaves were falling and you heard the lonely whistle of the Baltimore Express. That's when a school can seem like a prison.

Papa and I agreed not to tell Mama about my hair right away. It wasn't until I finally went home that Mama was treated to the exciting news. As I got off the train, she took one look at the vision of blonde loveliness that was now her daughter, and fainted. We managed to get her to the first-aid room, but it was ten minutes before she revived.

To Mama I was still a child, little Virginia Komiss, her baby. And it was thus that I had disgraced the whole Komiss family, my very first time away from home. We had to stop at the drugstore for hair dye, which Mama applied liberally when we got home. It was poured on my head in the bathroom, and my hair came out a kind of mahogany-black. When I was dry and combed out, I looked like a polished highboy. I was screaming with fury because the man of my dreams never even had a chance to see Lorelei Komiss, the new *femme fatale*. So I acted quickly. I headed straight for the peroxide bottle.

Well, Mama and I went to war. My hair changed back and forth I don't know how many times until Papa intervened. "One of you is going to have to give in or she'll be bald. We can't go on like this. There has to be a happy solution."

The happy solution was to wash out the dark and gradually lighten my hair. And the funny part turned out to be Mama. In later years if the subject came up (and it did), Mama would say, "Ginny's *always* been blonde. Whatever do you mean? Virginia's like my husband. David was a blond." Memory, or vanity, or pride, plays the strangest tricks on us all.

And I have to tell you the truth, doing no commercial for Clairol or Breck or L'Oréal, it did affect my entire life. It absolutely changed my personality. I felt with total confidence that I no longer had to be as aggressive in getting boys to look at me. I became more "helpless," more demure.

Thirty years later, everybody always tells you how pretty you used to be. You will meet men who will say, "Oh, I wanted to take you out but I didn't have the nerve." It's such a terrible thing. You wonder why you worried so about not being popular, when maybe you scared people off by your own insecurity.

I definitely felt more secure as a blonde, although I think I was probably prettier as a brunette. Now it's a big advantage feeling secure. Only someone who knows what it is to feel insecure can fully appreciate what a big help it is. Recently, a friend who's seen me in a number of different situations said, "Virginia, you were born with cool."

"I absolutely was not born with cool," I replied with some heat. "I developed it." Papa always told me I was born with the saddest, most vulnerable eyes in the world. I remember Papa saying to me, "Darling, you've got to cover up those mirror eyes." He said, "I look into your eyes and see so much sadness. I see questioning. I see hurt in your eyes when someone even raises their voice to you. Don't you see that you're asking the world to hurt you?"

The cool, when it finally came, was a cover-up, like the new hair color. Cool is often a cover-up for the way you really feel. I think people who are job hunting, men or women who have that certain aloof air of cool confidence about them, will, nine times out of ten, get the job instead of the eager beaver.

When we were children, Mama used to give Juddy and me enemas periodically. We were irrigated more frequently than the Sahara. To Mama, an enema was no more than a mouthwash. No matter what happened or what the problem was, that was Mama's cure. I thought it was the most terrible thing in the world that could happen to anybody. If I saw so much as a hot-water bottle being carried to aid the sick or the weary I ran to hide under the bed.

Once, when I was very young, I heard that the Queen of England had been given an enema. I don't know how this news came out—on the radio, I guess, or in the newspaper. But there was an item that a cathartic was administered in the royal palace. Well, at the time, that was my most vivid lesson in democracy. If the Queen of England was forced to submit to such an indignity, who was I to complain? One thing you have to admit about an enema. It's the greatest leveler there is.

Of course, if I ever met the Queen of England I'd have to be tutored in protocol, like nearly everybody else this side of the Atlantic. And the person who sent me the invitation should be present to edit me every second I was with her alone. My one ambition would be to be able to say something like, "Oh, Your Majesty, you have such a lovely figure. You've really kept yourself up, and I know from experience how much of an effort that is. And the agony you've had with your children, with all the restrictions on their freedom. You've paid such a big price, Your Majesty, for your royalty." That's how I am, I guess.

You know, I'd like to get right to the point and talk to her woman to woman. I think social pretension is one of the ugliest things in the world. I know one woman who puts on such airs, whose hauteur is so icy cold, you feel certain she would patronize the Queen herself.

So color me blonde, incorrigible, and patriotic. Now tell me why there are so many jokes about blondes. Brunettes can be brunettes without levity. There are no jokes about brunettes. Redheads . . . well, maybe an occasional joke or two. But blondes! The jokes never die.

Not that I have any regrets. As the saying goes, "If I have only one life, let me live it as a . . ."

After the rigors of National Park, I went on to the

University of Chicago and Northwestern. These were my third and fourth schools, and I'm not even counting the School of Life, which is the most difficult university of all, incorporating, as it does, that renowned institution of higher learning, the School of Hard Knocks.

In my mind, when I wander through the classrooms of my youth, trying to rediscover knowledge, friendship, the forces that shaped my life (which are otherwise known as destiny), my memory sometimes plays hooky. I remember Robert Hutchins and the learning philosophy he believed in, but I can recall only a few other teachers' names at the University of Chicago.

Hutchins talked to us about the responsibility of learning and his belief that it was not based on classroom attendance. A person could study alone for a whole semester, never attend a class, and then go in and get an A+ on the final examination. Classroom attendance, therefore, was not compulsory. Unfortunately, this didn't work for me, because I learn best by hearing. I don't learn well by reading.

The classes were enormous. There was none of the informal intimacy of Francis Parker and National Park. And the process of learning seemed much more forbidding. But there was a Mrs. Flint who taught Shakespeare wonderfully well, and my memory of her is vivid because I loved Shakespeare so much.

And Thornton Wilder came to us for a seminar. That was a fantastic experience, because we got to discuss with him *The Bridge of San Luis Rey*. If you ever want to read a novel about the forces of destiny, read *The Bridge of San Luis Rey*. Somehow, without even meeting me, Mr. Wilder, magical genius that he is, had managed to write the story of my life. It's also the story of yours.

I've often felt, see, that I was the last person to get off that bridge before it collapsed. Not just once, mind you, but many times. In the novel, the narrator asks "Why?"—just as we ask why in real life. Why were those three particular people on the bridge when it collapsed. The answer is destiny in every case, although of course the circumstances vary.

I'll give you an example of what I mean. Dr. Burgess (oh yes, the names are coming back to me) was a brilliant sociologist. He had done an incredible amount of research on personal characteristics and social strata. He had created this questionnaire for couples aspiring to get married.

Well, together with this young man I was very much in love with, I filled it out. Nowadays, these questionnaires are all over the place. But Dr. Burgess' must have been one of the first. And I'll vouch for the skill of his method, because my young man and I discovered that we were definitely unsuited for marriage. The questionnaire said no and it was absolutely right. So you see? Destiny can come in many guises, even the form of a questionnaire.

Suppose we hadn't filled it out! It was based on the theory of the attraction of similar types. "You're going to suffer all through your married life if you marry this boy," Dr. Burgess told me. I'm a very demonstrative person, and this boy was very cold.

I also remember these terrible geology hikes. Why, you may well ask, was I taking geology? Because I had to have a science course. I'm not gifted in math. In fact, Harry says that my expertise in math is limited to keeping track of how much money he owes me.

If I had it to do over again, I wouldn't take geology. But when the time for choice is past, hindsight is useless. I was a product of the liberal arts school of thought. Today, I think the liberal arts mean liberal parents. All knowledge is beneficial to a point, but I have not found too many practical uses for what I know about gypsum (it tastes like salt). I have no more needed geology than the man in the moon. Now the men *on* the moon may have needed geology, but not Virginia Graham. Nor did I need shorelines and glaciers, about which I can speak with some authority, should anyone request.

Once the geology professor stopped the whole class on a field trip through the Dunes when my high heel

broke. Which, of course, it did on its first encounter
with a rock. "There's one in every class," he said. I
could have killed him. I think I had worn my highest
heels in protest. My muscles have never recovered
from hiking barefoot through the Dunes from then
on, which I deserved.

Talk about destiny! Later, at Northwestern, I had
an elective course open and somehow, providential-
ly, I chose speech. As I recall, I only wanted to get
rid of any trace of a provincial accent I might have
picked up, in case I later decided to go into professional life. At the time, I hadn't thought too much
about what I was going to do.

Dean Dennis, who headed the Department of
Speech, was such a marvelous teacher. I knew I had
this powerful vocal instrument, this voice that could
be heard six miles away, and I think that maybe I
wanted to experiment with it a little bit, to see what
it could do. "Her voice is so delicate." I had heard a
certain boy say admiringly about a friend of mine,
and I remember being highly aggravated. I felt this
was a not-so-indirect criticism of me, a message.

I've always been certain that people were sending
me messages. When I'm reading a letter or a book,
I try to read between the lines for any hidden messages. When someone's talking, I try to read between
the *spoken* lines. Because when we're speaking, we
don't always talk about what's on our minds. And
that's what I like to know, what's really on people's
minds.

Now you'll excuse me again, I hope, because I
have to backtrack once more. When I was ten years
old, Alice Gerstenberg, who was a fine playwright
and director of a drama group at the Goodman Theater, had a writing contest for youngsters. I was always writing murder mysteries and killing people off,
but because Papa hated violence, I just let them die
a natural death. Whenever I needed to get rid of a
character for the sake of the plot, I'd write: "And so
he died."

I asked Papa if I should write a play and enter

the contest, and he said yes, just please make it a nonviolent play. So I wrote a two-character play (two or four, depending on how you looked at it) without any physical violence but perhaps a smidgen of mental. These two women, who haven't seen each other for years, meet on the street and talk. But they never say what they really think. Their alter egos say that:

FIRST WOMAN: Oh, how nice to see you again. You look wonderful. How's your dear husband?

ALTER-EGO OF FIRST WOMAN: I should have crossed the street. You're still as ugly as sin, I see. Did your husband ever return?

SECOND WOMAN: I love your dress. What a fascinating hairdo! Tell me about your wonderful life.

ALTER-EGO OF SECOND WOMAN: So the Salvation Army is still providing your clothes! You've got a perfect rat's nest on top of your head. I've always wondered what you look like off your broom.

The alter egos were draped in sheets back of the two women. The play was called *Shadows* and it won.

When the *Chicago Tribune* called to interview me, Juddy took the call and gave almost the entire interview. I finally took the receiver to state my goals in life: "To get married and have as many children as God lets me have. That is my destiny."

I hated deceit when I was ten years old, and I hate it today. Now back to Northwestern and the speech course.

Well, the speech course was wonderful, because I'm crazy about talking, alone or with other people present. I also enjoy listening, though I don't always hear what I listen to. And Dean Dennis was an inspiration. "I don't know what you plan to do with your life," he told me, "but your voice will be the most important thing. You have one of the most persuasive voices I've ever heard. There's a quality in it that can get you anything."

How's that for prophecy! I'd say that was rather astute, because it worked out exactly that way. My voice has been my blessing. What I feel, I'm able to put into my voice. A lot of people find this difficult. You never know what they're feeling unless they cry or display some other visible sign on their faces.

Now after this splendid education, you would think I could have landed at least a job as a secretary, but fate had something else in store—the Depression. It wiped Papa out, along with a lot of other people. Fortunately, Mama had put some money aside and she was able to help him make a new start.

Meanwhile, I was selling a cleansing cream door to door. I was a kind of Avon representative ahead of her time. The cream was manufactured, if that is not too strong a word, by two friends of my father, who had given up their real estate business for this new venture. I wasn't a bad salesperson, but it was not a red-hot outfit and the future prospects didn't look too glorious.

My next job, however, was hardly an improvement. It came about through political favoritism. In a precinct that was a Republican stronghold, I, the precinct captain, had singlehandedly converted our entire apartment building to the Democratic Party. I was therefore in line for some patronage. I was given a job in the County Building with a fine woman by the name of Laura Benkendorf. She was also a precinct captain. The two of us would sit for eight hours a day and read quit-claim deeds off to each other. You wouldn't have needed a kindergarten education to do what we did. I mean, kindergarten would have been too much schooling for this.

What we actually did was make certain that the titles to properties up for sale were clear. Working so closely together, Laura and I became good friends. Her childhood was nothing like mine, but whatever differences there were did not stand in the way of our friendship.

Thinking back, we didn't have one thing in common except that we were both trying to survive the Depression, like everybody else. I found absolutely no difficulty understanding Laura's problems and hopes. Nor she mine. We talked about our families, our complaints, our needs. We were one person.

I must say this: At no time in my life have I ever been thrust with a group of people with whom I could not identify. How I got this ability, I cannot tell you. I think it was Papa. I believe it was Papa telling me about his youthful experiences traveling from city to city selling his wares, buttons and needles and things. Notions.

He had all the obstacles except youth. Youth and those beautiful eyes and that beautiful face! He didn't even speak the language, but somehow he was able to communicate, and people understood. Of course, it was a young country then, and everybody was a greenhorn. It's a marvelous thing when everybody's green and people help each other out.

Eventually, I was promoted to the Federal Home Loan Administration office. By the time I became twenty-one, I was earning $125 a week, a small fortune for a young woman in those Depression days.

I was young and alive and happy, and the world was my oyster. That summer, my college friend June got married and asked me to visit her in New York City. Of course I accepted. And in the fall, I boarded the famous *Twentieth Century* in Chicago, little dreaming how far my trip to Gotham was to take me.

The Wonderful Town, the Movie Star, and the Naked Truth

The *Twentieth Century* was a *train!* Running from New York to Chicago, and then back again, it was famous throughout the world. The dining car was a gourmet's dream, and I will never again taste cornbread without returning there in memory. In 1933, Ben Hecht and Charles MacArthur even wrote a play called *Twentieth Century*. All of the action in their highly successful comedy took place aboard that train. It was the last word in comfort and elegance, and in its heyday, for many, it offered the most glamorous ride in the world.

The termination point of the *Twentieth Century* in New York City was Grand Central Station. In those days, there was a tremendous sense of achievement in travel, especially on trains and ocean liners. Our destinations seemed so much farther away, because it took us so much longer to reach them!

I believe there was also a radio show called *Grand Central Station,* announced on the air as though a conductor was calling out the train's arrival in the terminal: *"Grand Cen-tral Sta-shun!"* For movie stars aboard the *Twentieth Century*—and there were often movie stars aboard—a contingent of photographers was always waiting from the *News,* the *Mirror,* the *Journal-American,* the *World-Telegram.* The afternoon editions would carry pictures of Ann Southern or Carole Lombard, sitting on top of their enormous trunks, a peppy smile on their faces, and posed to display their shapely "gams"—to which the captions underneath the pictures always referred—to best advantage. A trip to New York seemed like the most thrilling thing that could happen, and to a great many of us it was.

How can I express, as we pass the Bicentennial year of our nation when so many of our cities are in trouble, how can I adequately express what it was like in those days to arrive in New York City from the hinterlands, which every place else was considered? Like all of America at its best, there seemed to be no limit to its attractions, its possibilities. To those of us with a certain zesty edge to our appetites, it was heaven on earth. It seemed to promise everything in endless profusion: people, adventure, excitement. Why, New York City never slept! It was the ultimate trip you could take.

There were opportunities here! New York is where all the Old World traits were transplanted. The emigrants came in and breathed the air of a strange new land. Then as soon as they could, they recreated the air of the lands they had left. Chinatown, Germantown, Africatown, Polishtown, Italiantown. Miraculous city! Never before were so many cultures blended together. There can never be another city like it. Surely, New York has been Mecca for more people than any other city in the world.

This was not my first visit to New York, but it was my first visit alone and grown-up. June Friend, now Mrs. Edgar Moses, and Judy Gaines, my cousin, met me at the station. I was born a city girl, but I must have looked pretty provincial in my orange, green, and brown outfit, dressed to kill. An enormous deep-yellow chrysanthemum graced my lapel.

Well, the girls took one look at my getup and ran. They refused to recognize me. I had to run through the tunnels of Grand Central screaming, "Here I am! Here I am!" to get their attention. As though they could miss me in my vivid colors!

June had arranged some parties. The first night there was a costume party at the Unity Club in Brooklyn. Eligible bachelors were present in abundance and I met a number of them, including a handsome, dapper young man about town named Harry

Guttenberg. Harry was to be my date the following
night. Everything had been arranged by June the
Matchmaker.

And June must have known what she was doing.
The next night, Thanksgiving Eve, Harry escorted me
to the Central Park Casino for cocktails. He com-
mented on my hair, which I had had specially done
that afternoon by a famous Italian hairdresser. Harry
thought it looked terrible—a foretaste of things to
come!

I made a quick trip to the ladies room to undo my
too stylish coif as best I could. It was important I
look my best, because the minute I laid eyes on
Harry, I knew I was going to marry him. Don't ask me
how, I just knew.

We went on to the Mayfair Club, which was in the
wonderful old Ritz-Carlton Hotel at Madison and
Forty-sixth Street. Harry was very good-looking, but
there was something else about him that had caught
my fancy. He looked *familiar*. It was almost as
though he was a member of the family already. I
felt absolutely comfortable with him.

Harry was, of all things, a native New Yorker. His
family had been theatrical costumers since his grandfather founded the Guttenberg business in 1869.
I saw him every night for the rest of my visit.

On my last night, Harry proposed. Of course, my
mind was made up already and had been since the
costume party at the Unity Club. But before I said yes,
it was very important that we discuss the subject of
children. Harry might want to change his mind.

At eighteen I had undergone very serious surgery
for the removal of an ovarian cyst. The surgeon told
me then that the chances that I would ever be able to
have children were slim. I've always loved babies,
but at nineteen that news hadn't affected me the way
it did now.

"Harry," I said, "you're thirty-four years old. You've
never been married. I'm sure one of the reasons a
bachelor marries is to have children, and I cannot have
children." I had to tell him.

Harry looked at me, "How do you know that I can?" he said. "If we can't have our own children, there's certainly somebody else's child we can have together."

I decided that this was the most liberated man I'd ever met. All my life, whenever a couple couldn't have kids, it was always because of the girl. It was always the girl's fault unless the boy was a roustabout or a ne'er-do-well.

Now you've got to allow me to digress, once again, otherwise I'll forget the story the word "roustabout" just reminded me of.

When I was a young girl, we always associated venereal disease with boys, never girls. Never "good" girls, at least. Anyway, there was a movie about venereal disease called *The Naked Truth*. It must have been one of the first. I mentioned to Mama that I wanted to see it.

"You're not to see that movie, Virginia," she said. "It's restricted."

Well, of course, she couldn't have found a less useful word for her purposes, because the very next day I was the first one in line. I was waiting in front when they opened the box office. I bought my ticket and went up to the balcony. After a while the movie started and I was just beginning to satisfy my curiosity when an immodest old man sat down next to me.

I got up and went downstairs to find another seat. It was an enormous theater and by now almost completely filled. And this is what was so fascinating about the whole thing. I saw one seat on the aisle, so I took it. Well, there were two women sitting next to me, and they turned out to be Mama and Aunt Celia. Aunt Celia always sat close to the aisle wherever she went, because it gave her a quick getaway to the ladies room. Her assets were very liquid. When she went to the theater, she spent more time in the john than watching the play.

So there I was sitting next to Mama, and I want to tell you something. It was an occasion which we shall not ruin by describing in great detail. I won't reprint what we said. Because I was able to explain the movie to Mama. Mama was confused. I was there in order to interpret *The Naked Truth* for my mother.

Now I'm back with Harry at the Mayfair Club in New York on the last night of my visit. Remember? Harry has proposed and I've told him maybe I can't have children and Harry says maybe he can't either. Who could resist such a man?

I went back to Chicago. During the winter, I met Harry's family, and Harry came out to Chicago to meet mine. Because Harry's mother was not well enough to travel to Chicago, we agreed to have the wedding in New York in May at the Hotel Pierre.

Mrs. Guttenberg was a beautiful lady. She had become ill after a son died of X-ray burns in World War II. From knowing her, I learned that no matter how many children you have (she had seven, two boys and five girls), you mourn the one who dies for the rest of your life. It isn't enough to say, "Well, thank God, I have six others." You lose one child and you can never fully recover.

It was a small wedding. Harry was more nervous than I was; I was almost calm. After the nuptials, we had a delicious brunch. Then Harry and I departed for a cruise to the countries of Central America.

However, that morning I made an unpleasant discovery. Every bride knows how special this one day is. Every groom knows, too. When I awakened, I discovered to my consternation that I was, shall we say, a little indisposed. Nature had played the trick that she sometimes plays on nervous young brides (is nature still a female?), causing something to happen that does not make fulfillment too pleasant. I remember Papa walking up to my husband, aged thirty-five, and saying to him, "My boy, you've been patient so long, do you mind waiting a few days longer?"

How, you ask, did my father know? Oh, my dear, I told him. I told my father everything. Absolutely everything. Then Papa, in turn, would run and tell Mama, who wouldn't believe it. Mama always thought I was making it up.

So Harry and I boarded our honeymoon cruise ship even though we were required to postpone the most important part of the honeymoon for just a few days. Soon, however, we thought, all will be well.

About two days out of New York, just when I thought Harry's patience was about to be rewarded, I noticed that he looked very green. In fact, standing against the railing, his face was the color of the ocean. So I asked him. I said, "Harry, may I ask you a very personal question?"

You see, I had been raised in an anal atmosphere. Mama believed that the healthy elimination of waste material from the body is as important as anything in the world. If we were having a telephone conversation, it was the second question she asked.

When I asked Harry the date of his last body function, he said, "When did we get married?"

"Do you mean not since then?" I asked.

Harry nodded his head.

"Okay, Harry," I said. "That's okay. I was given a little gift, and . . ."

You see, I didn't know how to be delicate about an enema bag, but that was the next thing Mama included in my trousseau after a toothbrush. She thought it was the cure for everything. If you broke a leg, if you had hives, anything. I don't know why our whole family wasn't paralyzed.

I said, "Harry, we're going to solve this problem." So I administered first aid to the proper nether region, and from that moment on, I think the honeymoon was over and our marriage began. I mean, nothing can make you closer to a human being than that.

Consequently, as the boat sailed deep into southern waters, everything was finally okay. All systems were go.

After such a troubled beginning—maybe because of it—the rest of the cruise came close to being idyllic. The ports were glorious, our spirits were high.

When the boat docked in Costa Rica, a special surprise was in store for us. You remember that platinum blonde, none other than Lorelei Komiss? Well, she's still present and accounted for. I'm still very blonde and now very thin once again.

There were newspaper reporters at the dock for

some reason, and as I walked down the gangplank, I heard a loud shout from below.

"My God, there's Jean Harlow!"

Then, suddenly, everyone was looking at me, and I'm waving back with my hand. And my foot had no sooner touched the dock than pandemonium broke loose. Everyone was shouting questions and smiling and reaching out to touch me. A way had to be cleared for us through the crowd. Flashbulbs were going off like firecrackers.

"May I have an interview?" "How long are you going to stay?" "Are you really Jean Harlow?" "What is the purpose of your visit?"

And I'm playing it very cool. "Please, please!" I say. "No discussions or interviews."

Can you imagine? "I don't want to discuss that," I say, when they ask me about my love life.

Poor Harry is going bananas. "Are you crazy?" he says. "What are you doing?"

Sotto voce, aside to Harry, I say, "We're going to have a marvelous time. Leave it to me."

Word spread like wildfire. We had to go from the dock at Port Limón, where we landed, up to the capital city of San Jose on a funicular, a little train. People were waiting for us all the way up the mountain, shouting, screaming, calling out questions.

And I'm sitting there calmly beside Harry, smiling, waving back with my hands. "Hello, hello, everybody. How are you?"

Harry is so mortified he's got his head between his legs.

The mayor of San Jose is waiting at our hotel to present us with flowers. That evening he takes us out to dinner. And never would I admit one thing. Not a word. "Please," I would say, "my name is Mrs. Harry Guttenberg. I don't want to discuss anything personal." And everybody is saying, "Isn't she modest? Isn't she sweet?"

The next morning the newspapers are full of us. Headlines, photographs, full-page spreads. "FAMOUS MOVIE STAR VISITS SAN JOSE." "JEAN HARLOW HERE

FOR VACATION. *Red Dust* Star Desires No Publicity or Fanfare. Longs for simple holiday."

We really shocked them. We made a little bit of noise in Costa Rica, and I never had such a good time.

We were really very, very new to each other. We were strangers. I had only known Harry for two weeks in New York, and a few weekends when he flew to Chicago. I had nicknamed him Lindbergh. When I showed my engagement ring to my father, Papa said, "Don't show me the ring, show me the man. It is a beautiful ring, but it's the man who's important, darling." He was very anxious to know about Harry's family because Papa was convinced of the influence of environment. After he met the Guttenbergs, Papa said, "You're going to have a man who's going to love you for the rest of your life." My mother-in-law was a matriarch; her personality was very strong. His father, too, was a kind and good man. And Papa said, "You will have a wonderful life, because that's what Harry's known at home."

Here's a piece of advice Papa gave me. Never, never talk against your parents to your mate. If you do, you may get over your anger or annoyance, but your mate will never forget what you said. This is especially true in the early years of marriage, when the separation from your family is so crucial.

The honeymoon came to an end. We returned to our new apartment in New York. One morning after we'd been back a couple of weeks, I discovered that my clothes were becoming very tight.

Overweight, I thought. I've got to cut down on calories. But I wasn't overweight at all. I was pregnant!

Lynn and Shared Beginnings

———————————>+ +<———————————

It was the biggest shock of my life. I couldn't get over it, after all our talk about not being able to have children.

I called up June and asked her what doctor I should see. She gave me the name of a good obstetrician, and some of the funniest moments of my life were spent in that doctor's office. You've all had the pleasure of visiting a doctor's office, I'm sure. First of all, there's the waiting room. The waiting room of an obstetrician's office is like an ongoing coffee klatch. The first morning I got there, nine expectant mothers were lined up in a row, one to represent each month, and each and every one longing to share with all and sundry how it was with her. Full of excitement, you might say. There's nothing like a shared experience. You learn so much.

I had become immense right away, and I carried it all in my bosom and midriff. Nothing in the stomach. The baby kept moving up. Every day it got higher. "Finally," I told the assembled ladies in the waiting room, "I'm going to have to switch to a dentist for the delivery."

I did not become lovelier. You know, when the husband is supposed to look at you and say, "You're so beautiful, darling. That wonderful expression has come into your face." Wonderful expression! The nose spreads from side to side, in a horizontal manner; the lips grow fat—with girl babies anyway. Girl babies make mothers' faces change for the worse. I can tell you, almost invariably, the sex of any unborn child by looking at the mother's face. Because girl babies take looks away from the mother. They fill the heart

38

later, but they take the looks away during pregnancy. You can see it.

I was so excited I would forget to ask the doctor the questions I wanted answers to. Most of the girls would come in with their questions all written out, like a shopping list. "Is there a discount on premature births, Doctor?" "What's the going price for heartburn?"

I had the most terrible heartburn of any woman who ever lived.

"Listen to me," one woman said. "Don't pay any attention. It's hair growing."

"What do you mean?" I said. "I'm supposed to be carrying in the pelvic area, and the baby is strangling me up *here?*"

"Trust me," she said. "I'm telling you. I've had five children. With three I had heartburn, and with two I didn't. The three I had heartburn with have gorgeous hair." I wanted to ask if the others were bald.

We would bring sandwiches and Mah-Jongg tiles. A newcomer was no sooner in the door than someone would ask, "Is it your first?" The answer everyone preferred was yes. This indicated that the new mother was on tenterhooks to learn about the pregnant experiences of one and all. She was a novice, one might almost say a virgin mother, unlike the regulars and eager to improve her standing with her peer group.

Sometimes you could tell if it was the first child when the woman sat down. Those mothers sat with knees tight together, legs crossed at the ankle. After the first baby, a little distance separates the thighs, and with each additional child the spread of the limbs became greater. One woman, with eleven going on twelve, looked like the entrance to the Holland Tunnel. She sat in a wishbone, or lotus, position. I wanted to pay her a toll. I don't think she ever had the strength to cross her legs again.

When it was my turn to go in to see the doctor, I would tell him all these funny happenings. Most of these women were very modest. They were ashamed to take off their clothes in front of the doctor, a man.

I wasn't, and I couldn't understand why. Then I finally realized. After you got up on the table to be examined by the doctor, totally disguised by a huge white paper-towel robe, you were absolutely alone. Now this doctor was a godsend—the answer to the modest, embarrassed woman. He was only five feet tall, maybe five one. So when you would lie down and look toward the end of the examining table, where he ought to be, he wasn't there. Just the top of his head was showing.

I remember, after the pregnancy was over, the doctor said, "You know, Virginia, your positive thinking and your attitude brought you through this."

"What do you mean?" I said.

"Well, you had that terrible operation when you had the cyst removed with a dormant infection still in your body, which could have been totally revitalized, energized by your pregnancy. You used to walk out of the office and I would say to the nurse, 'My God, I don't know if I'm going to save her or the child. Look how happy she is. She never seems anxious. She never asks questions or anything, and we don't even know if we're going to pull her through.'"

It never occurred to me to think of that. I couldn't conceive of having a child without four fingers and one thumb on each hand. It never occurred to me that my baby would be anything but perfect.

By the end of the ninth month I was gigantic. I'll tell you how I looked. I looked like the heftiest day laborer in the history of the labor movement. I no more looked pregnant than President Herbert Hoover.

I remember that I had to go to Brooklyn a week before the baby was due. A friend of ours owned Martins Department Store and she was going to let me get my layette there. Mama had come from Chicago to be with me, and I remember it was February and the sidewalks were icy. The doctor said the best way to get there was by subway, because there wouldn't be any slipping and sliding as in an automobile.

Well, the subway car was packed and jammed, and Mama and I had to stand. Finally, Mama couldn't take it any longer. She pointed her finger at the nice-looking man sitting in front of us and asked him to give me his seat.

He looked me up and down. "She's stronger than I am," he said, and refused. This was in the thirties, remember, long before Women's Lib. Mama was furious. "This woman is about to have a baby," she said.

He jumped up. "For God's sake," he said, "not *now!*"

When the proper time came, I went to Doctors Hospital. Next door to me, I later learned, was a woman who had given birth to a cerebral palsied child. It's funny how coming events have cast their shadow over my life in advance. I think that must be fate's way for preparing us for the future.

There are really no adequate ways to describe active labor. I just wish that every enemy I've ever had could undergo three labor pains. I always maintain that if Adam could have experienced any one of them, civilization would never have gotten started. And every single pain is an anticlimax. The baby seems to take forever to make any headway.

Finally, though, that great moment arrived when I knew that great things were about to develop. To emerge, as it were. The doctor was calm, reassuring.

"Now we're going to take you into the delivery room, and we're going to pass your mother, who's in the waiting room, on the way. And we know you're going to control yourself."

"Of course I am," I said.

So out we go into the corridor and then the waiting room, and there I see my mother. She is looking at a picture of a large family and smiling. Now my pains are coming regularly and fast. This is the time in labor when if you had a gun you would not only shoot your husband, you would also shoot the person who introduced you to your husband. We are not really filled with undying thoughts of love at this period of dilation.

As we passed Mama, I heard her say, ever so sweetly, to the industrious mother seated beside her, "Oh, what a lovely thing to have a family of six! That's just what my Virginia is going to have."

"*Help!*" I screamed, ruining the day, I guess, for Mama. My nurse, whose name, by the way, was Miss Payne, had to restrain me. A big family was not in my plans at the moment.

It was Thursday, February 6. At 8:45 on the dot, Lynn was born. They had given me only a mild anesthetic, and the second she was born I looked at the clock. Then glancing at Lynn, I took one look and said, "Put her back—she's not done." She was bald; she was all eyes.

"She's just seen the world for the first time," said the doctor. "Have a heart." He was so relieved, so thrilled that I'd come through the delivery so easily, that he said, "Let Virginia's parents come in." It was totally against the rules for grandparents to come into the delivery room.

The first thing Mama said was "My goodness! She looks just like Harry." Then she gasped. "David," she said in a loud voice, then borrowed a line from Aunt Celia, "the baby has kidney trouble!" She forgot that most babies are born with bags under their eyes.

"This way out, madam." It was the doctor. The next thing I knew, two nurses had lifted Mama off the floor and hustled her away.

Home we came, Harry, Lynn, and I. Mama and Papa went back to Chicago.

Soon, however, I found myself with time on my hands. I had help with Lynn and the housework, and I began to think of what I might do outside the house in the way of useful activity. So I became a Big Sister through the auspices of the Board of Guardians, who were involved in the rehabilitation of wayward girls. And I also became a worker for the Federated Charities and the National Council of Christians and Jews. But I needed brain food. I guess I had a hankering for new worlds to conquer.

A mutual friend arranged a meeting with Bert Le-Bahr, then head of WMCA, a New York radio station. Mr. LeBahr wasn't exactly impressed with my background in radio, but I told him I'd done a little writing in high school (who hasn't?) and he agreed to let me try to improve the commercials on a daily three-hour show called *Grandstand and Bandstand*. What did he have to lose? He thought the commercials were terrible.

I went home and listened. I thought the commercials were terrible, too. But improving them was not as easy as you might think. The format for *Grandstand and Bandstand* (doesn't the title grab you?) was sports, popular music, and—to tie everything together, I suppose—advice to the lovelorn! I guess they wanted to touch all the bases.

I tried rewriting the commercials. That helped a little bit, but I wanted to do something really impressive, dramatic. Finally, I had an idea.

The next day, I put it to Mr. LeBahr: Why not have the sports and music stars on the show present the commercials themselves? That way, listeners would identify the product with the star, both the voice and the endorsement. This kind of advertising was common in magazines, but I had never heard it done on the air.

Mr. LeBahr was impressed. He put me to work at $75 a week, a comedown from my Chicago salary, but in a much more exciting field. I wrote under the pen name of Virginia Gotham. And soon I was promoted. The advice to the lovelorn part of the program was presented by none other than Mae Murray, the glamorous silent-film star. Her writer was leaving, and I became the replacement.

I was thrilled. I had never even been close to a real film star. Now I would be putting words into her mouth.

Miss Murray lived up to my expectations. She used to arrive at the studio in a white Rolls-Royce with a leopard throw rug. On each side of the interior hung marvelous Waterford crystal vases, refilled with fresh flowers every day. Her chauffeur would spray the atmosphere around the car with perfume each time Miss Murray alighted.

She was blonder than I was. I remember seeing her years later at Versailles, a nightclub in New York where Edith Piaf was making one of her first New York appearances, dancing blithely around the floor in the arms of a handsome young man. She still had the skin of a baby.

My association with Mae Murray did not last long, however, because Mr. LeBahr offered me a new opportunity.

"Do you know anything about cooking?" he asked me.

Of course I did. And even if I didn't, I could learn, like the teacher going home to bone up at night, in order to keep one lesson ahead of her students.

I didn't hesitate. Overnight, I became Betty Baker, *chef extraordinaire*, a kind of companion to Betty Crocker. A second banana. My recipes, however, unlike Betty Crocker's, were not destined for posterity. You will not find Tuna Fish à la Betty Baker listed on the menus of gourmet restaurants around the world. No desserts were named after me. As a matter of fact, Harry and I may be the only people in the world who remember my debut as a paid performer. Which may be just as well.

I achieved at least a little fame, however, in this role. When I got in a taxi one morning, I said to the driver, "WMCA, please."

"Yes, Miss Baker," he said.

Miss Baker? He must recognize my voice, I thought. He must be one of my listeners. He couldn't have recognized my face, which was a pity. I had the perfect face for radio.

"Tell me," I said, "how come a fellow like you would listen to recipes?"

"Who listens to recipes?" he said. "You come on just before the horseraces."

But at the time, I was in heaven. Why, just the knowledge that so many people were *possibly* tuning in to what I had to say thrilled me to the bone. And, at the same time, I was being paid for it.

The art of cooking is laden with potential pitfalls. List the wrong ingredients in a recipe, or give incorrect amounts, and your Fondue Orientale will turn out to be an oriental disaster. All it takes is one little blunder. But there is no record that even one of my listeners was poisoned. The WMCA switchboard was never deluged with phone calls protesting my instructions, so maybe I was okay.

If I was improvising my recipes, I was also learning how to handle a show of my own, modest though it was. I was already in touch with a lot of wonderful people—my family in Chicago, Harry, Lynn, my friends, my coworkers and, last but not least, My Audience.

Sunshine

One day I was having my hair done when my hairdresser started talking to me about this marvelous suburban house a friend of hers had bought. A small down payment. An eight-room house with $72 a month carrying charges. A big lawn, a community swimming pool, playgrounds for children, and a clubhouse.

I began to think of all the advantages to us of country-style living, especially for Lynn, and the more I thought about it, the more appealing the idea became. We'd have fresh air and plenty of sunshine. Within a few days, Harry and I had arranged to drive out to Great Neck, Long Island, to see a very attractive development there.

One of the first questions we asked was if any of the neighboring houses had children. Dozens, was the answer, and I thanked God for this blessing because subconsciously knowing Lynn would probably be an only child, I didn't want her to know the loneliness and ever-present selfishness that can often be the "only child" syndrome.

Well, it was a marvelous, very small development. Eleven homes, a few still under construction. Some had been purchased, but the people hadn't moved in yet. The model house was on the corner and Harry and I walked in. What a house! A twenty-eight-foot living room, twenty-eight-foot bedrooms, a beautiful dining room, a sunken bathtub in the octagonal master bathroom, gorgeous closets, front and back lawns. I don't think there will ever be another house buy as full of value as that one was.

We made up our minds immediately. We decided

46

to buy a red brick Georgian, and it was one of the happiest decisions we ever made. The first thing I did was purchase toothbrushes for the guests I knew were going to come, now that we had so much room in which to make them comfortable.

When the demand for Betty Baker came to an end, as I'm forced to report that it did, I found life in the suburbs completely absorbing. I joined the local Red Cross right away.

We had been living happily in Great Neck for two years. One day I was visiting my friend Lucille Herbert when we heard fire trucks rushing down the street, sirens screaming, "Oh my God," I said, "that's the most terrible sound I ever heard in my life."

Lucille had no sooner said, "Yes, it is" than the phone rang. Lucille answered. It was a neighbor. "Tell Mrs. Guttenberg to go home at once," she said. "Her house is on fire."

I rushed home. When I got there, smoke was coming through the roof. I saw Lynn sitting on top of the car, perfectly calm and perfectly safe. I went over to her at once. She had been in no danger, and I thanked God for that. Harry was at his office in New York.

Fires always attract people, in the city or in the country. The firemen were doing everything they could to put out the blaze and townspeople had gathered to watch. I was trying to assess the extent of the damage.

"Maybe someone was smoking in the attic," Lynn said in a loud, clear voice.

Now Lynn had never been a talkative child. There were times when it was difficult to get her to say anything at all. But during the heat of the excitement, in one grand burst of detective zeal, she almost invalidated our insurance policy.

In the end, we were able to establish that the fire was the result of spontaneous combustion in the attic. Lucille asked Harry and me to stay with her while the house was being rebuilt, and Lynn stayed with our marvelous neighbors next door, the McIvers. That's one of the wonderful things about starting out in married life—the feeling that people are eager to help you. As we grow older, I think, this sense of community lessens. We grow less generous, more crotchety, less able to adapt our daily lives to the needs of others.

Soon after joining the Red Cross, I found myself completely caught up in volunteer work. I wasn't just involved. Most volunteers gave one day a week. I gave five. Most volunteers stuck to one branch. I was in them all. I was a nurses' aide, a motor corps driver, a Grey Lady; I taught first aid.

I have always been civic-minded, even as a child. When I was ten and Juddy was twelve, we held a benefit for the underpaid bellboys at the Grand Hotel in Mackinac Island, Michigan. Juddy and I felt that the bellboys were getting substandard wages, so we rounded up all the guests and organized a benefit. We had people sing, we had people play the piano, we had a dancer, and we had one harmonica virtuoso. It was my first telethon, you might say.

We loved living in Great Neck. It was a typical suburban life. Lynn was growing up in healthy country air, Harry commuted to New York five days a week, and I was busy with my family, our new house, and the community.

Meantime, Papa wasn't well. He was a heavy cigarette smoker—four packs a day—and he and Mama had moved to Arizona for the climate. He had developed emphysema. When I heard how sick he was, I left Lynn and Harry in Great Neck and went to Phoenix as fast as I could. Nothing else even occurred to me, because I knew what I had to do.

When I got there, Papa said, "I must be very sick. I see it in Bessie's eyes." Mama walked into the room and he saw the reflection of his death in her eyes. So I made sure that whenever Papa saw me I was always smiling and cheerful. Papa said, "My Ginny couldn't be laughing if I were dying."

To add to his misery, my darling father underwent a prostate operation. And I learned something then about male philosophy. Papa thought this operation was the end of manliness, in much the same way as those women who cringe from the thought of the de-feminizing aspects of the hysterectomy. "I'm never going to live through this," he said to me. My father's father had died after a prostate operation, and I al-most believe Papa willed himself to die after his.

After the operation, Papa got a little better. I stayed in Phoenix three months. I wouldn't come home until the doctors assured me that he was out of danger. There was one thing I knew for certain, above all else. Papa *couldn't* die, ever.

Back home in Great Neck, which is situated almost right on the Atlantic Ocean, I felt a lot closer to Eu-rope. As Red Cross volunteers, we heard the reports of tragedy unfolding there. Because storm clouds were gathering, and much of the world was already at war, male ambulance drivers at the Red Cross were being drafted or joining the navy, and women had to replace them.

On Sunday afternoon, December 7, 1941, Harry had gone to a football game. I had gone to see some friends in New Rochelle. A cousin of mine was mar-ried to Ivan Annenberg, then heading the *Daily News* circulation department. Around three o'clock, Harry called me. Ivan, who was also at the ball game, had been paged by his office. He had given the news to Harry: Japan had attacked Pearl Harbor. The country was going to war.

The news was all over the radio. When I tele-phoned the house to ask about Lynn, I learned that she was fine. I also learned that the Red Cross had called a Yellow Alert.

As quickly as I could, I got to Mineola and joined the other volunteers at the Red Cross office there. We were assigned to railroad stations throughout that part of Long Island, where trainfuls of young men were already arriving for emergency duty at Mitchell Field. We worked in relay, back and forth from the stations to the field. That work went on all night.

From that time on, the whole community—and the rest of the nation—began mobilizing resources. It was an enormous undertaking. In retrospect, it's awe-inspiring. Everyone helped, everyone contributed.

Time, money, energy. USO clubs were formed. Scrap metal was collected. War bonds were sold. Rationing began. But whatever was done here, on this side, reports of casualties abroad grew longer and longer.

Civil defense was fervent. People living in coastal areas felt especially vulnerable to attack, not only from airplanes, but from submarines—in those days one of the most menacing of all enemy vessels. I can still remember the eerie, scary feeling that raced through us when battered tin cans and pieces of metal washed ashore on the Long Island beaches. They told us more eloquently than any words that a submarine had been sunk. Was it ours, we wondered, or was it the enemy's? Mysterious . . . out of sight, yet oh so near.

Harry was not eligible for military service because of his age and his back. He became an air raid warden. He always felt an added sense of responsibility because of his draft status.

What a miracle is necessity! You never saw such capable people. What we didn't know how to do, we learned to do. We changed tires, we cleaned pistons, we repaired cars. We minded the children. Everybody did something.

Through it all I was smiling, determined to be cheerful. I got the nickname Sunshine. They even gave me a rank, making sure it was suited to my managerial ways: Sergeant Sunshine. And that's the way I was sometimes addressed when servicemen sent their cards to the only name they knew me by. Through some miracle of communication, I received them, for which I should like to salute the Great Neck post office, among others.

It was fashionable at this time to wear a flower in your hair. But one wasn't enough for me. I wore garlands. Like a cloche, they covered my upper head. It was not unusual for Sergeant Sunshine's crew to report for drill duty resembling the Hanging Gardens of Babylon.

Eventually, the casualties began to arrive, damaged in body and mind. Mason General Hospital, where I was a Grey Lady, did wonderful rehabilitative work with the mentally disturbed. Music has always been therapeutic for me, so I organized a singing group there. There was one young veteran who had begun a singing career before the war. Then, during combat, he had gone into shock. That stopped his singing altogether. One day I was leading all the men in the group with my own bountiful contralto and the veterans started yelling, "She's terrible. Get her off!"

They may have been mentally disturbed, but they were very truthful. "Enough, enough!" they shouted. Finally, to keep us quiet, this boy came up and began to sing like an angel. Later he had a great success as an entertainer.

A year later, when he was headlining at the Copacabana, New York's ultimate nightclub, I was sitting with Harry at a front table. This talented performer was kibitzing with the ringsiders, flattering them, when he looked at me and said, "Hi there, beautiful. I don't know who you are. You do look familiar, but if I had been familiar with you, I'd remember."

And I said to Harry, "Isn't that marvelous? He doesn't remember me at all. But there was that one glimmer."

Finally, after the war, I had to stop my Grey Lady work, because so much of the brain damage to the men was incurable. It seemed to me that I could only be effective when there was some hope of improvement. And when I saw the vacant looks in the eyes of those heartbreaking men, and knew that they were going to be there forever, I had to leave.

Harry's brother-in-law, who was in the beauty-supply business with the Bonat Company, soon sounded me out on a new project. Some friends of his heard me emcee a fashion show for Cerebral Palsy and told him how funny I was. He wondered if I might be able to talk to the hairdressers at the International Beauty Shows held in New York once a year.

"Certainly," I said. No background whatsoever.

So I went into New York and met Joe Burns, who was putting on the shows, and he explained what he wanted me to do. "Do you think you'll be able to handle it?" he said.

"Oh, certainly," I said. "This will be a cinch."

The shows went on for three days—and the days could last as long as fifteen hours. All the big companies—Clairol, L'Oréal, Breck—were displaying their wares downstairs, and we were upstairs. Mr. Burns allowed me to hire a secretary and I chose a girl named Marie Monell, who was a Smith College graduate and had a terrific sense of humor.

The first day I got up to introduce all the hair-stylists, and I suddenly began to look at these people, especially the women. I noticed that many of them were gray-haired. Also, many of them had figures that looked dumpy, and their clothes were unattractive. These details were distracting me as we proceeded with the show.

Finally, I could stand it no longer. I let them have it. "How can you people profess to be vendors of beauty," I said, "when you look like this? I want everyone to take out a mirror, and we will all look at ourselves in the mirror.

"Tell me. If you were a saleslady, would anyone look at you and say, 'I want you to help me'? If you worked in Personnel and were interviewing yourself for a job would you deserve to be hired?"

This was really and truly the first time many of them had been asked these questions. I made them aware of the fact that if you're in the business of selling hair color, your own hair is your best advertisement. And while I don't think it's healthy to put too much emphasis on physical beauty, we can all improve our appearance.

It worked. There was immediate rapport between the hairdressers and me. All the people downstairs were rushing upstairs to see us. It became a floor show. And all of it happened in the blinking of a false eyelash. I had added a new role to my ever-expanding repertory: I was not only Sunshine; I was Virginia, the Beauty Consultant.

Waiting to Be Born

On the day before I went to be interviewed for the beauty show, I had gone with a friend to Billy Reed's Little Club, a very popular "in" spot. We'd been told about a wonderful fortune-teller who was giving readings there, and I wanted to see what the future might hold in store. At the Little Club, your fortune came with the chicken salad. Order one and you got the other.

Well, the fortune-teller was uncanny. First, she predicted my recovery from a debilitating, incurable illness. That, I had heard years before. Then she came up with something new:

"My dear," she said, "you are going to be internationally known. You are going to be a great woman in the world of entertainment."

I was dumbfounded. It had never entered my mind, even remotely. The Search for Beauty contest was a lark, not a serious bid for a career.

While my mind was reeling under the impact of this new piece of information, the fortune-teller asked my name. I told her. She thought I should decide on a new name for professional use. I was taken aback.

She went into a kind of spell, rearranged her cards on the table, and summoned up all her powers to produce my elusive new name. Lines of deep concentration appeared on her forehead.

I waited. I had lived thirty-four years without knowing who I was destined to be. I could afford to wait a little longer.

Suddenly I thought of something important. "I have everything monogrammed V.G.," I said. "I'd like to keep that."

Duly noted, then back into her trance. At last she raised her head. "The name is Graham," she said. "Virginia Graham."

How often since that day have I scolded the fates for conspiring to present me with so forgettable a name. But I didn't know it was forgettable at the time for the simple reason that I had had no previous experience with it. Nor, to the best of my knowledge, had anyone else.

When I got home, I thought of everything the medium had told me. Sickness. Well, that could happen to anyone. That I would have to deal with when the time came, like everybody. Then I thought of the rest of her forecast. It seemed ridiculous. Virginia Guttenberg? I couldn't sing, I couldn't dance, I couldn't act. I couldn't play a single musical instrument, not even the tambourine. How could I possibly entertain?

She must be crazy, I finally decided. There was no way I could ever be an entertainer. But the next day, when I was introduced to the guests at the beauty show, it was in the company of my new name. To the assembled audience, I was Virginia Graham, somewhat dazed by my new identity, but game. If fame was on its way to greet me, I would try to meet it halfway.

In 1950, there was a completely new look for women. Cosmetics manufacturers had gone all out and prescribed dazzling new ways for women to become beautiful, beginning with their faces. The man handling public relations for the beauty show put in a call to the office of Dave Garroway. Would Mr. Garroway be interested, the PR man wanted to know, in having someone explain to his viewers the wonderful new look for women.

The answer was yes. "We have a girl here who is very clever," said the PR man. "Her name is Virginia Graham."

If you're ever on the *Today* show, chances are you'll have to rise before dawn. I had to get up at four. Looking at myself in the mirror, I was my own best example—a living testament to the value of looking new. There ought to be a law against anyone's appearance at that hour.

People had gathered three-deep on the sidewalk, as they used to do when *Today* was presented in the street-level studio on Forty-ninth Street in Rockefeller Center, to look in the big picture window. And when the time came, I was introduced to Dave Garroway. He began our little talk by asking me a question.

That was all I needed. It was like the signal to begin a marathon race, because I was off and running. With no self-consciousness whatsoever, I proceeded to explain the new cosmetics, demonstrating as I talked. At length. Cosmetics are wonderful; I don't know what we'd do without them. But applying them, putting them on, can be one of the funniest things in the world to behold. And I was making the most of those at hand. All else was forgotten as I improvised, mimed, grimaced, and quipped.

It must have been funny. Everyone in the studio was hysterical, and their laughter spurred me on. Dave Garroway was astounded. One question! All he had done was ask me one little question and I had taken off like Secretariat at the Kentucky Derby. Who was I? Who was my trainer? Where had I come from?

As I was leaving, the director told me he'd never laughed so hard before. "May we have your name and address?" he said.

Yes, he could. I wasn't bashful about giving it to him, either. Coy, I'm not, nor ever have been, nor ever will be.

Of course, I was pleased with the response in the studio. And it was a satisfying boost to my ego that they asked for my address and phone number. I got a nice feeling every time I thought of it. At the very least, I thought, I had done a good job for the beauty show.

Then, a few weeks later, the telephone rang. It was the *Today* office. Dave Garroway was going on vacation. Would I be interested in taking over for him for a week?

I had to say yes because no never crossed my

mind. It never does. No, at best, is a local stop on the express train to yes. Besides, the fortune-teller at the Little Club had already told me what was going to happen. Did I have the moral right to make a liar out of her?

Remembering my brief interlude discussing beauty on the *Today* show, I said to myself, This will be a cinch. The only difference was in the amount of time at my disposal. My first stint had been brief. This appearance would last much longer. Otherwise, there was nothing to it.

But that wasn't the way things worked out. To begin with, I failed to take into account the simple fact that being a guest on a show is an entirely different responsibility from being a host, or hostess, or emcee, or anchorman or -woman. A guest is only along for the ride. A host is the *driver*.

Well, for one solid week on the *Today* show, I was the worst driver you have ever seen in your life. I ran over everybody. Paying no attention to traffic signals, red lights or green, I talked myself into one collision after another. My "interviews" were monologues—my own. My guests were lucky if I let them open their mouths to yawn. I was in the driver's seat and I definitely believed in power steering. By the time the week was over, the ground was covered with the bodies of the slain. Corpses lay everywhere.

It was Disasterville. The simple truth was that I tried too hard. I tried to control everything and I wound up out of control myself. That week taught me a lot of lessons, though I didn't know it at the time.

Not long afterward, I was given another opportunity. Ed Herlihy was host on a daily television show originating from Tavern on the Green in Central Park. He devoted a portion of each show to charitable causes, sponsoring a different one each day. Cerebral Palsy, for whom I had provided the commentary at many fashion shows, asked me if I would appear on the Herlihy program and do the rundown on hats, the focus of fashion that day.

Yes. Y-e-s.

It was a one-hour show. After three quarters of an hour, I was still waiting to go on. Impatient, irrepressible, impetuous me. Finally, with only seven minutes to go, I was introduced. When Ed Herlihy finally got around to ask me a couple of general questions about suburban life, I took the bull by the horns. "Listen, Mr. Herlihy," I said, "you've been on for forty-five minutes. It's my turn now. Let's not waste time on chitchat. I'm here to do a fashion show. It was good to meet you. Here goes!"

I'm mortified every time I think of that speech. Of all the gall! I then proceeded to make mincemeat of the millinery, too. But the hats, at least, were funny, and I made the most of them. At the time, there was nothing more stylish than an outrageous chapeau. And because many of them were very pretentious indeed, hats were natural targets for ridicule and sarcasm.

Humor, praise the Lord, redeemed my performance that day. When the show was over, I tried to find Ed Herlihy in order to thank him, but he had left for the day. How could I blame him? We are good friends today, but no thanks to my behavior on his show.

The program was hardly off the air when Ted Cott, a young man at NBC, put through a call to me. He wanted to talk. Could he have a limousine pick me up?

Need I tell you my answer?

He didn't waste any time.

"What have you done?"

"I'll be very truthful. I haven't done a thing in my life."

"Why were all those women laughing at you? I've never heard such laughter."

"Women like me. They think I'm funny."

"Okay, I'll find out if they really do. We have a woman who's doing a show that bores me stiff. Do you think you could do a cooking show as funny as that hat show?"

"Yes."

Well, I thought, I'll just get out my old Betty Baker routine. I've got a head start on this one already.

Ted Cott was very enthusiastic, and a kinescope was quickly made. In those days, a kinescope did essentially what a pilot film does today: It sold the program to a sponsor—or not, as the case may be.

And, dear reader, lest you think that fortune was waiting demurely around the corner to crown me with stardom, let me quickly disabuse you. It was an expensive, well-produced kinescope. But while we were making it, the woman who bored Ted Cott stiff acquired a sponsor. What television station is going to cancel a performer with a sponsor?

My kinescope had a clever format. Viewers were to send in recipes, from which we would choose the most interesting. Step by step, we mixed the ingredients and cooked the food. Then a jury sampled it and gave their opinion of the recipe, and the best recipe won a prize.

But my kinescope was relegated to wherever dead kinescopes go at the National Broadcasting Company, to languish there in its dusty tin can. I don't think Ted Cott ever saw it. With the exception of one person, I don't know that anyone on the NBC staff ever saw it. That one person, however, happened to have a very adept hand in the shape of things to come, though at the time I didn't even know who he was. His name was Morgan—Monty Morgan.

In the fall of that year, I went with Harry to a party in Great Neck. During the course of the evening I was introduced to a man named Zeke Manners. I did a double take. The name was hauntingly familiar.

"Could you," I asked him, "be the same Zeke Manners who had a radio show on WMCA in 1937?"

Well, he could be and was. I told him that I had been Betty Baker, the ulcer queen, and we proceeded to take a nostalgic stroll down Memory Lane.

Then he told me he had a television show. I must have expressed interest, because the next thing I knew Zeke had asked me to appear on his show as a guest.

It was a daily afternoon show, two o'clock to four, on WJZ, which eventually became WABC. Zeke, of course, was the host, and provided entertainment on a number of fronts: fashion, food (he took viewers to restaurants all over New York), nature classes, the horses, telephone calls from viewers, and music. The works! Zeke himself played the ukelele, casual in the extreme. The name of the show was no slouch: *Zeke Manners and His Beverly Hillbillys.*

I must have made a good impression on some of the viewers during that first appearance, because the phone started ringing. Zeke would take the phone calls right on the air, and gab with the callers. I wish I could see a tape of that show today, and hear both sides of the conversations. Would they be a treat for sore ears? I wonder. Might they have given an indication of the Virginia Graham to come?

Afterward, Zeke asked me if I'd like to start doing the same thing every day. "Only as soon as possible," I replied. "Make me an offer."

To say that the monetary offer was peanuts would be to place too much value on the offer. It would amount to an overstatement. And peanuts in those days were cheap. They cost a nickel for a good-sized bag. But I was young, and Zeke was enthusiastic. It was arranged that Virginia Graham would join the regulars. The other girl on the show was Vera Massey, a victim of multiple sclerosis, and a brave and valiant lady who sang songs of inspiration.

Picture us, if you can—a kind of entertainment grab bag, clowning around the studio, live and uncensored. There was a freshness and spontaneity about television then, before the practice of taping set in. Television was in its infancy. All the shows were experimental. And I think it's fair to say that none of us quite knew where we were going, from one show to the next.

Six months after I began, I ended. The termination came when AFTRA, the American Federation of Television and Radio Artists, established a union scale. After Zeke Manners learned that my minimum salary would have to go from less than peanuts to eight hundred dollars a week, he chose to sever our relationship.

Back to being a housewife in Great Neck I went.

Back to the daily routine of suburban living. But somewhere inside Virginia Graham nee Gotham nee Guttenberg, nee Komiss, a fledgling performer was now struggling to survive. Somewhere inside her body, a star was waiting to be born.

And now I come to that part of my life that offered the greatest challenge I had ever faced. It is, in many ways, the most painful to recollect. Yet it will always be vivid in my memory.

But before I begin that story, let's pause for a chapter break.

The Power Within Us

There are few words in the English language that strike such fear in the human heart as "Cancer!" Looking back at my medical history, there was every indication that it would happen to me. At the age of nine, I had typhoid, which was a rarity. Forty people took a drink of water out of a well in Excelsior Springs, Missouri, and I was the only one who got typhoid. Every hair on my head fell out. I prayed it would grow back blonde, but my prayers were in vain. If I was the only one struck, however, I was also the only one to recover, and recover I did. Color me lucky.

Now I'll tell you a very interesting thing. When I was still nine years old, we were in Hot Springs, Arkansas, at the Arlington Hotel. Mama and Aunt Celia heard from the floor maid about a gypsy fortuneteller there. They decided to go.

I had always been interested in the supernatural. If they were going, I quickly decided, I was going, too. "I'm going, too," I said. I don't remember now why Mama didn't have more control over me. I must have been the irresistible object. I was absolutely determined.

Mama decided not even to try to be the immovable force and took me along without a murmur. She really had her hands full with me. What nine-year-old should have her fortune told by a gypsy? Aunt Celia was horrified.

But I remember everything the gypsy told me. She looked in my eyes and said: "When you are thirty-five, you're going to be pronounced incurably ill with a terminal disease. Everyone around you will think that you are going to die. But you are going to be one of the few people to survive this disease, and you are going on to be a very great person."

I give you my oath that this is the truth, because I will remember it until the day I die. The fortune-teller at the Little Club had repeated the prediction.

Later, when I was in my late teens, I developed a ruptured cyst on an ovary and had a partial hysterectomy. It was excruciatingly painful. Gynecology was then in its infancy. I think the first hysterectomy was performed at Johns Hopkins Hospital sometime around 1900. My operation was a long time after that one, but there was still a lot of ignorance, self-consciousness, and false modesty about the invasion of a woman's body—as there is to this day, though nothing like what there used to be.

Walking up Madison Avenue one day, I saw this beautiful sculpture of a Chinese woman reclining nude. Now remember that the Chinese are famous for their modesty. For the sake of curiosity, I went into the gallery to ask the price (astronomical!). I had always wondered, if Chinese women were so modest, why they were always lying around the house undressed. The gallery owner said the figure was called a "doctor woman." I said, "What does that mean?" He said it meant that when the Chinese women would go to a doctor for an examination, she would point to the spot on the nude statue that was her area of complaint. Very often, if she was not candid (and how could she be?), the doctor would take her appendix out. This method was not only modest, it was barbaric. But as long as she didn't talk, she was still modest. That's what I could call prognosis by remote control.

Anyway, by the time I was born, there still hadn't been a tremendous invasion into that area. And an ovarian cyst in a young girl of eighteen was somewhat out of the ordinary. When the cyst ruptured, I had peritoneal and uremic poisoning. I was absolutely incapacitated for eight months.

They took out a fallopian tube and an ovary. I remember the doctor saying to Papa at the time, "You know, Mr. Komiss, I really should perform a total hysterectomy on Virginia, because the invasion of infection could happen again. But I have to make a bigger decision. She's so young and full of life, and she has a tremendous love of children, of babies." And Papa said, "Do whatever you think is wise."

And the doctor did, leaving one tube and ovary, and I recovered. Chicken pox, measles, whooping cough, I got everything that came along except the common cold. Never the common cold, never the influenza viruses. And what happened each time? Instant recovery. I was really and truly a leader in disease, a pioneer. I often felt that my body had a monopoly on the homesteading rights of bugs. They invaded; I repelled. Call it fate, call it heroic endurance, call it masochism, call it what you will. I call it simple survival.

Simple? I believe that when the doctor who delivered me gave me a swift slap on the behind, when he gave me that resounding smack, he infused in me the will to survive. From that point on, it was up to God and the doctors and me. How can that be simple?

Of course, my family only consulted with doctors when my cousins' telephones were busy. Aunt Celia had an immediate—one might almost say extrasensory—diagnosis for every known illness (and a few that are yet unknown). And she loved nothing better than sharing her knowledge by telephone with members of the family with the admonition "Pass it on." So a kind of round-robin chain reaction of information would develop from Aunt Celia's instantaneous reaction.

"What does Aunt Celia say it is?" a cousin would ask. Or, "What is Aunt Celia's opinion?"

"Either a ruptured appendix or an incipient hernia," the answer might be. "Aunt Celia is waiting for further developments."

It might be a stomachache. Aunt Celia carried a complete medical record of every member of the family to two generations back in her head. Complete in every detail and highly inaccurate. Her favorite follow-up to a new diagnosis was, "It runs in the family."

In our family, hypochondria reached an all-time high. Some members are in their eighties now, and nineties. When you talk to them, they say, "Can you imagine? We should have been dead sixty years ago. If we'd only known we were going to live, how much we could have enjoyed life."

I survived all these different things. And from the time of my ovary operation, I had severe menstrual pains. My monthly periods were often accompanied by hemorrhaging, though I never let it incapacitate me. I was never the kind to go to bed or to take a lot of pills, but when I had a certain amount of discomfort I was smart enough to go to doctors for a checkup.

Frequently they would say, "You're overtiring yourself. You've got to stop working so hard." Well, during the war years, I was lifting stretchers, I was driving Red Cross ambulances, I did a lot of physical work. How do you stop doing these things when you're living in a country that's been attacked? How do you thank God and thank your country? Someone has got to serve. Someone has got to equalize the score. So I overdid, the way I do everything. I'm very intense.

Perhaps I did weaken my system, but I don't think that brings on a malignancy. And all during those years, when the Pap smear was first being given, I would go to doctors and I would have the Pap smear. Negative, negative, negative. There was never, in all those tests, an indication of anything. But in my heart, I knew something wasn't right.

Then, in 1947, my father died, and that was the most devastating experience of my life. I can't even talk about it now, to this day. Strong as I am, I'm very vulnerable to loss. No one would think it of me, but I have a private time for crying almost every day of my life for the people I love who are gone. It's private because I think grief is a very private thing. Grief is the hardest of all the emotions to endure, because there seems to be nothing to hope for, nothing to do, nowhere to turn to ease the pain. There are many grieving people who go into a house of worship to say a prayer for the dead, or to mourn, or to light a candle. But I am absolutely destroyed if anyone sees my grief. It has to be personal and private. When I'm by myself, I acknowledge my grief, shed my tears, and then go about my duties of the day. But that's just my personality; that's just the way it works for me.

When Papa died in 1947, my body suffered a terrible shock. I loved him very, very much. Most people love their fathers. Still, I think Papa meant a little more to me because the bond between us was so close. And when he left, it sometimes felt as though a part of my own body, a part of my own mind, had been ripped away.

It was a difficult, challenging year, 1947. During the course of it, fourteen women, as volunteers, began the Women's Division of Cerebral Palsy. I was one of them. That experience came about this way:

Two of my very good friends in Great Neck had children who were victims of cerebral palsy—Ethel Houseman and Betty Levinson. They asked me if I would help them. Of course I said yes. The affliction had only recently been recognized, as such. Only the symptoms were known. Doctors could at least diagnose the symptoms of a child suffering with it, and try to find a cure. But the children were only part of the problem. Because their parents were also victims. We had to learn how to deal with the parents, too.

The first task was getting the parents to recognize the fact that their child suffered from the palsy. Some of these children were in mental hospitals! We struggled to collect the money for new institutions, where the children could go for proper treatment, where their muscles could be retrained to make up for, at least temporarily, their imperfect nerves.

They were heartbreaking, those children. Their poor heads hung down, only partly because their neck muscles lacked the strength to support them. Even worse, the children couldn't bear to watch the horrified faces of people who saw them—children and grown-ups alike. Their eyes expressed their misery. They couldn't talk coherently, but the look in their eyes was steeped in misery.

We were all volunteers. And I can never give enough credit to the volunteers of America, wherever they work. Because it is through their dedication that so many inroads have been made into the treatment of cerebral palsy, cancer, multiple sclerosis and so many other diseases. Look what was accomplished in fighting infantile paralysis. Let that be an example to us.

It was hard work getting the Women's Division started. After a strenuous week of lecturing to volunteer groups I went to visit my father in Phoenix and had a severe hemorrhage while I was there. After an examination, Papa's doctor told me to go home and have a hysterectomy. "If you don't," he said, "you're going to have cancer."

Well, you can imagine how I felt. But I had to stay in Phoenix until after Papa's operation was over and his breathing got better. Weeks later, when he was well enough to go, he and Mama returned to Chicago, and I came home. Mama had told me to go to a doctor as soon as I got back.

I did. When I entered his office he again gave me the Pap smear and examination. When it was over, he said, "I understand your father's been quite ill."

I said, "Yes, but he's much better now. He'll soon be fine."

"Well, Virginia," he said, "people don't live forever."

"What are you talking about? Don't say such a thing. My father's only seventy-four years old. He's brilliant, and he just has a prostate condition, that's all."

So the doctor said to me, "Well, Virginia, everybody has to go."

"Doctor," I said, "I don't appreciate this conversation. I'd like you please to just finish your examination, because I want to go home. Mama's with Daddy in Chicago. And I've just gotten Lynn all ready for camp, and I want to go home."

"All right," he said, "let's finish the examination."

He took the test and finished the examination. Then he asked me into his office and said, "I have to tell you something, Virginia. Your father died this morning."

Well, I have to tell you something now that I am mortally ashamed of. I screamed as you have never heard a person scream in all your life. I found out later that I almost cleared his whole waiting room. The patients out there didn't know what was happening. I screamed with all the terror and heartbreak of a barbaric cave woman. It must have been a terrible, primitive sound.

Finally, the doctor had to slap me in the face. I had never believed that Papa would die. No matter what onslaughts he faced, Papa would live forever. After being with him so recently all that time in Arizona, I was totally destroyed because I hadn't been with him at the end. But to the day I die I will thank God for this, because his passing was not a pretty one or a tranquil one. God spared me an image that would have been with me, I'm sure, the rest of my life.

The doctor explained that when my family had called me at home to notify me of Papa's death, they learned I was at the doctor's office. They had told the doctor that my father would have wanted nothing more than for me to be examined. To take the Pap smear first, please, and tell me afterward.

That was thirty years ago. At that time, the Pap smear was almost 95 percent effective. I was in the ineffective 5 percent. The test was negative.

Four years passed. I continued to hemorrhage. I was subject to periods of depression over Papa's death, I was always tired. I went from one doctor to another, including four famous specialists. Some told me my problems were psychosomatic; some told me they were due to nerves. Some told me my problems would disappear with the change of life. One doctor was willing to bet money that I would never have any trouble.

Finally, a friend sent me to her doctor, and he said, "If things don't get better, I would like to do a

D & C on you, which is a diagnostic curettage." Then something came up and I never went back.

It got to be 1951. At the same time my physical problems were increasing, I was aware of a renewed desire to be around people, to communicate with them. I had always enjoyed people, and sought to make friends. When I graduated from Francis Parker, the yearbook prophesied: "Virginia . . . is vitally alive and willing to participate in all the functions of the community in which she moves. Her numerous friends are her only drawback for she is only one person and cannot devote herself enough to each one."

I was a teenager then, fifteen and a half years old, which is not the most unselfish period of life. But in me was this desire to be loved and to have friends. Friends have always meant a great, great deal to me. Strangely, looking back, I remember this foretaste of destiny. You have to believe me, please. I beg of you to look for the signs of destiny in your life, because they are there.

Alfred Adler, the great associate of Sigmund Freud, spoke to us at Francis Parker when I was eight. He looked into the eyes of those little children, and spoke to them in a tongue foreign to him, with a heavy, guttural accent. "Look at you, my liebchens," he said. "Every one is a talent, a power." And a little eight-year-old girl named Virginia Komiss heard him and remembered. This power is in us. I don't care what it is. If you cook in your kitchen, if you make patch-work quilts, if you read to the sick and elderly, if you write letters for a blind person, you have the power in you to serve, to do something for life.

I feel it every day, this power, it doesn't matter what I'm doing. I feel it when I'm addressing the Junior League, and I feel it when I'm pushing a vacuum cleaner. There are big moments in your life, and there are lesser ones. It doesn't matter. The power is always there. I felt this power, this sense of destiny, when Papa died, and I felt it during the International Beauty Show that year, when I was hemorrhaging so terribly it was almost impossible to finish.

After I finally got through with the last appearance,

I went to lunch with a friend, Pearl Vale. She took one look at me and said, "Ginny, you look terrible. What's the matter with you?"

"I was already feeling rotten enough," I said. "I want to thank you very much for making me feel worse."

"You have black rings under your eyes," she said. "You usually have such pep, and today you can hardly move. What's the matter with you? Have you been to a doctor?"

"I've been to a dozen," I said. "And every single doctor I'm sent to is the head of a hospital. Don't doctors work under anybody anymore? The maharajah's wife goes to my doctor. Or the Aga Khan, or the Duchess of Rochefort. I'm ready to take pot luck with an intern. I mean, apparently the maharajah's wife doesn't have my condition."

"Stop kidding, Virginia. It's not funny. You're going with me to my doctor. I'm calling him this minute." Then what she did was the most wonderful thing a person could do. She went right to the phone.

Now let's talk about destiny. Let's follow the finger of destiny.

We went to the doctor's office that afternoon. You remember the doctor who delivered Lynn? Well, here's another short one. Dr. Virgil Damon, five feet two. This was one of the most fascinating repetitions of my life, never having to be embarrassed by a physical examination. Afterward, the doctor said, "You may have had a hemorrhage, but I don't think it disturbed your pregnancy."

"My *what!*" I said.

"Relax, dear. There's nothing wrong. I think you're pregnant!"

The Will to Survive

"Oh, my God," I said. Lynn, our only child, wasn't yet a teenager. "I'm ashamed for the neighbors," I said. As a matter of fact, I was thrilled to death. Employing that strange reasoning we sometimes use when we lose someone we love, I thought, Well, maybe Papa will come back to me as a child.

The doctor took a test, to be on the safe side, but he was convinced I was pregnant. Three days later, he called to say that the test came back negative so they retook it and it came back positive. I had waited to be sure before letting Harry know. When I told him, he said, "This is impossible."

"Now you can be a proud father again," I said.

"They'll think I'm the grandfather," moaned Harry. "How can you do this to me?"

I didn't know. Lynn was incredulous too. What could she say to her friends? This was living, undeniable proof that her parents had done it twice. Once was more than enough. Besides, the first time, before she was born, didn't count. That was all a mistake. But twice! Twice was mortifying. What could she tell her friends?

I was delighted. This was the most youthful thing that had happened to my body since I had to wear braces. Just when Lynn was growing up and becoming an adult, there would be someone to take her place when she left home. In the meantime, Lynn decided, I ought to be confined to the attic. There I would live out the remaining months of my pregnancy. No visitors would be allowed. My food would be left on a tray at the door. I could go out at night for a breath of air—joking, of course.

During the night of June 12, in the third month, I started to hemorrhage badly. I knew I was losing the child. I woke up Harry. We called for an ambulance. When it came, it was staffed by women I had trained for Red Cross during the war. And there I was, giving them instructions. My back-seat driving takes a back seat to no one. One thing about it: When the dear Lord takes me, I will still be trying to tell the driver which way to go, how fast, how slow. I am the worst, the *worst*. I admit it.

The doctor, who was waiting, told me if the pain wasn't eased by morning, he'd do a D & C. A D & C is a therapeutic procedure which can justify an abortion as legal in certain cases. Afterward, when the doctor told me I'd lose the baby, I felt that maybe God was protecting me from what might have been a maimed child. Nature, however cruel at times, has a wonderful way of safeguarding us.

I had never thought I'd have Lynn. When she was born healthy, it seemed like a miracle. Now, I knew it must be better to lose this child. I believe I was born with the power to accept the inevitable. Thinking back over all the catastrophic experiences I've had, my response to necessary things has been to accept them. What are you going to spend your time crying about? It's only when you know there's a fighting chance to change things that you can do otherwise.

They took me into surgery. I entered the operating room with the faith that the doctor, with the help of God, would finally make me well. All my physical troubles, all my travail, would be taken away, and I would be healthy again.

That was all I knew until I came out from under the anesthesia. The sun was waiting to greet me. It shone through openings between the slats of the Venetian blinds at the window. I was alone and my body and mind felt tranquil. The shafts of sunlight were like a ladder to heaven, a harbinger of peace.

As I lay there testing my senses, adjusting them to the knowledge that I had undergone an operation, the doctor entered. He was one of the handsomest men I knew, but his face was whiter than the walls. I could tell from his expression that something was amiss, but it wasn't until he had talked for a while that I knew it was serious.

"We have found something up there," he said. "You are a bright woman who can live with truth. I know you are in the professional world and you want to get your house in order."

"Get my house in order," I said. "For what?"

Then he told me. "We have found cancer."

Cancer? I leaped out of bed. My surgery had been over no more than two hours, but my anger was so fierce I wanted to shake him bodily. I do not know to this day what kept me from it. I became absolutely wild. I said, "What do you mean, I have cancer? What are you trying to tell me? Are you trying to tell me that I'm going to die?"

He ordered me back to bed, but then I became hysterical again. I don't think I ever acted like that before or since except when Papa died and later when I lost my brother.

"Please, please control yourself," the doctor said. "You must calm down. If I'd thought you'd be like this, I'd never have told you."

"You told me I'm going to die," I cried.

"I didn't say you're going to die," he said. "I thought you were intelligent. I thought you'd want to get your house in order."

"What house?" I shouted. "I haven't even built a house yet. I've got the basement and maybe the floor of the first story, but everything else is waiting to be built." Then I began to shout for Harry.

Later, I found out that Harry and my wonderful friend Nan Goddard had been waiting in my room for my return from surgery. When the doctor gave Harry the news, giving me from three to six months to live, he had fainted, breaking his fall by toppling against Nan. As it turned out, that was, for Harry, the beginning of a long and complicated nervous breakdown that continued for several years. He went into total nervous shock.

There will always be speculation, pro and con, on

whether a doctor should or should not tell the cancer patient of the condition? Who can know for sure? Some patients hasten the dying process the moment they hear the news. Others fight back.

In the back of my own mind at the time was the certain decision to take my own life, to do it myself instead of letting cancer do it for me. If I had cancer and was going to die, it would be by my hand and not the hand of time.

As I became more rational, I decided that there must be at least a chance to survive, that if my life had any purpose or meaning, there had to be a fighting chance that I could live. "Maybe it isn't all over," I said. "Maybe it isn't. And holding on tight to that almost certain impossibility, I began to make plans with the doctor for the second operation.

Dr. Damon was a giant of a doctor. He sought the services of a man he thought was the most qualified.

He wanted Dr. Howard Taylor to perform it. When I asked him if he could hold out any hope for me, he replied, "We're going to do the best we can." The next day, June 14, I met Dr. Taylor. He told me to stop worrying and put myself in his hands, the way a good student does with a good teacher, and I was reassured.

But later, alone in my room, my confidence wore thin. Suppose I died. Who, I wondered, would come to my funeral? How would I be remembered? In my mind, I tried to picture the chapel, to hear the words to be spoken in my behalf. I began to grieve for all the unkind things I had ever done, to atone for my shortcomings. I thought of all I wanted for Harry, for Lynn.

Time diminishes the outline of memories, and I'm not certain now exactly when this took place in the sequence of events that followed, but one afternoon not long afterward, I knew without question what I was going to do. Suddenly, aloud to myself, I made my decision. By then my confidence had vanished altogether. "I'm not going to live," I said. "There's no point in dragging Harry and Lynn through the terrible suffering of a long terminal illness that might even kill them. I am going to the window and it will be over in a minute."

I felt bereft and abandoned, completely, hopelessly alone. I called up Harry and told him what I was going to do.

I walked to the window and looked down. It would be so easy. . . . And as I stood there, on the threshold of what I thought would be an easier death, I waited for some sign from God to tell me what to do, to show me the way of His will. Where are You, God? I asked. Won't You tell me the right thing to do?

Suddenly, Papa's voice came back to me again. "Ginny," I heard him say, as clearly as if he were standing beside me, and as he had when I was a child, "God talks to you all the time."

Then where, I wondered, was God now? What had I done to be forsaken by Him? What were my sins? Were they so great as all that? Papa, I wanted to shout, *where is God now?*

And then I heard Papa's voice again. "If you listen and don't talk," he said, "you'll hear Him."

I listened. I did. I put my trust in God, as Papa had always taught me to do, And that was what saved me from jumping. By the time the nurse reached me, I was calm again. "Please call Harry," I said, "and tell him I'm all right." They made sure, however, from that time on, that I had constant attendance.

Lynn was told that I'd had a miscarriage. Fortunately, she was soon to leave on a cross-country tour anyway. I wanted, above all, to spare her this terrible ordeal.

Expressions of sympathy poured in, from strangers, from people I'd worked with, from friends. Flowers arrived by the basketful. I couldn't smell them. My senses were paralyzed with terror. People would come and go. I was aware of them and deeply grateful for their sympathy and presence. But it wasn't people I lived with during those terrible days and nights as I prepared for surgery, it was fear. Fear was my constant companion.

When I tried to joke with the parade of technicians who came to check my blood, or my metabolism, or whatever, they had an invariable response: "In a case like yours," I'd hear, "we have to take every kind of precaution possible."

"Thanks a lot," I would summon up the humor and fortitude to reply. "You're very, very good for the nervous system."

On the day before the operation, I asked Dr. Taylor to grant me one favor. "Of course," he said. "What do you want to eat? Chocolate cake?"

"No," I said. "I want to go to the beauty parlor. I don't know what tomorrow may bring, but no one has ever seen me dark at the roots when I'm standing up, and they're not going to see me that way when I'm laid out."

They sent a nurse with me to David Roberts, who was my hairdresser then, and he had a packed house. I had no sooner walked in than I told everyone present my whole predicament. Well, it was pandemonium, because no one had ever heard of anyone living through cancer. I remember that Betty and Jane Kean were there with their mother. And my college friend June Moses came to meet me with her sister Georgine, who brought me two ounces of Joy. "That's a hundred dollars," I said. "One ounce would have been enough."

It was not quite like a party. No one was laughing. I had a manicure, a pedicure, the works. "Oh my God," I kept saying to June and Georgine, "do you believe this is happening to me?"

For a little while, I was able to forget my fear, to pretend that things were the way they used to be, that time was on my side. It was almost as though I would never die. Sometimes, when fear and pain are too much to bear, God provides us with insulation. And I think that talking it out is one of the best kinds. Talking with those girls, I was able to push the thought of tomorrow's operating room far, far away.

When I left, I figured at least I'd have the best dressed face at Forest Lawn. I learned later that they closed the beauty parlor for the day soon after.

By the next day, the day of the operation, my light-headedness had vanished to be replaced by that old menace, deadly fear.

I pleaded with the doctor to give me sodium pentothal to prepare me for the main anesthesia because I was so mortally afraid of it, and he did. As a child, to prepare me for my tonsillectomy, Mama had told me I was going to have my picture taken. And when the mask came toward my face, I thought they were trying to kill me. Since then, anesthesia had become more frightening than the operation itself.

Perhaps it was the drug, perhaps it was inner fortitude, but when I went into surgery for either the end or a new beginning, I went without fear. I felt at peace with God, because I knew I was a part of His will.

And right after the operation itself, I felt no pain. When I asked a nurse later why I had felt no pain, she told me she believed it was due to the delicacy of the surgeon's hands. All of Harry's sisters had volunteered to give me blood, should I need it, and when I came down from the recovery room ten hours later, they were waiting. Harry's face was a white blur, I know, and he must have kissed me, but for another day and a half *everything* was a blur.

When I came to at last, it was the twenty-third of June. My operation was performed on the twenty-first, my mother's birthday, a kind of miraculous coincidence.

I felt no recovery pain whatsoever. And when I got up to walk, I stood absolutely straight, as straight as a ramrod. That was almost unheard of, and I've always believed that my body was obeying the will of my spirit then. I know my spirit was unbent.

The doctor was confident that he'd removed all the cancer, but he wanted to give me radiation anyway. What they did was strip me naked and have me lie down on a table. Then they marked off my stomach with a blue pencil. It must have looked like a subdevelopment, like a housing project. "Tell me," I said, as they measured me off, "do you think the waterfront property is any more valuable? I'd like to invest."

Well, they were hysterical, those dedicated scientists. Altogether, I had thirty-five intensive X-ray treatments and they never made me sick. A little squeamish sometimes, but nothing more than that.

That was an ordeal, that was a mountaintop of an experience. Climbing up, sometimes only half aware of where I was and completely unsure of where I was going, I don't know what kept me from falling off. Looking back, I think it was destiny, that God was with me every step of the way, that He was preparing me for a job He wanted me to do. That's why I feel a sense of mission about those who suffer from that terrible disease. That is why, I believe, God granted me a second birth.

Because I was reborn. I know that as surely as I know that the stars are at home in their courses, the tides at home in their ebb and flow, the baby at home in his bed. We are, all of us, engaged in His work, each in his own way, and in all the world I could ask for no greater opportunity to serve.

Triumph from Despair

Harry's health was not good. A period of depression followed my battle with cancer. He too had been plagued with physical illness, and had undergone serious plastic surgery in recent years. All of these operations failed to call forth the fortitude Harry usually displayed in the face of physical pain.

Now, however, his problem was emotional. He consulted a psychiatrist who suggested shock treatments. Harry agreed to undergo such a program, and after a series of treatments he seemed to improve considerably.

Then, once more, fate took us firmly by the hand. The building in which Harry's business was located —the Guttenberg costume collection, containing hundreds and hundreds of historic, irreplaceable theatrical costumes—was bombed by arsonists, resulting in a fire that virtually destroyed the inventory. What fire didn't destroy, in large part, water damage did. A tenant in the building had hired men to burn his floor to collect insurance. Several people died in the fire.

We struggled to save what we could. Harry and I even took up a daily vigil on the sidewalk outside the building in hopes of preserving what was left. Eventually, we were able to reopen the business in another location, but Harry's already frail nerves were severely damaged by the disaster. He wanted to be hospitalized, and we arranged for him to enter the Institute for Living in Hartford.

Meantime, I was getting six-month checkups following my cancer surgery, and would continue to for a total of five years. I don't know what we would have done without our good friend Tom Bosley, my first cousin, who had come to New York from Chicago to become an actor and was staying with us. He was a wonderful companion to Lynn, and an antidote for gloom to everyone. Tommy was full of his experiences working at a series of odd jobs. Eventually he created the role of New York's Mayor LaGuardia in the smash musical *Fiorello*, for which he won a Tony, and went on to have a great success in the role of Howard Cunningham, the father, in *Happy Days*.

Finally, Harry was able to come home to continue his successful recuperation with us.

All my experience with illness—to quote Aunt Celia, "It runs in the family"—had convinced me that I had a responsibility not ever to refuse help to charity. One day a man named Sol Schwartz called to ask if I would agree to speak at a telethon for arthritis. He knew of me through his wife, who had heard me speak at luncheons for Cerebral Palsy.

I said yes at once. Then I asked him what a telethon was. He explained that we'd be on the air seventeen nonstop hours, and that we'd need an additional twenty or so for preliminary work in the studio. All the big stars—Milton Berle was prominent among them—were volunteering their time and talent.

I had always thought arthritis was a disease brought on by age, but Mr. Schwartz made it clear that youth was no barrier. Many children would be present, he said, who had never known what it was like to live without pain.

Backstage preparation for a telethon, no matter how well organized it is—and most are very well organized indeed—is sometimes frantic. It was a completely new experience for me and I was interested in all that went on. I was fascinated by the challenge, and only disappointed that the studio audience seemed apathetic and listless, as though they were there to sit back and be entertained. Not only that, the telephones were not ringing. There was a depressing lack of response from tuners-in.

When the time came for me to speak, I stood at

the microphone and looked at the audience. I didn't know what to do. My problem wasn't nervousness. I've never been nervous talking to people. I just didn't know how to get them concerned about the millions of people who suffered from arthritis every year, every month, every week, every day. Finally, I decided to tell them the truth.

"If you were suddenly to meet the angel of death who asked you what you have done in this life that was wonderful or even worthwhile, what would you say?" I began. "If you had only one week left to live, what would you do with this week?"

The audience seemed to be more attentive. I sent up a prayer to God to help me stay on the right track.

"This was the question I asked myself when I looked into the mirror after the doctor told me I had cancer."

Suddenly the audience was completely quiet. I could feel the silence, sense it; it was almost tangible. Even the backstage staff had stopped at their labors to listen. Gathering strength from this response, I continued: "The doctor told me that I had cancer and had only a few months to live."

There was an audible collective gasp from the audience. The word "cancer" was verboten, not to be spoken in the never-never world of life, because it was a synonym for death. Yet I was filled with the truth of my own experience, and I suddenly wanted desperately to share it with the millions of unseen viewers who might never have another chance to learn about the miracle of hope, when everything seemed hopeless.

I told the audience what had happened to me. I couldn't help myself. It was almost as though a force was telling me to, forcing me to relive the terrible pain of my own ordeal, which had turned the tables on negative thinking, on hopelessness. I wanted to show them that people everywhere, in all walks of life, however they are afflicted, have the opportunity to help conquer disease, to wrest faith out of anguish, triumph from despair.

Finally, I did something I hadn't done since I was

a child: I wept. I completely broke down in front of a group of people and cried.

The response was galvanic. Phone calls deluged the switchboard. The telephones, whose silence had been tomblike, were ringing with a joyous message of reassurance and hope to arthritis victims all over the country, all over the world. They were saying that people cared. Indifference had been replaced by a resounding affirmation of love and support. The pledges of money were like the promise of spring after the bitterest of winters.

And I, too, was altered. I will always believe that the wonderful response to my message helped me to get well. Somehow, my body also was strengthened by this bond. Along with the victims of arthritis, I had new reason to hope.

I went on to do many telethons for a number of charities—Multiple Sclerosis, Mental Health, Muscular Dystrophy, among others—and I learned a lot about medicine during those experiences. I also learned a lot about television. But the most important lessons those telethons taught me were about people. They are wonderful. There is nothing else in the world like them. United in a common cause, people everywhere will open their hearts to their fellow human beings.

Many friends in show business have told me that I damaged my career by identifying myself so closely with disease. That may be true. But I felt then exactly the way I feel now. I had no choice. If I could help call the world's attention to those terrible killers, and what research can do to increase the victims' chances for life, I had to do it. For me, there was no other way.

My own recovery was proceeding well. Lynn was growing into a beautiful young lady, and Harry, too, was thriving.

Then, in September 1952, the telephone rang again. The caller was a stranger, but his message had a familiar ring. He identified himself and then asked me a question:

"Have you ever seen a TV show called *Food for Thought?*"

I hadn't, and told him so.

"We have a girl on the program who has to leave. Do you think you could take her place?"

I didn't say yes right away. I'm not completely without shame. I told him I'd like very much to watch the show and see. Could I let him know? That was no problem.

Then I asked him how he had happened to call me.

"My wife used to see you on the Zeke Manners show. She thought you had a terrific personality."

Well, that made me feel good. I watched *Food for Thought* the next time it came on.

Then I said yes.

It was a terrific show. This time we weren't preparing food to eat. This time we were preparing food to think about, fodder for the mind. Viewers wrote to the program outlining problems they found most difficult to cope with. Experts in the given field were invited to the studio to discuss the problems and offer advice. The best letter of the year won a prize.

Our goals were modest and so was our budget. My agents had wisely had the forethought to make it a contractual provision that if my first month was successful, the show would be rechristened *Virginia Graham and Food for Thought*. Well, that was the name of the show from 1952 till 1957.

We tackled subjects in many fields: health, politics, education, science, entertainment. My secretary from the beauty shows—marvelous Marie Monell— was with me again and we had some wonderful adventures with people in all walks of life. After President Eisenhower suffered his coronary, four doctors came on the program to talk about heart trouble. And do you want to know something? In New York City, *Food for Thought* outpulled *The Kate Smith Show!*

It was during those years that eighty cured cancer patients, including me, went to Washington to demonstrate for the total cured-of-cancer population, which even then numbered 800,000 remarkable people.

It was also during those years that Ralph Edwards, a remarkable man himself, chose me to be the subject of his program, *This Is Your Life.* Women's clubs around the country had persuaded him. That show was noteworthy for many reasons, and very high among them, I'd place the element of surprise.

One day Ralph Edwards called me to say that he was presenting the life of Jack Hausman, who was highly instrumental in founding the Cerebral Palsy organization. Would I agree to introduce Jack on the program? He was moving the show that one night from California to New York just to honor Jack.

I had been invited to speak at a dinner at the Waldorf on the night of his show, for the New York State Commission Against Discrimination. It was a subject I had very strong feelings about, and I told Ralph Edwards about the conflicting date, but agreed to see if we could work something out. The Commission people were cooperative. They'd put me on first; then I could get to the television studio in time for the introduction.

So far, so good. Then Harry refused to go to the dinner with me—something he'd never done before. Well, I was very perplexed with him but went on alone, figuring everyone has the right to say no once in a while, even a loyal husband. (Today, I'd say *especially* a loyal husband.)

When I got to the theater, there was Harry, waiting for me. That seemed peculiar, too. Why should he be at the theater when he refused to go to the Waldorf? Shaking my head at the vagaries of men, I took his arm and we went inside and took our seats.

I recognized some of Jack Hausman's friends, who were already seated, and we gaily waved to each other. Meantime, I was rehearsing in my head my introduction to this fine man. Now remember: This is live television. There is no tape in the cameras. Never before in history had it been possible to make a fool of yourself in front of so many people at one and the same time—so quickly, so to speak.

Ralph Edwards had told me I'd have forty-five

seconds. I wasn't nervous, but I was excited. I felt honored to introduce Jack. My biggest problem would be trying to do justice to him in such a short time.

Then I saw Dr. Laurance Jones. He was the head of the Piney Creek School for Nergo children in Alabama, where segregation was still the rule. He'd done a tremendous job with the children there, and he'd been a wonderful, very articulate guest on *Virginia Graham and Food for Thought*. I was a little puzzled that he was in the audience tonight, but there were any number of ways he might have known Jack Hausman. When Dr. Jones pointed at me shaking his head in the yes direction—up and down, I was even more puzzled. Maybe he thought I didn't recognize him.

Then the minute hand of the studio clock was on the hour. It was time. Ralph Edwards was walking toward me. As he approached Dr. Jones, he stopped in his tracks and I was puzzled afresh. That wasn't on the agenda; I was supposed to be first.

"Dr. Jones," Ralph Edwards said, "I know the audience of America wants to know how much money you've received for your school." Dr. Jones rose to respond, and as they talked I decided that the good doctor had been trying to tell me before that he was also an early part of the program.

Yet I couldn't help wondering why Ralph Edwards hadn't told me, though he must have his reasons, whatever they were.

Then Dr. Jones sat down and Ralph Edwards approached me.

"You're Virginia Graham, aren't you?" he said. "You have a television show."

"Yes," I said. "But if you see it in California, you have to have a good tailwind because I'm a local yokel and my show doesn't go out of New York."

Nothing was going the way it was supposed to, that was for sure.

"And you've worked for Cerebral Palsy," he continued.

"Oh, yes, as has Mr. Hausman," I said. I was wound up tight to begin my gem of an introduction. You know, get ready . . . get set . . . I had barely opened my mouth to go, to let out the first glorious pearl, when I was rudely outmaneuvered.

"And you've . . ." As Ralph Edwards began to detail my small accomplishments, an eerie feeling crept over me. It was unlike any eerie feeling I'd ever felt before. Cold shivers coursed through every nerve in my body. I was one big electric shock, because, suddenly, I knew what was happening.

"Brace yourself, girl." This was Ralph Edwards speaking. "Virginia Graham, *this is your life.*"

"Did I Find a Girl for You!"

Oh, I became a human waterfall! My eyes poured out enough cascading tears to fill a reservoir. Everybody was there: Mama, my brother Juddy, Lynn, who had come in from Endicott Junior College, and, of course, Harry. The people I had worked with: Kenny, the incredibly fine cerebral-palsied young man who had loved me so much as a boy that I had been enabled to help him walk; Kathy Thieme, from *Family Circle* magazine—an early sponsor of *Food for Thought*, who was also a cancer survivor; Ruth Curtin, from the very first arthritis telethon. She and three handicapped friends were now the Fourdettes. In a Ford automobile, they traveled everywhere, raising money for artificial limbs, reading to the blind, doing whatever they could to minister to human suffering.

And friends galore. It was an emotional experience that is with me to this day. In a word, it was unforgettable. Later, at the party at the Essex House, I learned of the incredibly complicated subterfuge that Harry and the other participants had engaged in, to assure my complete surprise.

People from all over the country called up at the party and during the days that followed. Twelve thousand people wrote letters. Ralph told me later that up to that time the only person on the program who received a bigger response was Lillian Roth.

It was an exhausted but strangely exhilarated Virginia Graham who finally went home with Harry that night.

Early the next morning, the phone rang. I picked up the receiver and said, "Hello?"

"This is Mitchell Benson calling, Virginia. How are you?"

I allowed as how I was fine. "But I haven't been to bed yet. Last night was the most thrilling night of my whole life."

Mitchell Benson produced a radio program called *Weekday* on NBC. It was, essentially, a forerunner of *Monitor*. Two weeks earlier, I'd talked to him about the possibility of replacing Margaret Truman, who was cohost with Mike Wallace, and who was rumored to be leaving. Mitchell Benson had been very polite during our talk, but when I left, the feeling I got was very much don't call us, we'll call you.

"What time can you be down at the office?" he said. "We think you're just the right person to replace Margaret Truman on *Weekday*. She's definitely retiring from radio next week. Can you be here this morning?"

"I can make it at eleven-thirty, before I go to the studio for my TV show."

"Fine," he said. "And if you have a lawyer or an agent, bring him with you. We're in business."

When I got to his office I met Mike Wallace, and also Allen Ludden, who had become associated with the show after *College Bowl* went off the air. It was March 1956. This was my first staff job at NBC, and the salary was my best so far. I was very pleased.

That night, after I'd told Harry and Lynn, I called Mama to report the good news. I gave her all the basic facts about what I'd be doing in the new job, and told her I was thrilled.

"Oh, isn't that sweet," said Mama. "I'm so happy for you." End of conversation.

Later that night, Mama called back: "Cousin Dora wants to know. Is this another charity that you're doing?"

"Yes," I said. "NBC—No Better Charity. It put Milton Berle through school, and now it's paying for my postgraduate course."

It was very hard for her to grasp the idea that anyone would pay me for talking.

Still later, another call from Mama: "You're taking Margaret Truman's place?"

"Yes," I said. Just imagine!

"Well," said Mama, "that's terrible. How can the network do that? How can they take the President's daughter off? Aren't you ashamed? People are going to hate you. Since when can you replace the President's daughter?"

They might be paying me, but it would come to no good. There was no winning with Mama.

Mike Wallace was an incurable practical joker and I love him dearly. He subjected me to the most appalling series of practical jokes, both off the air and on. Hotfoots. Burning my scripts as I read them to our audience on the air. Throwing paper clips into my décolletage. I thought he was absolutely hilarious; I couldn't stop laughing. We would always be united by a deep bond of affection, but meantime Mike enjoyed watching me break up over the airwaves. He knew he was funny. That was the joy for him. I was a natural target for his humor.

Finally, one producer had seen enough. He cooked up a plan to help me get even with Mike. One of our features was reading letters from listeners aloud on the air and talking about the problems they raised. This producer dreamed up a situation in which I would tape the feature in advance. When that part of the program went on, the next day at three, the tape would be playing, unbeknownst to Mike. He would think we were broadcasting live, as usual, whereas in reality no one could hear us except the people in the studio.

Here's what happened:

Three o'clock approached on the day in question. We were talking quietly during a break in the broadcast. "Now, Mike," I said, "today I'm going into a very delicate subject." Remember, these were the days when the networks were very sensitive about any allusion to sex.

"You are?" said Mike, somewhat surprised, since he was aware of my deep moral convictions. This particular part of the show always demanded concentration and was one of his favorite times for horse-play.

"Yes," I said. "I'm answering a letter from a woman who's written that she is terribly worried because her husband either has lost interest in her or has another woman."

"You wouldn't dare," said Mike. "You just wouldn't dare on the air!"

"Listen, Mike," I said, "don't start with me because this woman is in trouble. She needs help and I'm going to handle it delicately. But don't you laugh. If you laugh . . ."

"Virginia! Me laugh?" He was warming up already, the soul of innocence. "Would I do anything like that to *you?*" The very idea!

"Of course you would."

A producer quickly intervened to reassure Mike that we had cleared both the letter and my response to it with the NBC continuity department, and please to behave himself.

The "On the Air" sign lighted up. From this point on, Mike thought we were broadcasting live, but we weren't.

"Dear ladies and gentlemen," I began, "I'm about to talk about something that could be a little touchy, but I feel we are all mature people. This is the letter:

Dear Miss Graham,
    I have been sharing for twenty years a double bed with my husband. We've had a good life. But of late I've noticed a tremendous change in his attitude. No matter how attractive I make myself and how much I perfume my body, he turns coldly from me in the bed and I am lying frustrated and full of questions. Is he finding me undesirable or is he robbed of his manhood?"

Mike was turning blue with combined shock and moral outrage. He couldn't contain himself. Strange choking sounds emerged from his throat.

"Now I must say to you," I continued, deadpan,

"the troubled woman who wrote this letter and all others with the same problem, that men do go through a difficult period called the—"

"*Hru-hurff-urgh!*" It was Mike, unable to restrain himself any longer.

Turning from the microphone, I let him have it: "Mike Wallace," I shouted, "this is the last time this is going to happen. Ladies and gentlemen, he's driving me crazy. He's done nothing but harangue and harass me. He's the most evil man. He's made me laugh. He's tried..."

Mike had turned white. All the color had left his face. Making a grab for the microphone, he struggled to undo my damage:

"Ladies and gentlemen," he pleaded, "ladies and gentlemen..." Then quickly to the sound booth, "Go to music, go to music!"

My goodness! The sound engineer couldn't hear him. Either that, or the sound engineer was no longer able to understand plain English. Mike was gesticulating wildly. If his voice couldn't send the message, maybe his body could.

But I wasn't through. "He's a devil, that Mike Wallace," I continued, "the meanest man I ever..."

Clearly, through the glass, we could see a technician lift the telephone from its cradle. Then we heard his loud voice answering the call. "I'm sorry, General Sarnoff. Yes, General Sarnoff, we'll get them off the air right away." General Robert Sarnoff was President of the National Broadcasting Company.

Mike was in an advanced stage of hysteria. "Ladies and gentlemen," he beseeched, "Virginia Graham is a fine woman. She's devoted her life to charity. But overwork—"

"Don't apologize for me!" I screamed, glaring at him. "Apologize for *yourself*. You cad. You no-good ...you've ruined my life and I hate you!"

"Oh, ladies and gentlemen," groaned Mike, "I've pushed her too far. It's my fault. You've got to forgive her. Don't listen..."

Poor Mike was now tearing around the small, enclosed studio like a caged wild animal, pounding his fists on the soundproof glass. Not one single person would come to his aid. All the technicians seemed strangely preoccupied.

Finally, I could stand it no longer. I laughed. And laughed. And laughed. They had to pound me on the back to stop my laughter. Finally, dawn broke and Mike realized that he was the butt of a practical joke. He was so sick with a combination of relief and exhaustion and outrage, he had to be taken home.

The tape of that episode, made by one of the technicians, is still played today as one of the classic examples of *faux pas* on radio.

There was no more practical joking. Mike Wallace had received his comeuppance. Perhaps he had met his match at last.

Allen Ludden and I often discuss that incident. We adore Mike Wallace and have only the highest regard for his ability. He is the finest sight reader, and has the purest diction and a mind to match. Best of all, he has a divine wife, Lorraine. I used to say to her, "Pray the show stays on forever. He takes out all his shenanigans on me, so you only get what's left."

For a while, I was doing both *Weekday* and *Food for Thought*. How I managed such a heavy work schedule, I'll never understand. But manage I did. For one thing, it was a heck of a challenge. And when *Weekday* went off the air in 1956, I set my sights on the phenomenal new adventure in late-night viewing, the Jack Paar show.

The Paar show was the first real talk show to reach such an incredibly wide audience. It was a new concept in television and it was a smashing success. It was changing the bedtime habits of millions of people. It was a daily subject of conversation, even for people who didn't watch it. "Did you see the Paar show last night?" became the status question of the next day. It was always a good subject for coffee-break rehashing. Nothing quite like it had ever been seen before. And little wonder. It was outrageously entertaining.

Thinking back, I'm sure I must have recognized very quickly that I had a natural affinity for talking—

in front of a camera and microphone, on the telephone, at a bus stop, undergoing surgery, anywhere.
There's some of the exhibitionist in all of us. It may
be deeply buried in some people, but nonetheless I
believe it is there. And talk shows are a kind of magic.
They give us instant access to some very interesting
people.

I wanted to be one of them. I talked to my agent.
"Please get me on Jack Paar." My agent could not
make much headway. He was having trouble getting
through to the producer. For weeks, I beseeched him:
"Do something. Do anything. But get me on that
show." I knew it was right for me.

Then, when my agent was finally able to make a
pitch for me, the reaction wasn't encouraging. Paar's
producer had been pleasant but firm: "Listen. I'm
sure Virginia Graham is a lovely woman. I know she
does a lot of good work for charity. But I don't think
she'd be interesting to Jack. She's a do-gooder, and
when people are up at this hour they want a more
provocative personality. I don't think she'd be right
for Jack."

But I refused to be daunted. I pestered my friends
and anyone else who might have an entrée to Jack's
good graces. It did no good whatsoever. But I was
determined to discover some way to get on that show.
There must be one somewhere, somehow. All I had to
do was find it.

Came a certain Monday. Harry and I had tickets to
the biggest hit on Broadway—Anne Bancroft and
Henry Fonda in *Two for the Seesaw*. We had sold our
house in Great Neck and bought a co-op on upper
Fifth Avenue very close to the Metropolitan Museum.
That made it not only easy to get back and forth to
work, we could also enjoy the luxury of an occasional
night on the town without having to worry about the
long drive home.

Then I got an emergency call to do the commentary for a fashion show at the Waldorf, to benefit
Boys Town of Italy. Jinx Falkenburg had been sched-
uled to appear, but Jinx was ill.

How could I say no? The people calling me were

friends and, as always, I felt I had an obligation to charity. We could see Anne Bancroft some other night.

Now if you don't remember, or weren't around in those days—or old enough to be interested—1956 was not a banner year in fashion. That was the year designers invented the Sack. It was an experiment in maternity for everyone, single or married.

I was regaling my audience at the Waldorf on the peccadillos of fashion in general, and that year in particular, when someone sent me an urgent signal from backstage: A model had fainted; kill time until the patch-up was made.

Wing it, as they say in showbiz. Well, I fastened my seat belt and took off into the wild blue yonder. I was going to see how far I could fly. Taking my whole enormous family, my work, my opinions about everything under the sun as my traffic pattern, I improvised fifteen minutes of nonstop in-flight chatter, jokes, and wisecracks. And the audience went wild. They laughed at everything I said. If they didn't laugh, they applauded. I was in heaven. That's where my plane had landed.

Now, unbeknownst to me, in the audience that night was a fabulous woman named Elsa Maxwell. To those of you who may not recall her, Elsa Maxwell was an elegant but completely unpretentious woman who met royalty and us with the same down-to-earth aplomb. She was famous for her parties and her friends, and she had a lot of both.

Every Tuesday night, on the Paar show, Jack would say, "Well, Elsa, what have you been doing?" And she would amuse his listeners with tales of high life and low. She was, in essence, a kind of town crier, like the old village watchmen who used to call out, "Twelve o'clock and all is well"—if such were indeed the case. She knew everybody and had done everything. My friend Monty Morgan once described both her commitment to charitable causes and her appetite for living when he said: "She did anything you wanted as long as you brought her a pastrami sandwich on rye with a pickle."

At the end of the fashion show, to my complete surprise, Elsa Maxwell came up to me when the show was over and said: "Virginia, I don't remember when I've been as entertained as I have been tonight. Tomorrow when I'm on the Jack Paar show, I wish you would listen. Because I'll tell Jack all about it."

I was enormously grateful for her reaction, but I felt certain nothing would come of it. In any case, however, I didn't intend to miss that show.

Came the time. "Well, Elsa," said Jack, in his own inimitable way, "what have you been doing?" (I can still hear that incredibly urbane voice of his.)

Elsa said, "Did I find a girl for you!"

"What do you mean?"

"I was at a fashion show last night. A woman said the nicest things about you. It was the best fashion show I ever saw. She would be a divine guest."

"What's her name?"

"Virginia Graham."

One week later, I was a guest on the Jack Paar show.

Warming Up for Girl Talk

But my debut was less than triumphant. Quite a bit less, in fact. I had come on the show prepared to talk. Instead, I was forced to listen. My fellow guest was Jack E. Leonard, an extremely funny man. And champion talker that I am, I couldn't compete with him.

During the early part of the show, the audience had laughed at my stories—a little. Later, when I was planning to have them in stitches, I didn't get a chance to open my mouth. Jack E. Leonard put on a one-man show. I was completely shattered. All my hopes had come to nothing. As a guest on the Jack Paar show, I'd turned out to be a dud.

My terrible disappointment was somewhat assuaged by one man on Jack's staff. He booked the talent for the show, and his name was Monty Morgan—the same Monty Morgan who, as an NBC staffer, had seen the kinescope of the cooking show I'd done for Ted Cott, the one that wound up on the NBC shelves years before. When Monty told me he'd seen it, I asked him how it was, because I never got a chance to see it myself. "Virginia," he said, "I said to one of the boys, 'See that girl? Brother, she's going to make it.'"

That was a kind thing for Monty to say, and I appreciated his confidence, but I certainly hadn't made it with Jack Paar.

Through my agent, I asked for another chance. The prospects, we were told, were anything but promising. A big-budget talk show is not the fitting place for second chances. That kind of show can't afford a first strikeout, let alone a second. Jack himself, however, must have had second thoughts. Maybe it wouldn't hurt to have me try again. Maybe, my second time up, I might get to first base on a scratch single. When I got the news, I was ecstatic.

This time I was better—much better. I was more relaxed, the atmosphere was more congenial. This second Paar show was the show on which I told how an old beau had recognized me on the first one. He had not seen me since I was eight. But he knew it was Virginia Komiss, he wrote, sitting up there beside Jack, because "After all, who else could look like two June Allysons?"

This was also the show that caused my career to change directions. No longer was I just the chronic tearjerker appealing for funds to support worthy causes. People must have been somewhat fatigued watching me in that role. I sold a lot of Kleenex. The minute people saw me open my mouth, they'd start to cry. It was a conditioned response, like Pavlov's dog. They didn't even have to know what sickness I was representing. Cry, then give her money. That was their sequence of events. I was a pioneer in alerting the populace to new diseases. The Mayos used to call me for the latest information. Maybe I, not Elsa Maxwell, was the true Town Crier.

Now, finally, another side of Virginia Graham could be seen at last. And in some ways, it was the most important side of all. Not only could I make people cry. I could also make them laugh. Furthermore, I could do this not only in New York City on local shows. I could do it coast-to-coast, on national television. I had always feared that my funny side might appeal to only one region. Now I had reason to hope that my humor, like laughter itself, might be universal.

Jack Paar was a wonderful man. He did a great deal for me. Two years later, I did his show while he was on vacation. But he not only helped my career in very big ways. He increased my self-esteem. He helped me grow as a person. And that, it seems to me, is what helping people is all about in the first place.

Harry and I, meantime, were growing as a couple, too. We celebrated our twenty-fifth wedding anniversary with a fabulous trip to Europe. It was incredibly exciting—London, Paris, Rome and other Italian places, including Positano. The worst language barrier was in England. I think the English, who are—and have been for hundreds of years—perhaps the most restrained people on earth, were somewhat taken aback by my high spirits. I am ebullient; they are somewhat reticent, to say the least.

Before sailing, I'd been offered a job promoting hair color for Clairol. I made the decision to take the job on the trip coming back from Europe. That job was one of the most exciting things that ever happened to me. I was their goodwill ambassador (ambassadress, excuse me). For four years, Harry and I traveled all over the country, meeting people in all walks of life and promoting the revolutionary new Clairol products.

At one and the same time, Clairol sold both the beauty parlor and the drugstore, who encouraged the woman to do it herself. I was sort of the Henry Kissinger of the hair waves. I would go to the drugstore and promote the do-it-yourself hair color. Then in one fell swoop I would go to the hairdresser's and say, "You should be grateful to us because when these people make a mess of their hair, you'll get customers." As handy as I am with my own hair, coloring is beyond me. In an emergency I might try to remove my own appendix, but I would never think of coloring my hair by myself.

Wearing my Clairol halo, I talked to people everywhere. My adventures on those journeys would fill a book. Once, in Newburgh, New York, I was about to speak to about eight hundred hairdressers. The man who introduced me was unstinting in his praise. "Now, folks," he said, "tonight we are very honored to have with us a woman who has done more for humanity than anyone else in the twentieth century." That was just the opening remark, mind you. What woman—or man—could live up to that kind of billing? Who does he think I am, I wondered. Madame Curie? Albert Schweitzer?

But he wasn't through. As I'm bracing myself to deflate such a ridiculously overblown image, he delivers his clincher: "Ladies and gentlemen, I give you Virginia Graham, the woman who invented cancer!"

Now I would like to describe exactly what happened to me at that moment. After a stunned silence, there was a smattering of applause—maybe seven people out of eight hundred were clapping. You know what that sounds like. We were in a hall that was longer than two bowling alleys built end to end. I had to rise from my seat in the rear and advance—walk—to the stage. Jack the Ripper would have felt more wanted, more pleasantly received than I did. Or Frankenstein. Every eye was on me and I have never seen such mixed emotions on the faces in any crowd. Some people wanted to laugh and others were absolutely aghast. Welcome, Virginia Graham! Welcome, sweet savior.

I went up to my beneficent friend and tried to make amends, though what I could say was nothing compared to what I could think—and did. Getting that audience to laugh was almost an exercise in futility, they were so embarrassed, but I managed to do it.

It was a demanding job. I remember at the time that a young woman called me an overachiever. We'd just been introduced. She looked me up and down and said, "So you're Virginia Graham?"

"I think so," I said, and we had a little chat. Then she left, and when she thought I was out of earshot, she said, "My God, what an overachiever!"—as though it was either a disease or a handicap.

I went back to my hotel and sat down and thought about it. Then I said to myself, "Well, I guess I am." I decided it must be some kind of ongoing role in my life—Virginia, the Overachiever, never late, always willing, nothing's too hard or too frightening for me.

I decided that it must come from Mama. Mama often made me feel that I was not quite adequate at all the things I was trying to do. Even as a child I was willing to tackle almost anything. At the same time, Mama wanted me to compensate for the liabilities of my physical being, by which I guess I mean my womanhood. Mama really and truly thought that I was in no way connected with anyone she had ever encountered before. If I wasn't some kind of throwback, I was nonetheless an enigma. She couldn't make heads or tails of me.

I think part of this was competition. While I was going to Northwestern, Mama went back to school with me. I have to report that she was thrown out of class because she got there late every day. So, on that last day, the professor told her to turn around and leave.

I went all over for Clairol. I went to women's prisons, and we talked about the grooming that is necessary for "habilitation." So many of those women weren't being rehabilitated. They had never been habilitated in the first place. I went to underprivileged areas. Those young people would come in dragging their feet and gaping at me, wondering what in the world we could have in common, and in no time at all we'd be communicating. They knew I could laugh at myself.

I especially love working with young people, because I really love anything that's growing. So often when you see people later, it's too late. You think uh-oh, nothing else is going to happen there for a while. Their terminality is not just a malignancy of the flesh, it's a sickness of the spirit, the mind. We put a time bomb inside us, sometimes, that explodes within us and stops us from being productive. So when you see young people, you think maybe one word might launch them into a productive life.

And it gave me special satisfaction to realize that I wasn't a young subdeb arbitrarily changing the color of her hair, but a grown woman whose hair, at periodic intervals, was dark at the roots. I always felt that my own hair was the best possible recommendation for buying Clairol. A young girl can always use hair color, but she doesn't need it the way we older girls do.

We went to colleges, department stores. And we worked with every race God put on the face of the earth. I will always be grateful for those experiences because whenever I go into another city and have to search for the proper rollers and setting lotion, I find someone who remembers those years and understands how much I admire good hairdressing and all that goes with it.

During those years, I gave a lot of thought both to the past and to the future. I'd done a lot of interesting things in my life, and all of them were stimulating, or useful, or educational, but I felt that the time had come to point my career in one direction. And the direction that appealed to me most was television. Television, I believed, offered me the opportunity to be most fully myself. Nowhere else, it seemed to me, would I find a more compatible medium.

The opportunity when it finally came, was a humdinger, though it took a long time to get the humdinger humming!

ABC wanted to produce a new show for women—a talk show on general topics. Monty Morgan, my old friend from the Jack Paar show, had recommended me to Armand Grant, director of programming at ABC, for emcee. He himself was going to try his hand at producing. Quickly, we made a pilot. Abbe Lane, Ann Shanks, a photographer, Rona Jaffe, and I discussed younger women falling in love with older men. We didn't pull any punches; we said exactly what we thought. I remember that we corraled our audience from passersby on the street, and they were wonderful. Their laughter kept us at our liveliest. Everyone who saw that show thought it was fabulous.

Then quickly, too, absolutely nothing happened, just as before. I was beginning to think that nothing in the world happens more quickly, and often, than nothing. Even the Clairol people, who were interested in sponsoring the show, were unable to persuade the network to let them see the pilot.

Finally, after literally months of corporate inertia, we had given up hope. And once again the telephone rang. It was ABC; the show was going on. Henry Plitt, president of ABC Films, had resurrected it. Its title? *For Women Only*. At the eleventh hour, we found out that there was a local show in Boston using that title. Someone came up with the title *Girl Talk*, and I remember crying like a baby because I thought it was a trite title, implying chitchat instead of more worthy topics of discussion. How wrong can you be! If we had searched the world over, we couldn't have found a better title.

The plan was to coproduce the show with ABC Films and then syndicate it. Syndicated shows are sold to local stations individually. Unlike the basic network shows, the local stations have no obligation to carry them. *The Lawrence Welk Show* is one of the most successful examples of syndication today.

The year was 1962. It was fall. Monty had booked the new show's first guests: Rona Jaffe, once again, Lisa Howard, a news commentator, and Eva Gabor. The women. The topic was whether or not wives and husbands should take separate vacations. We had been waiting for a program of our own a long, long time. Now we had it. The girls were going to be able to talk at last.

Talking to the Girls

There is something innately vulnerable about a woman. It's a quality that is built into her sexuality. In the most basic sense, she is built to receive. And I've often thought that if you took the biggest female bore of all time and had her compete against the biggest male bore of all time, the male would be more boring. The man would win the boredom contest.

This is because of the woman's essential vulnerability. Being more vulnerable, more open, if you like, a woman knows from birth—or she learns soon after—that she has to clothe her body, her mind, and her feelings in some kind of protective coloration, some kind of defensive armor. She cannot afford to be smug. She cannot afford to be infinitely self-righteous and superior. The things she has to learn are much more subtle than what a man has to learn.

Now, thanks in large part to today's women, the roles a woman can hope to play are increasing. And glory be to God for that. Man or woman, don't ever let someone force you into playing a role you don't want to play. This is something we sometimes have to do as children, but once we reach the age of consent, I believe we have a responsibility to ourselves and to the people we love and who love us to suit our repertory of roles to our own individual needs.

It isn't easy. Often we have to fight *ourselves* tooth and nail because we're frightened of failing or, even worse, we're frightened of succeeding. I firmly believe that a fear of success, alone, has created more failures than any other force in the history of the human race.

Now these are terrible oversimplifications, and

there are variables and exceptions enough to last us till kingdom come, thank the good Lord once again. But they do not invalidate the basic truth of that idea. Every woman knows I'm right. So do most men. That is why Leonardo da Vinci chose a woman to be his subject when he painted the *Mona Lisa*. That is also what Women's Lib is all about. I think.

It is, too, why *Girl Talk*, from the very beginning, was such a rich and rewarding experience for me. I was not only the hostess of a talk show. I was the hostess of a talk show for women only. It was a new role for me—and yet it wasn't. That's the thing about roles: When the right time comes to play a new one, you suddenly find its outline already inside your body, where it's been hibernating for years, waiting patiently (or impatiently) to emerge.

It's destiny again is what it is. Daily living is basic training for what lies ahead. Because suddenly, after years of studying women, getting to know them, working with them, finding out what makes them tick, I was assigned the job of talking to them five days a week on every subject known to man and woman, and getting them to talk to each other— which was not always a simple task. It was a thrilling job for me. I love the other parts of my life. I love my family. I love my friends. But *Girl Talk* didn't happen in the normal course of things. It was unexpected. It was a complete surprise. It was also a challenge, and I was determined to make the most of it.

But if it was women only on camera, it was men, too, behind them. Monty Morgan did the work of half a dozen men, and did it brilliantly. So did Bob Delaney, our director. No problem was too large; no detail was too small. To cite just one example: From the first, Monty insisted on footlights. These are the lights that mask and hide shadows. And their value was not only cosmetic. It was also psychological. Our setting became warmer, more alive, more intimate. And our theatrical guests, especially, felt much more at home. There is nothing like flattering light to put a woman at her ease.

I would like to fill this book with the names of our guests on *Girl Talk*. I would like to follow the lives of each and every one of them and tell their stories—what they have done in the years since we met, and what they are doing now. Each of us has a different story to tell, and yet our similarities are so much greater than our differences, our bonds so much stronger than the weak links in them.

Women are ageless. We are. Especially as we grow older, especially then. And even more than men, I think, women are the same all over the world. We're united by our sex and by our humanity. Touch us, and we all respond. Wound one of us and you are wounding us all.

Girl Talk took place mainly in New York. But we also traveled. And never was our common bond more evident, I think, than when we went to Rome and interviewed the granddaughter of Mahatma Gandhi.

I have to believe in karma. I do. Because I'm certain that I knew this woman in another life. Otherwise there could not have been this same warmth and instant attachment to one another, this *reunion*. Tara Barta Charga was a young girl with a marvelous face, sloe-eyed and beautiful. She just radiated charm. And by the way, folks, the red dot is cosmetic. When you see Indian women with the red dot on their foreheads, that's like eye shadow for us, or painted fingernails. It's strictly cosmetic. There is no mysterious message in the red dot.

There I was in Rome on top of the Cavallieri Hilton talking to the granddaughter of Mahatma Gandhi and having tea. Little Ginny Komiss. Imagine! And I've got to try to tell you what it felt like, because it's important. All our lives, I think, when we watch people in the entertainment world, in the arts, in sports, in politics—in any form of public life—we ask, "What makes them a star?" What qualities of charisma and talent and drive does it take? When does someone who's less than a star *become* a star?

All the time I was up there, with the television cameras grinding away and zooming in and crowds of onlookers watching us, I was thinking to myself and wondering, Is this what a star is? Have I become a star? "Am I a star, Mama?" I would flash the question to her. "Have I made it yet?" It was almost as though I was still a little girl. I was so excited, I couldn't get over what was happening to me.

I'll have to reconstruct our conversation from memory as best I can. We were talking about womanhood and I asked her who she would choose for a wombmate if she could be born again.

She said, "A twin sister who was beautiful and more intelligent than I."

This was a subtle and modest answer, and when I pressed her to explain, she said such a twin would give her so much to aspire to.

Then I asked her where she would choose to be born, if it could happen again, thinking to myself that of course she would want to be an American woman.

"In India," she said.

"Isn't that interesting?" I said. "Why?"

"Because in India," she replied, "the men want us to have rights. They are fighting for us."

I asked her who her best friend was, thinking she might say Singelina Rossellini, the film director's wife. I knew they were close. But she didn't.

"My mother," she said.

I was surprised and told her so. Your mother knows you at every different phase of your life, I said, and maybe your mother loves you more than anyone else. Were those the reasons she described her mother as her best friend?

"No," she said. "The reason I say that is because she is the only person I can go to with happiness."

At this point, I thought we might be having a language problem.

"Isn't what you mean," I said, "that your mother is the person who stands by you in trouble and in grief?"

"No, I don't mean that at all, Virginia," she said. "For example, my child got the best grades of anybody in class. I certainly couldn't call my neighbor whose child was in the same class and got lower grades. The best person to share our happiness was my mother. And when my husband got a position instead of our friend who was applying for the same appointment, our friend's wife was certainly not going to call to share our joy."

And I thought, Isn't this true? There can be times when our closest friends don't want us to succeed, because they fear that if we do we'll reject them, we'll consider ourselves superior. I think that's also why many people get so much satisfaction from funerals. It's sometimes more of a comfort to share someone's grief than to share their joy.

One marvelous and joyful guest on *Girl Talk* was the British writer, Barbara Cartland. Barbara will stand out in my mind forever because I owe her an enormous debt of thanks. She came to New York in 1965, already a success in England and beginning to acquire a wide readership in America.

She writes these marvelous romances, full of adventure and excitement. They're full of ordinary people and royalty and drama and suspense and wonderful happy endings. And they're eaten up like popcorn by millions of readers.

Barbara looks like a porcelain doll, she is so beautiful. She looks like an enchanted creature out of a fairy tale. Her clothes are made by this famous dressmaker to the Queen, and after her appearance on *Girl Talk*, the American people besieged us with phone calls asking where could they buy her books.

It was Barbara's own enthusiasm that's responsible for getting my publisher and me together for this book. We met at a party in Los Angeles in 1976. We had not seen each other in over ten years, but she recognized me at once and rushed up to say hello. Chances are, we'd never have met had I not had a show called *Girl Talk*.

I was never so happy. Oh, we had fantastic guests on that show. We had Joan Crawford, Barbara Walters, Olivia de Havilland, Carol Channing, Margaret Mead, Leslie Uggams, Phyllis Diller, Luise Rainer, Margo Champion, Jolie and all the Gabors, Phyllis

Kirk, Betty Friedan, Shelley Winters, Helen Gurley Brown, Hermione Gingold.

We had Bette Davis, Dr. Virginia Apgar, Gypsy Rose Lee, Inger Stevens, Betty Furness, Georgia Gibbs, Michele Lee, Jane Withers, Leatrice Joy, Merle Oberon, Doris Lily, Marion Preminger, Marian Javits, Rosemary Clooney, Virgilia Peterson, Maxine Messenger, Margaret Whiting, Ruby Dee, Roberta Peters, Candice Bergan, Jan Miner, J. P. Morgan, Katherine Murray, Martha Roundtree, Maggi McNellis.

We had Totie Fields, Margaret Truman, Lily Daché, Sybil Leek, Dorothy Kilgallen, Angie Dickinson, Julie Harris, Ruta Lee, Gwen Davis, Pauline Trigère, Kirsten Flagstad, Kitty Carlisle, Lynda Byrd Johnson, Arlene Francis, Dr. Claire Weeks, Anne Bancroft, Jane Morgan, Della Reese, Shirley Knight, Constance Ford, Dina Merrill, Barbara Feldon, Thelma Ritter, Perle Mesta, Georgia Brown, Eve Merriam, Jessica Tandy.

We had Irene Worth, Lucille Ball, Dr. Mary Calderone, Cornelia Otis Skinner, Vanessa Redgrave, Radie Harris, Anne Baxter, Melanie Kahane, Dorothy Rodgers, Lisa Minnelli, Joan Rivers, Coral Browne, Adele Simpson, Mollie Parnis, Peggy Cass, Agnes De Mille, Dr. Rose Franzblau, Maureen Stapleton, Amy Vanderbilt, Gloria Swanson, Ann Landers, Jean Dalrymple, Sylvia Porter, Charlotte Curtis, Erma Bombeck.

We had Dewi Sukarno, Sylvia Miles, Liz Smith, Judith Crist, Maureen O'Sullivan, Maggie Daly, Cindy Adams, Mia Farrow, Marlo Thomas, Pearl Bailey, Estelle Parsons, Rosemarie, Goldie Hawn, Alice Ghostley, Glenda Jackson, Ruth Preston, Mary Margaret McBride, Eugenia Sheppard, Cloris Leachman, Dorothy Manners, Rona Barrett, Kay Medford, Muriel Humphrey, Rosemary Prinz, Rita Gam, Jo Anne Worley, Selma Diamond.

We had Gael Greene, Linda Goodman, Lee Grant, Arlene Dahl, Mercedes McCambridge, Nancy Walker, Suzy Parker, Eileen Ford, Mimi Benzell, Hazel Scott, Polly Bergen, Alice Pearce, Elizabeth Montgomery, Bibi Osterwald, Edie Adams, Jill Haworth,

Lilo, Candy Jones, Kaye Ballard, Dody Goodman, Lynn Redgrave and, last but not least, many, many more.

We talked about extrasensory perception, proper methods of birth control, men, the possibility of having a woman as president, organic gardening, karma, the effect of television on the quality of American life, men, the right age to teach children about sex, the right *way* to teach children about sex, books, the decline of the hat, assassination, which animals make the best pets, mercy killing, the best recipe for pound cake, men, impulse buying, Martin Luther King, how to remove ink spots from velvet, *The Feminine Mystique*, Laurence Olivier, the importance of women in the clergy, infidelity, faith healing, mysteries, Alcoholics Anonymous, transvestites, health foods, men, *Hello, Dolly!*, the Catholic Church, wedding ceremonies around the world, affection and the infinite ways to express it, the Kennedys, hippies, the best way to save money, military uniforms for women, the Peace Corps, hit-and-run drivers, how to give good parties, needlework, the Museum of Modern Art, dolls, the best way to exercise, Christmas cards, looks that could kill, jewelry, men, letters of condolence, Elizabeth Taylor, suntans, duplicity . . .

Stop me, please, before I run out of space. I believe it would be easier to compile a list of things we *didn't* talk about. No, I take that back. It wouldn't. That would be like looking for a needle in a haystack. I'm not certain that I could ever find that needle, because I'm not sure there was anything we didn't talk about. I believe it's possible that we may have talked about everything under the sun.

Now some of our talk was frivolous. And some of it was once-over-lightly. And I don't maintain that we provided the last word on anything. We did not solve all the problems of the world. No one will ever do that. Some of our talk was serious, and some of our talk was light and amusing. But one thing I can say: We did ourselves proud and gave ourselves plenty of food for thought. Sometimes, I must admit, we gave ourselves mental indigestion, but it was food that fed us nonetheless.

We listened. We disagreed. We took exception. We shocked each other and ourselves. We clashed. We struggled to find the right word. We asked questions. We probed. We sparred; we feinted. We got mad; we made up. We apologized. We tried not to talk all at once. We raised our eyebrows a couple of times. We argued. We came on too weak and we came on too strong. We talked as we had never talked before. For eight wonderful years, we aired our goals and shared our roles and bared our souls.

I want to tell you a story about Harry and about *Girl Talk* and about Jockey shorts. One thing we tried to do on *Girl Talk* was make it appear to be originating in each of its syndicated stations. That helped create an intimacy, and also kept us from becoming a New York show. We definitely didn't want to put a regional stamp on it, because we wanted to identify with women everywhere, not just provincial New Yorkers.

So I would travel to various cities to do local spot announcements promoting the show. Well, Harry went with me to Minneapolis. Merv Griffin is always teasing Harry about how much he likes to sleep. And we had to get to the station very early. I took my position and was waiting for the camera to be set up when I looked at Harry. Poor Harry was snoring already.

I told the director to turn the camera on him. "Ladies and gentlemen," I said, "you've got to watch *Girl Talk*. It's such an up show. It fills you with pep and energy. Everybody loves it."

And there was Harry, snoring peacefully away, the perfect underscoring to my message.

Tippy Huntley, Chet Huntley's widow, who was in Minneapolis at the time, happened to see that promo. She knew someone in the advertising agency handling the Jockey shorts account, which was building up a campaign using unusual people, and she called to suggest me for a Jockey shorts commercial.

When the agency interviewed me, I suggested using Harry, just as we had on the promo, and they liked the idea.

Here is the scenario we worked out. Harry would stand like a statue, a portly, well-built statue, wearing his usual white under and outer accessories. I would say, "Harry, every time we go traveling on the road, the maid goes snow-blind looking at your underwear. Everybody else is wearing colored shorts. If you enjoy color television, you've got to switch to colored Jockey shorts." Harry was to just look at me. "Are you listening, Harry?" I'd say. And his one piece of dialogue was, "Yes, dear."

We had to do twenty-nine takes before he got it right, because Harry was always looking somewhere else, or saying something else. That's one reason why Harry was the most talked about husband on television.

I always felt that the special value of our show was its completely feminine point of view. That was our trademark. That was our strength. That made us completely distinctive, unlike any other talk show on television. And in our sixth year, when the decision was made to include men among our guests, it was over my very strong objections. Because it was my opinion that we lost our unique function then. When *Girl Talk* went coed, we became, I think, just another talk show.

And in my eighth year as emcee, I had to make the agonizing decision to leave the show, or to continue under a contract that was patently unfair to me. I chose to leave the show. That decision caused me great heartache at the time, and the special poignance of that heartache will always be with me.

My friends were wonderfully loyal and I'll always be especially grateful to Cindy and Joey Adams. Some of them felt that I should have stayed on the show, but none of them ever blamed me after I left. I love my friends but I depend upon myself. I am my own last resort.

Should I have stayed on *Girl Talk?* Rarely a day goes by that I don't ask myself the question. Three answers are possible. No. Yes. I don't know. I've lived with yes and I've lived with no. Injustice is a terrible thing to live with. So is regret. Perhaps it's a toss-up between the two. Today, I find it most comfortable to say to myself that I simply don't know.

I like what has happened to me in the years since then. I think that change is one of the greatest stimulants in the world. Without change, I think we have a tendency to become stagnant and stale. Without change, I don't think growth is possible.

Still, my heart is full when I think of my years with *Girl Talk*. They brought me friends. They brought me fame. Here's a little story that will illustrate both. On a game show called *Stumpers*, panelists were asked to identify a person from three clues of one word each. As best I recollect, the first clue was "talk." Then "gabber," then "girl." Then Betty White, who is surely one of the most delightful and richly deserving people of the female persuasion in all of showbiz—and was, herself, a marvelous guest on *Girl Talk*—Betty White said, "Virginia Graham!" After all these years off the air, Virginia Graham is still talk-gabber-girl.

We often reminisce, Monty, Bob Delaney, my wonderful director, and others associated with the show either as guests or staff, about those wonderful happy days. A week never passes that people don't come up to us and ask when *Girl Talk* is coming back on the air. We thank them. It's so gratifying to keep getting that kind of response after such a long time. And we always answer, "Soon, we hope."

But this time around, we'll call it *Ms. Talk*.

Hooray for Hollywood

Not for one second have I ever been able to forget my illness. Such is the price of survival. It is brought home to me in manifold ways each day of my life. The experience of surviving cancer is both a victory and a responsibility—not only to myself, but to stricken people everywhere.

I absolutely would not accept the definition of terminality. That is one of the reasons I was asked to be chairwoman of the Cancer Crusade for the American Cancer Society in 1969, and that is one of the reasons I accepted.

At the time, Steve Barry was in charge of public relations for the society. He was one of the finest people I've ever known, and when he passed away he was mourned by people all over the world. I worked with him from my earliest involvement with the society, which was a couple of years after my operation. We'd go all over the country to conventions and I would meet these brilliant doctors. Because we need them so much, I think we have a tendency to view doctors as superhuman beings, gifted with life-and-death powers. Well, I would treat them as no one else had ever treated them. If they were at the wheel of the car, I'd put on my back-seat-driver act. If they were single, I'd kid them about their love lives. I especially enjoyed telling them what they should eat and putting them on a strict diet. And I discovered that doctors do not like to be treated as gods. They like to be treated as people.

Cancer has never had a telethon for fund-raising. This is a policy I've never approved of and, ever true to my basic nature, I didn't hesitate to make my views heard. I think a cancer telethon is needed, and not just to raise money. A telethon is one of the best ways to inform the public and disseminate information. Look what Jerry Lewis does with muscular dystrophy—one of the most fantastic education jobs in the world. It's as well organized as a university.

Every trip we made that year with the American Cancer Society was a crusade of love. We went to over fifty cities. And through my own experience, I was able to bring the American people (and, ultimately, people all over the world) a message of joy and hope. It was a God-sent opportunity for me, because it gave me something wonderful to do the year after I left *Girl Talk*. In the best possible way, it was a chance for me to serve.

Then, in 1971, came the marvelous opportunity to do *The Virginia Graham Show* on the West Coast. Now I was born a Chicago girl, and after my marriage I became a New York girl. Both these cities are blessed with four different seasons: winter, spring, summer, fall. That means you have lots of good weather and lots of bad. You may never know from one day to the next what the weather will be—with or without the aid of the weather forecasters—but one thing you can be sure of: The weather will change. If not for the better, for the worse. In fact, studies have shown that New York City weather is more changeable than any other weather in the world—a conclusion that I would never attempt to refute.

But the new show would be produced in Hollywood. I was thrilled with the prospects of having my own show again, but somewhat doubtful about leaving New York. Harry was retired now but his roots were still there. Lynn and her husband Sye now had two wonderful children—an older girl, Jan, and a younger boy, Stephen, and it was especially painful to say good-bye to them, even though I had it put in my contract that I could return to New York every five weeks to see them.

You never know when you make a move whether the change will be good or bad. But it took me no longer than the drive from the airport to the Wilshire

Holmby, where we were going to live, to know that Los Angeles was my garden of Eden. Everything about Beverly Hills I loved. I loved the climate. I loved the pace and I loved the space. I loved the ease of moving around.

I loved being able to park indefinitely, without having to garage the car or tend to a parking meter. I loved pulling in to a gas station and getting a friendly miniature car wash in the bargain. You don't even have to ask. Some of them even vacuum the car. And always, when you leave, "Have a nice day!" Now I'm happy to observe that this is happening all over the country.

I'd never seen hospitality like that in my life. Lucille Ball had sent me flowers enough to cover the whole coffee table. Fruit baskets were everywhere. Our trunks had been sent ahead, and when we walked into the bedroom, every piece of clothing had been unpacked and put away.

I've never met nicer people. My show was not even on the air yet. I could have closed in three weeks. But so many women in Hollywood had known me on *Girl Talk* and knew I was coming out. They had been guests on *Girl Talk* and they had all been a part of my success. My success was *them*. A building is built of bricks, and each brick helps to make that building tall and strong. They were the bricks that made my career tall and strong. And I adored my guests and will always be grateful to them.

I didn't make *Girl Talk*. At my best, I brought out the best in my guests, whom I was lucky to have on my show. Any guest who ever comes on with me knows that I feel privileged to have them. They are paying me a great compliment in coming on. They are honoring me. I'm not doing them a favor; they're doing a favor for me.

We hadn't been in Hollywood one whole day when I knew that Harry was miserable. He doesn't like change. And he knew that this was a show that was going to make many, many demands on my time. On a day-by-day basis, we couldn't be as close together as we had been during *Girl Talk*.

When we were in New York, I would go crosstown, across Central Park, do my five thirty-minute shows, and come home. All in two days. But this was different. *The Virginia Graham Show* was a one-hour show. Five hours a week. And I would be gone more. I would be having interviews and doing public relations and having fittings.

When you are lucky enough to hit it rich, see, everything comes to you free. When you've got the teeth, you can't afford steak. Then, when you can finally afford the steak, you're wearing dentures and can't chew it up. It's just . . . I don't know. It's not an inequity, it's just a fact of life.

Now I was finally in Hollywood, the fabulous city of everyone's dreams, at a marvelous salary, and with my car paid for by the company. And this darling friend of mine, Bea, introduced us to everyone she knew. I have known Bea and Irv Citron since I was a bride. We met on Long Island when our children were growing up together. She had moved to California and when Harry and I went out there, she just opened up her heart and introduced us to everybody. She is one of the most popular women I have ever known.

Pamela Mason gave a marvelous party for me. So did Frenchy Allen, Marty's wife. I never felt strange. And from the minute the show went on the air, it was a success. It was a knockout. It went on in the summer at six o'clock at night, and it was the only new show of the season. Everybody else was on reruns. And we knocked them off their feet because it was a lively show with a fantastic group of young people helping.

When I stopped to look back, I thought, Oh my God, how is this possible? Consider what Monty Morgan did *alone* when *Girl Talk* started. Not even a secretary. And then, at the height of our run, a booker and a secretary. And I believe our staff for *The Virginia Graham Show* must have been between fifteen and twenty.

I was so happy. Marvin Hamlisch did the theme song for me again, as he had for *Girl Talk*, and we had an orchestra. It was more than I had ever dreamed of.

And the thing I'm forever grateful for is, at the moment of happiness, I always know it's happening. I'm aware. I know that it's really and truly me feeling happy. That's one thing I want to impress on people. When you are happy, if you're having even five seconds or five minutes of happiness, or five years, and you have that marvelous euphoric feeling that flows through your body when you are relaxed and full of pleasure, stop what you are doing for just one moment and say, "Oh, how wonderful to be this happy. Oh, how glorious to be alive."

Now I must tell you something. When you go to Hollywood, it takes three things to prove you're a star. Number one: There's a standing order for flowers in your dressing room. Number two: You have a star on your door. Number three: there's a heavy rumor that you're sexually perverse. If you're lucky enough to be the latter, you will get your own series or primetime show. (Naturally, it just seems that way.)

So I arrived with one big strike against me. Both Harry and I are the soul of middle-class respectability. I'm not bragging. That's just the way we are. We can't help it.

But my promoters wanted a swinging Virginia. Wasn't there a scandal buried somewhere that they could resurrect and fan into a rumor that spreads like wildfire? I racked my brain. On her interview show, Helen Gurley Brown once asked me if I found women more attractive than men. "I'll answer in a minute," I replied. "In the meantime, do you have a cigar?" Was that heavy enough, provocative enough?

Then I remembered something else. The summer I was ten years old I was sent to camp and an older girl made advances to me. I didn't know exactly what she had in mind, but I did know it seemed wrong. When visitor's day came, I told Papa. Had I done the right thing in rebuking her, I asked him. "Always trust your instincts," Papa said. Would that do?

They looked at me disgustedly.

Suicide! That's always good for human interest.

My
Album of
Memories

Top, left and right: My brother Juddy and I
sat for these studio portraits.

Bottom: Little Ginny Komiss (center) with friends.

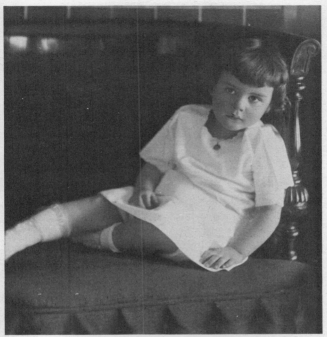

Above: An informal photograph of Mama, Lynn and me, sitting at the pond in Great Neck.

Top: *My beloved Papa.*

Bottom: *Here I am in my Sergeant
Sunshine uniform for the Red Cross.*

Top: *Yours truly singing the praises of Clairol.*

Bottom: *Adela Rogers St. John and Joan Crawford trying to get a word in edgewise on Girl Talk.*

Top: Anna Moffo, Hermione Gingold, Gwen Verdon, and yours truly laughing at girl talk.

Bottom: *Harry Hershfeld, Monique van Vooren, Selma Diamond, Virginia Graham, Marty Allen, Dodie Goodman, and Ella Logan when I was named Woman of the Year by AGVA, the American Guild of Variety Artists.*

Top: Artist Don Kingman had just presented me with this portrait, in celebration of the AGVA honor.

Bottom: With the inimitable Carol Channing, just before going on the air.

*Top: Four of the girls at a posh dinner party.
With Jolie and Zsa Zsa Gabor, and Cindy Adams, standing.*

Bottom: Harry and I on our way to the theater.

Top: A tense moment with Mrs. Gilman in
Late Love *at the Pheasant Run Playhouse.*

Bottom: Bob Delaney, myself, Monty Morgan and the
anniversary cake, following Girl Talk *show number 1000.*

Top: With Michael Hennessey in Butterflies Are Free *at the Chateau de Ville Theater in Saugus, Massachusetts.*

Bottom: Lynn and Sye, Jan and Stephen Bohrer, cavorting in the snow.

Top: *Enjoying an outing with Jan and Stephen.*

Bottom: *Senator Barry Goldwater autographing a copy of his book,* Conscience of a Majority *on* The Virginia Graham Show.

Top: At a restaurant with Joey Adams, Father Parella,
the famous priest of show business, and Louis Armstrong.

Bottom: A relaxed moment with Muriel Humphrey.

Top: At a party for Irv Kupcinet (third from left),
host of Chicago's famous Kup's Show and columnist
for the Chicago Sun-Times, with Marshall Field III
and Bailey Howard, owner of the Sun-Times.

Bottom: Sharing the spotlight, uneasily,
with a visitor from the zoo.

Top: My wonderful friend, the great Totie Fields.
Bottom: Harry and I outfitted in period costumes.

Top: *The Bohrers and the Guttenbergs,
on the occasion of Jan's bas mitzvah.*

Bottom: *Virginia in Virginia. My Act IV curtain speech
after* Any Wednesday *at the Hayloft Theater in Manassas.*

Would I agree to jump from a window—nothing too dangerous, say the third floor? "We'll catch you," they said.

"Let's do it the other way around," I said. "I'll catch you."

These were the people who helped all the stars get to the top. They were supposed to know everything about everybody. If they didn't know it already, they could find out.

I tried to picture their operation. I decided they must have every mattress in Hollywood wired for sound. Somewhere, there must be a Central Receiving Station where daily results were tabulated and analyzed before release to the general public. The reputations and careers of the stars then moved up and down in direct relation to the rhythm of the mattresses.

The Rumor (or Rhythm) Machine. There are only two ways to cope with this machine without brain damage. You can believe everything you hear, or you can believe nothing. And I must say that Harry is a model of virtue. He has never believed a rumor. I used to wonder if he was just trying to protect me, but no, that's not his method. And he's absolutely right. He says, how do they *know?*

Well, those promotion people gave up. But if they couldn't unearth some scandal, at least they could change my image. I guess they figured there weren't enough Virginia Grahams already. They wanted more. Well, this was flattering, if only in a left-handed kind of way. And I obliged, I said all right, okay. I'm game.

They had me riding elephants. They had me at bat at Dodger Stadium with Willy Mays throwing the ball. They had me watching this Indian who was throwing hatchets around a person standing sideways without hitting him, would anyone volunteer? Well, a young woman who was pregnant arose and went to the stage and said, "My husband will kill me if you don't, but my friends have dared me to come down and do it."

I sat there in my seat looking at her and thought,

My Lord, we can't allow this to happen, so I stood up and said, "My dear, I want you to go back to your seat. I shall allow him to throw the hatchets at me."

Then someone cried out, "No, no, don't let her do it." But I walked down the aisle and got up on stage and stood there in profile and let that Indian throw six hatchets at my body. And it gave me the greatest satisfaction to let my promoters see that I did not flinch. Not once. I didn't wince. I didn't move a muscle. It was one of the most dramatic moments in all of history. Afterward, Harry told me that he would absolutely have me committed if I ever did such a crazy thing again.

This was all part of the concept that young is new, new is good. Progress is change, is what this ballyhoo was all about. That is one of the most naive misapprehensions in the whole world. "Change" and "progress" are two different words. Progress can only be for the better. But change may, or may not, be for the better.

"We're going to change you, Ginny," I was told. "We're going to make you real hip."

"I'm the hippest person you know," I said. "Whether you know it or not. What do you mean you're going to make me hip?"

You see, some people think I'm square. After all the outrageous things I've said and done in my life, I don't see how they can, but some people actually think that Virginia Graham is a synonym for four equal sides and four right angles. I love to watch their faces, I love to observe carefully the change of expression, when they find out that such is not the case.

Listen, I'm not through. One day at Sea World, I had to jump into the water with a porpoise. Over my head and fully clothed. They took pictures of the porpoise and me doing some kind of acquatic getting-to-know-you routine.

But that's the new Hollywood. Do you remember the old Hollywood? Do you remember the great days of the movie magazines? All during the years at National Park, we used to sit and read movie magazines. Janet Gaynor and Norma Shearer. Fredric

March and Robert Taylor. It was such heaven to imagine the fabulous lives these people lived in some magical, mythical, impossible place called Hollywood. If you were over seven years old, you knew such a place could never really exist, and yet sometimes you believed it did. Sometimes you were positive you were wrong the other times when you thought such a place was ridiculous.

I received my sex education from movie magazines and Elinor Glyn. They were such marvelous fluff. I remember they used to refer to "erotic zones," which I thought were something created by city ordinance, like a school zone or a hospital zone, where there had to be a fire hydrant or a "No U-Turn" sign.

Television stars will never be as glamorous as movie stars. Never, no matter how successful they are. And one reason is that the myth of privacy and secrecy and mystery no longer applies. Sometimes it was real, with the movie stars, and sometimes it wasn't. With Greta Garbo, it was real. It still is. With Gloria Swanson, it was real.

Nowadays stars and studios hire press agents, whereas in the old days they didn't. In those days, *sup*-press agents were the people to get. The magic consisted of keeping your extracurricular activities *out* of the newspapers, not in.

One of the most wonderful guests on *The Virginia Graham Show* was Adela Rogers St. John. What a survivor she is! She was a pioneering newspaperwoman in the days when that field was almost totally dominated by men, and she is also a distinguished author. She came on the show and bared her soul. When you're in the newspaper business, or any other where there is a lot of tension and competition, you often begin to take a cocktail just to relax. This sometimes leads to another and then another, and of course in many cases it results in a dependence on alcohol.

Nowadays, some of the finest people in the world, both in show business and other fields, make a point of using their own experience to help and strengthen other people. Because our weaknesses, much more than our strengths, are our bonds. I think we love each other because we're human, not because we're invincible.

Adela brought more spiritual nourishment to my show than almost anybody. She managed to find comfort from some deep inner source when her son died. She was able to embrace her religion more fervently than she ever had before. Somehow, she felt, her son would continue to live through her.

I had marvelous guests from all walks of life. Alice Cooper was a fabulous booking for me, and I had a wonderful time with him. It is our differences, I think, that make us interesting to each other, and Alice has a personality all his own.

Now I must tell you something very funny that happened to Harry and me. Somehow, Hollywood is more public than New York. It may be the warmer climate. It may be the ease of moving around. But Harry and I can never have our differences except at home. It doesn't matter what city we're in. We can't fight in an elevator, we can't fight in a restaurant, we can't have words in any enclosed public place if other people are present. So one day we were driving along in our car on Sunset Boulevard in Los Angeles, and we were having what is lovingly known as a heated discussion, because we had been . . . we were giving it to each other good. And at every red traffic light I'd say, "Smile, Harry, smile! The people in that car are watching us." Then we'd both stop shouting and smile and drive on.

But once I forgot, and later I got a letter from this woman who said, "I will never look at you again. I have never been so disillusioned in my life. That poor man you were yelling at was cringing." She wrote, "You have lost me forever."

Do you resent being in a goldfish bowl? Then don't be in this business. Someone once asked me if I thought people had the right to ask for autographs. You bet they do. But the one thing I beg of them if they see me in a restaurant, please, come over before the food is served. They wait to attack, like commandos, until the waiter is bringing hot soup. I love hot soup. Not warm, or room temperature, or cool. Hot.

Come, dear autograph hunters, I love you all, before I am served. Or after. But come, because that is contact, too.

I like being in a fishbowl. I enjoy being known, because it brings me closer to people.

Hollywood diets all the time. I think they don't even swallow their saliva if they've had a Certs. They can be totally disciplined about everything except sex, but they'll do anything to gratify their sexual appetites. I think they should eat bread or have a Danish. Maybe that would take care of their inner hunger.

The older some women get, the more rigorously they diet. And the older they get, the younger the swains they like trailing behind them. Some of those women look like sticks with a slipcover on. Jan, my granddaughter, says, "Nana, they look fine from the back. Then they turn around and you see all those grandma faces."

I think when you diet obsessively, and wear hairstyles and dresses that are suitable for someone thirty years your junior, you look twice as old. At least. That's not sour grapes. It may be flavored with a little carbolic acid, but it's really not sour grapes.

One day in 1975 I was at Gucci buying a Christmas present when Mary Livingstone came rushing up. "Oh, Virginia," she said, "when are you coming back. I've loved you since *Girl Talk*. So did Jack." That made me feel wonderful, because I'm crazy about Mary, and Jack Benny was always one of my idols. Then she introduced me to her companion, Leonard Gershe.

"I want to thank you so much," he said. "I hear you've done such a good job with my play."

Oh dear, I thought, here we go again. He's confusing me with Sheilah Graham or Martha Graham or Gloria Grahame or somebody.

"What is your play?" This is one of the dumbest questions I've ever asked.

"*Butterflies Are Free*," he said, without an ounce of hurt pride that I hadn't recognized his name. My pride was hurt, though, because I had interviewed

Leonard Gershe after *Girl Talk* went coed. So I tried to make amends.

"*Master!*" I said. I got down on the floor at Gucci at Christmastime, when they're so busy they're giving you numbers to get in—you have to stand in line, the same as the supermarket—I got down on the floor and said, "Master, master."

This wonderful, modest man got down on the floor with me and said, "If you're on the floor, I've got to get down on the floor and thank you."

Before we knew it, a whole crowd had gathered: "What's going on? Is anybody hurt?"

"Oh no," somebody said. "Don't worry. It's just Virginia Graham."

So many of the sightless people have more vision than anybody. There's a bravado they all possess—Leonard, Ray Charles, George Shearing, Stevie Wonder. They put us to shame, because they're determined to be cheerful all the time. Even I am not always cheerful. But they do that so we won't be uneasy about them.

I used to know a girl who was involved with Fight for Sight. She used to come to my beauty parlor every week. She had her hair washed. She had her hair set. She had a manicure. She was always immaculately groomed. But she had something even more important than grooming. She had inner beauty.

Christmas in Hollywood is a seasonal impossibility. There are none of the outward trappings an Easterner is used to: fir trees and icicles and shopping in the cold. The perfume of Christmas to me is the smell of an old-fashioned Christmas tree in front of a roaring fireplace. There's nothing like that in Hollywood. Maybe, if you're lucky, you'll see a few pieces of tinsel at a stoplight.

The late Agnes Moorehead decided to do something. She decided to give a party at Christmas. To start with, she lived in a magnificent home, and when the guests drove onto the grounds, they left their cars with valets dressed as Santa's helpers. Then they entered this incredible mansion with ceilings thirty feet tall domed with the boughs of evergreens. And in an enormous grotto stood a Christmas tree the size of the giant tree in Rockefeller Center. There were gifts under the tree for everybody. And throughout the evening, carolers were singing.

There's something legendary about Hollywood parties, the biggest ones especially. There's something about the beautiful famous faces, and the opulence and the wealth. Some extra excitement. You sense it during the Academy Awards. There is a special presence that goes with fame and legend and beauty, a kind of grace, a kind of aristocracy. In some cases, it may be only skin-deep, but Hollywood, after all, is the birthplace of illusion, on the scale that we know it.

Probably the thing I will cherish most was my finding Sandy Carter. She came to *The Virginia Graham Show* under the sponsorship of Woody Fraser, my producer, and if I had been blessed with a second daughter, I couldn't love her more. When our show was discontinued, she went into business—Country Elegance, wedding dresses with Romance. Then she and Sherry Grant, a darling who was an integral part of *Girl Talk*, went into TV production. I predict they will be the Goodson-Todman of tomorrow, and our dream of a new show for me is with Monty Morgan, Sandy and Sherry.

I loved my three years in Hollywood. It was very gratifying to have a show of my own in the land of the stars. And I realized two lifelong ambitions—the kind you dream about forever and think are really impossible—when I finally met those two distinguished gentlemen of the cinema, Mr. Cary Grant and Mr. Fred Astaire. Color me Ginger Rogers.

Virginia and Harry "At Home"

At the end of the three-year run of *The Virginia Graham Show*, we came back to our apartment in New York. Lynn and Sye and their children, meantime, had moved to Hollywood where Lynn now has her own television show.

When I visit them now, as I do from time to time, I get an entirely different impression than when I lived there. Then, perhaps, I couldn't see the forest for the trees—almost all of which are transplants. Very few movie or television stars were born in Hollywood. And very few live there their whole lives through. It's a constant turnover. Anyone who relies on Hollywood as a permanent address without investments in real estate or some other business, has to be absolutely fearless on the subject of financial security. That is why Martin Milner has avocado farms, and Allen Ludden does marvelous things for a manufacturer, and so on. Everybody has to do something else.

Maybe this is equally true of New York City. Yes, I think that perhaps this aspect of Hollywood is more of a statement—a warning for all of us in every walk of life—that you can't depend on any one business. Even the modest man who just wanted to be his own boss and have his own grocery store was probably eaten up by the supermarket. The supermarket came to his neighborhood and ate him. The whole world is a blob. I don't know, readers, if you remember the movie where the blob came in and just ate up and absorbed everything around it, but I think we are living in a blob age.

Actors never know what the next ringing of the

telephone will bring: a new show or the cancellation of a series. A hiring or a firing.

So now it's time to catch you up on the million and one occupations that comprise my daily life from our home in New York. I'll tell you about my continuing adventures in the world of the theater on a musical comedy tour. I'll tell you more about Mama and Papa and Juddy, Lynn, Sye, and the children. I'll tell you more about Aunt Celia. I'll tell you about my movies. I'll introduce you to some rare and unusual fans. I'll tell you more about myself—including my guest appearances on television game and talk shows. Because even though I'm currently "at liberty" as a talk-show hostess, I'm often a guest on other talk shows, expressing my opinion on a wide range of subjects.

I'll tell you the truth. I even talk to myself. I count my worries like beads, praying over each and every one whether it's the welfare of a relative or a friend or myself. People used to say that if you talked to yourself, you were crazy. Well, we're all a little crazy anyway. There is some crazy in everybody.

Talking to myself is therapy for me. I really and truly cannot overemphasize the value of this. When I feel that God has deserted me, I find out by talking that I have deserted God. I cannot blame Him for my problems. Because there's one thing I know: From the beginning of my life, I have been to blame for everything that has happened to me that was wrong.

I had a rare experience once when a psychoanalyst told me a joke about his profession. Said the patient to the analyst: "Doctor, I have a confession to make. I talk to myself a lot when I'm alone."

"That's perfectly all right," the analyst said. "In fact, it's all right to answer yourself. But when you find yourself saying '*Huh?*,' call me."

Now let me tell you about our apartment. To do this right, I must turn back the clock about five years, to when Sye and Lynn were still in New York. (By now you know that I have an eight-track mind. The secret is out. That's how many trains of thought are fighting in my head for the right of way. Nobody, including me, ever knows for sure which train will come speeding out next, nor when. Sometimes the tracks are connected, sometimes not. Sometimes there's a wreck. I'll try to spare you the worst of the wrecks.)

So one morning at the beauty parlor, Eva of New York, some five years ago, I decided that the time for refurbishing our apartment had come. With my usual lack of impulsiveness, I engaged a decorator whom I met while under the dryer. I was not acquainted with her qualifications, but I liked the way she dressed. I liked her style. If she could look that chic, she had to be a good decorator.

So I had her come up to the apartment. I told her the only thing I really wanted to do was change the window treatment. You know, do something about the windows? Well, if you have ever brought a decorator into your home for a simple window treatment, you understand that ultimately you will wind up maybe holding on to your electric light bulbs, but everything else has to go.

Almost everything else. My decorator and her partner decided that I could also keep a few basic pieces of furniture, which they had completely rearranged in less than ten minutes. I never saw magic like that in my life. And I suddenly realized that those pieces did need recovering.

Well, while all this was taking place, while the transformation was in progress, I went back to Pheasant Run to appear in Neil Simon's *Barefoot in the Park*. My maid and the decorators worked together. The apartment was to be finished on a Saturday. Sunday I was to do my last performance and we were to come home on Monday.

Early Sunday afternoon, along about ten past two, there I am, savoring the prospect of returning to our newly glamorized apartment the very next day. Twenty minutes before I'm to go onstage, I get a phone call. I have to take it at the box office, where people were queueing up to buy tickets for my last performance.

There's one thing about ardent fans. If you're talking on the telephone, that doesn't bother them. If you're eating hot soup, if you're talking on the phone, if you're in a hospital being wheeled to the operating room for major surgery, it will not stop a fervent fan from running up and asking, "How are you?" They may not remember your name, but they will never forget your face.

"Hello," I say into the mouthpiece. Two dozen pairs of eyes are gazing at my face. Four dozen ears are hanging on my every word.

"Hello, Mother. This is Lynn."

"How are you, darling? How are your children?"

"Everyone is well."

"Then why are you calling?" Dreading the answer, but wanting to know the worst because it has to be faced.

"What is the name of your insurance man?" Lynn asked.

"Warren Weisberger. Why would you want to know?"

"He handles your fire insurance, right?"

"What has happened, Lynn? What is the matter?"

"Now I don't want you to be upset, Mother, but your apartment burned down."

"What?" I shouted. "My apartment burned down?"

As I finish my yell, a fervent fan can no longer resist. She wishes to join the small cast onstage for the climax of that mesmerizing one-act play *Her Apartment Burned Down*, by the indefatigable playwright William Makepiece Fate. She rushes up to me.

"Oh, Miss Graham," she exclaims, "I have always admired you. May I have your autograph?"

"Lynn," I say, trying to keep my voice calm. "In a minute. Let's talk about the fire in a minute. Right now, I have to give this lady my autograph." At least she remembered my name. I can do no less.

I get off the phone. I sign my name in the lady's notebook. She says, "I've always loved your show." She smiles. I hand her back her notebook. She won't go away. She is looking very hard at me. Ah, she is worried. She is waiting for me to smile. I smile. We both smile. Then the lady goes away.

I return to the phone. "Now what are you talking about, Lynn?"

"There was a terrible storm, Mother. Your apartment was hit by lightning."

"Well," I say, "how bad is it?"

"Mother, how can I tell you? Remember the blitz in London?"

"You've got to be kidding!"

"I have to tell you the truth, Mother. It's totally destroyed. The living room, the dining room, the kitchen. But no one was hurt."

"All right," I said. "Call Warren right away." I told her the number. Then I said, "We will be home tomorrow."

I gave my best performance, don't ask me how. In emergencies, when you're under pressure, you have to try to be better than ever. You have to try to outdo yourself. This is what we call our medicine. I did my curtain speech. "I want you to know," I said, "that lightning has struck again. Everybody says it doesn't strike twice. This is our third fire. But you know what? No one was hurt. When Harry's business was destroyed by fire, Harry might have been burned, but he wasn't. When our home in Great Neck burned, we were not inside it. Our child was not hurt. I have to go home now to rebuild again. How incredible that most often, the things we rebuild cannot be bought with money. We're all safe. Thank you for this wonderful visit. Wish me luck."

When Harry and I got to New York, we immediately checked into the Stanhope Hotel, two blocks away from our apartment. Harry would not have to see the apartment until it was redone. After the burning of his business, he could not bear to smell the cinders of destruction again.

When I went up to see what remained of that apartment, I didn't cry. My attitude must have been stoical by that time. The apartment was ravaged. The marble window sills were pulverized. There had been a violent electrical storm, and our air conditioner had been left on with the curtains pulled over it. It was a defective air conditioner. We were going to replace it. The air conditioner shorted when it was hit by lightning.

Everybody was so upset. Lynn was crying her heart out. She said, "Mother, your beautiful things." I said, "Darling, money will replace this. There are a few things I didn't do before that I see will have to be done now, and if God gives me the ability to make money, I will do it again. We'll refurnish. It's an inconvenience, but it's not going to kill us."

Now I'll tell you something fabulous about the New York Fire Department. The fire chief was about to leave for home when they got the call: "Virginia Graham's apartment is on fire." It was a special occasion of some kind, so he called his wife to say he'd be delayed, that my apartment was on fire, and she said, "Now listen, I know she loves her things and I want you to be careful. Don't you break anything." I had priceless antiques. I can't tell you how beautiful. Not one ashtray was broken.

The new rug was ruined. It had been woven in Europe. I had chosen different shades of sea blue, like the Mediterranean. It had just been delivered on Friday. When the decorator called up to reorder it on Monday, the man said, "Are you crazy? We just laid it on Friday." The decorator said, "Lay it again, Sam."

We had to live in the Stanhope for three months, and it was a terribly difficult period for Harry. We hadn't insured the new furniture because the apartment had just been furnished, but we got a very equitable settlement from our broker. We lost, but we didn't lose as much as we could have. So what are you going to say in a case like that? We were wiped out? Or we were lucky? I say we were lucky.

The apartment is beautiful. I love my possessions. I love our home so much that when I can't sleep at night, I get up and look at it. I drink in the beauty. When people ask, "Where are you going for the summer?" I say, "To my bedroom." This absolutely fabulous artist, Ricky Esposito, came in and painted the gardens of Versailles on my back bedroom wall. And I sit there stunned at the beauty.

The texture of the fabrics, the pink silk roses, the curtains, everything was duplicated. Not one thing was changed. The only thing we hadn't redone was the dining room. We had decided to wait to redo that. A great Hungarian artist, Paul Fried, who has since passed away, had done my portrait. It burned. At the time I cried, but *maybe* I'm glad. The difficulty of having a portrait painted is that as you get older, the face in the portrait doesn't. It's a continuous, omnipresent reminder of the frail mortality of your pores.

One woman, with the fine characteristics of a blue-ribbon loser at the Westminster Dog Show, came when I was showing the painting and said to the artist, "Is that the way you hoped she would look?" Definitely one of the sweetest reactions of all, wouldn't you say?

Lynn's portrait didn't burn. Lynn hates it. I love it more than anything because it's the way I love to think of her. When it was painted, she was just entering college. The dew was on her eyes, a radiance on her face; life hadn't touched her, except for the joy. She never knew how popular she was. But then, they never do, you know. I remember that the most. She was fun to be with, and cute and adorable, and her picture had the baby innocence that a mother and father love to have in a picture of their child. That was saved.

Some pictures were marred by smoke. But Harry loves them so much I can't change them. There's one in the living room that I don't like anymore because the color's gone out of it, and I liked the original color, but Harry loves it so much I could never change it. Paintings bring such pleasure to people. I always used to think that a love of art might in some people be an affectation, or a bid for status, but no more. Now I'm willing to give anyone the benefit of the doubt.

I'm not in love with the modern schools, because I don't understand them. What I want is to look at a tree and feel the bark and know the boughs are being burdened by the heavy leaves. Or snow, in winter, with blossoms soon to come. Or fruit. I am in love with natural things. I am, I'm nature's child. I like still lifes. I could have flowers in every room, on every wall.

I'm happiest close to nature. The whole natural world is a garden of delight to me.

I love to entertain. When I have a dinner party, I'm the most ridiculous woman. I'm like a little girl on her birthday. I set the table two days ahead of time. I'm well organized because I'm always working in advance. When all is in place, I put sheets of cellophane over the table. I will not have anyone in my house unless I set the table myself. My father taught me this when I was twelve years old. He and my mother were magnificent hosts. When they entertained, the table was something. When I put a knife on the table, Papa could tell I did it.

I go all over the city, getting candy in one place, nuts in another. I do my flowers. I pick out everything myself. It's a great tribute to your guests. I think they know when you've fussed like that. As I've said before—and I will say it to the end of my days—I love housework. I love my home. My home is my castle.

I'm not really crazy about cleaning up after dinner, and thank God for the dishwasher. It would be heaven after dinner to just have someone else clear the table and get the dishes put away. I find that and cleaning an oven very disenchanting.

New York is our home base. We love it. The summers are hot, the winters are cold—this one, 1977–1978, especially so, and spring and fall are much too short, but New York is where our hearts are. It's still the place where anything can happen and usually does. I definitely love New York, and I hope New York loves me.

God Bless My Public

New York must be the birthplace of the Fan. We are all fans, every single one of us, of someone or something, but probably because there are so many of us bunched up here, we tend to make a little more commotion about it than people spread out more comfortably in other parts of the country. I think the crowds who used to gather at the Paramount Theatre and scream for Frank Sinatra and Dean Martin and Jerry Lewis set the modern trend. Later on, it was the Palace Theatre for Judy Garland and Shirley MacLaine, and Madison Square Garden for the Rolling Stones and many, many others.

The New York fan is an ardent fan, both loyal and selective. New York is a tough town to crack, and the New York fan appreciates the effort that goes into an honest-to-God try by an entertainer, an athlete, a politician, or whatever. If a New York fan thinks you have what it takes, he won't hesitate to let you know. For above all, he is enthusiastic.

I learned about one of my fans in the funniest kind of way. Harry was having an examination at the hospital, and the doctor suggested that I use the hour the examination would take to shop or do whatever I liked instead of just sitting around.

Well, that was terrific. So I told Harry good-bye and took off for my favorite brassiere shop, a couple of blocks away. This shop is no longer in existence, but I have to pay tribute to the quality of its sales personnel. Their poise under stress was remarkable. They displayed extraordinary endurance in the battle with displaced (or misplaced) weight. Always. They were not, any of them, in the Junior Miss department.

They had the hypertension that goes with concerned maturity. Any bravado had long since departed.

The shop was on chic Madison Avenue and the ceilings were low. The average saleswoman was five feet tall. This is a very smart thing to do: If you have low ceilings, hire short salespeople, invite short guests.

Decorously, I was shown to a little dressing room, a cubicle. There, I made myself unfettered and free. Lovely knee-low curtains separated me from other customers, and them from me. Everyone's identity must be kept absolutely secret when you're having a brassiere fitting, because it is a moment of truth that must be shared with no one. In fact, I would sometimes prefer the fitter herself to wear dark glasses.

I had just gotten two beautiful bracelets which Harry hadn't seen yet. I'd kept them carefully hidden at the hospital, but I'd told him that morning that he was getting them for me. I showed them to Lily Dale and my fitter. Lily Dale was one of the owners; Irma was the other. The bracelets were Indian—silver, studded with little semiprecious stones. Lily Dale and the fitter admired them and then went out to get my master size. They had a file of their customers' sizes that no one else could see.

I waited, looking around me, feeling like a pigeon in a pigeonhole. There is not much to see in a fitting room, as you no doubt know, and I soon exhausted the possibilities. Then I heard a series of strange noises. There was a flurry of muffled voices.

All of a sudden, Lile Dale dashed into my fitting room, grabbed my bracelets, said, "We're having a holdup, but stay calm. Everything is going to be all right," and ran out.

Well, a holdup in a brassiere shop! What a clever play on words. I was curious, so I drew back my outside curtain somewhat to see what was going on, but all I could see was Lily Dale. She was ashen white and running downstairs. Wasn't it clever of the burglars, I thought, to know where to go.

What are you supposed to do nude in a brassiere shop during a holdup? I wondered what Amy Vanderbilt would suggest.

Meanwhile, Lile Dale rushed back in and said, "Listen, stay calm. We have a little window downstairs, and I just shoved the fitter through it. She's small and we've pushed her through the opening and she's gone to get the police. Irma has fainted and we're not going to allow her to recover."

How were they going to keep Irma from recovering? But before I could ask this question, Lily Dale had departed again. (I only learned later that when Irma's large brown eyes had first opened, they were quickly closed by the woman bending over her, and saying in Hungarian, "For God's sake, keep your eyes closed. The police are coming.") The burglar needed the unconscious Irma to open the safe—only she knew the combination.

Then, under the curtain to my left, I saw a body being pulled by the legs into the dressing room next to mine. Lifting up that curtain, I inquired, "What has happened?"

The woman had fainted. Two women had fainted so far. She was sufficiently recovered, however, to murmur softly in a kind of refrain, looking at me all the while, "Digitalis, digitalis."

Meantime, I'm still standing there in all my nude glory, so I pulled my half-slip up over me. That way, I looked modest, but I also looked nine months pregnant."

"Take it easy, dear," I said to the poor woman, "everything will be all right."

Now there were little murmurings from the other pigeons in their cubbyholes, and they were getting nervous. So in a firm, clear voice I said: "The only thing we can do is remain calm. Let's sing." Because when the *Titanic* went down, everyone was singing.

We began with "The Star-Spangled Banner," but I was the only one who knew all the words. Well, what else to do? I decided to dress and venture forth ever so cautiously to see what was going on. I mean, this had to be the dumbest thing in the world.

I took a peek around the corner and saw Irma, in her deep coma—from which she had recuperated all of twenty minutes before—and the thief, who is rummaging through the merchandise. I walked up to the man, held out my arm and said, "Take my watch. I'll give you anything, but don't harm us."

He looked at my watch. "I don't want it," he said.

This is the watch Harry was looking at when he told me I have the most marvelous jewelry in the world; no one else has such wonderful jewelry as I do. My word of honor, the burglar didn't want my watch. It relieved and disappointed me both.

Chastened, I returned to my cubicle and resumed waiting, wondering why this holdup was taking so long.

Finally, Lily Dale rushed back to bring us the news. "You can all get dressed now," she said. The fitter had returned with the police at last.

We gathered our belongings, emerged, and proceeded to the front of the shop. Sure enough, there were the policemen. Two of them. "Oh, Miss Graham," said one, "we didn't know you were here. It's been so quiet."

"Well, I tried to lead them in song," I said. "But I'm fine. None of us was touched."

At which point the vandal, now handcuffed to a policeman, looked up and said, "*Virginia Graham!* Oh, Miss Graham, my wife loves your program. She thinks you're wonderful."

"Thank you," I said. You never know when you'll need a character reference.

I picked up Harry at the hospital and we took a taxi home. During the ride, I reported my adventure. By that time, I must say, shock had set in. The driver was hysterical. Taxi drivers have given me my postgraduate course in humanity. What they have to put up with! If you want to know who's going to win an election, or the latest word on human nature—pro or con—ask a veteran cab driver. And I want to warn everybody who's ever in the public eye to behave and be a good tipper. Even if you're paying a public relations man, tip a taxi driver, because he's going to tell one and all: "Guess who I had in my cab yesterday. ——— ———! And boy, is she tight." Be nice. Tip big and never fight with your husband in restaurants and taxis.

Fans in Toledo, Ohio, are fervent, too. Here's what happened to Bobby Vinton and me.

I had a speaking engagement there, and afterward, on the way back to the airport, the driver of the courtesy car said, "My Lord! The fans you have, Miss Graham. The people who were waiting for you to arrive in the lobby! Have you ever had an incident?"

"I recently had a robbery," I said. This is always a safe and true answer to that question. I've been robbed five times in the past six years. I'm in the Hall of Fame of the United Burglars of America. "The police think that maybe fans took a lot of the stuff because what they chose was so unusual. It may have been a man and a woman and the woman was my size."

"We had something here," he said, and proceeded to tell me all about it. Bobby Vinton had given a concert in Toledo and the name of the hotel he stayed at was publicized. The day after he left the hotel, they got a very urgent call from a woman saying, "Has Mr. Vinton left?"

"Yes."

"Has his room been rented?"

She was switched to the room clerk and the room clerk said, "No. The room hasn't been rented."

"Put me on to the housekeeper," the woman said. "I want to talk to the housekeeper."

The housekeeper came on and the woman said, "Has anybody been in Mr. Vinton's room since he left?"

"Why, did he lose something?"

"No, but I want you to tell me what you did to Mr. Vinton's room."

"We changed the sheets, madam. Why?"

"I want to buy his mattress."

And she came over to the hotel and bought the mattress.

Later I met Bobby at O'Hare Airport in Chicago. He had a package with him.

"Look, Virginia," he said.

In his package were two of the most exquisite cups made in Poland.

"I never thought stars carried packages," I said, "only me." I always have a brown paper bag with a big fruit stain, or something. I never have the dignity of entering an airplane without having a terrible package that I manage to acquire at the last moment.

So Bobby asked me, "Do you like the cups?"

"They're priceless, Bobby," I said. "You'd better give them to me. I collect porcelain." They were beautiful.

"See this outfit I'm wearing?" said Bobby. He had on the most stunning dungaree outfit, with insets of leather. Absolutely gorgeous. A fan gave it to him.

I love all my fans. I wouldn't trade them for anything. Still, I sometimes yearn for the golden days of Lillian Russell and Marilyn Miller and the Ziegfeld girls. The age of the stage-door Johnnies.

One of my most wonderful fans is Verna Corsi, who lives in Philadelphia. She first wrote to me when I was on *This Is Your Life*. In those days, with Harry to help, we tried to make sure that each and every letter received an appreciative response. Verna's letter was especially warm and generous, and Harry replied in kind. Well, Verna wrote again and Harry responded again and soon Verna and Harry had become pen pals, Harry always signing my name on the letters. For ten years or so they corresponded regularly. And Verna would call me from time to time to make sure I was okay. When Lynn was married, she received a wedding gift from Verna. When Lynn gave birth to Jan and to Steven, congratulations. And every Christmas, Verna sent homemade breads and cookies and presents.

Then one year I was going to Philadelphia to speak. Harry said, "Virginia, Verna has been so marvelous to us, you must invite her to have dinner with us. We must try to repay some of the kindness she's given to our family."

So I called Verna up and told her where we'd be staying and asked her to join us for dinner. "Oh," she said, "I'll have to go on a diet and go to the dentist and have my hair fixed."

"I don't want any excuses," I said. "Meet us in the lobby."

When we got out of the elevator, there Verna is, this darling woman who looks just exactly the way her voice sounds, the way I had always pictured her. She came up and shook my hand and said, "I'm very happy to meet you, Virginia, but the person I want even more to meet is Harry."

"Well, that's very nice," I said.

"Never in my life," said Verna, "have I heard a wife rave so much about a man. All your letters about how wonderful Harry is, what a marvelous husband, have made me feel that you must be the luckiest woman in the world."

"Without a doubt," I said, light suddenly dawning. No wonder Harry had enjoyed the correspondence so much.

We had a very pleasant dinner with Verna and asked her back to our suite afterward. Meantime, Harry and I had a few minutes alone and I cornered him. Since Harry always signed my name, he said, "What was I supposed to write her about?" he said. "I'm not very good at girl talk, so I just told her how I would do this for you and I would do that for you."

"Harry," I said, "you know that this woman is going to ask for my autograph, don't you?"

"Oh, no, no, no," said Harry.

Sure enough, later in our suite, Verna said, "My grandchild instructed me especially to get Virginia's autograph. Here's a piece of paper."

"My dress needs fixing," I said, taking the piece of paper. "Harry, would you help me unzip in the bedroom?"

"I'll help you," said Verna.

"No," I said, "Harry will do it."

So Harry and I go into the bedroom where Harry signed my autograph.

Last year, two decades after Ralph Edwards did my life, I was talking to Verna on the telephone. I'd never been able to tell this story on the air because I didn't want Verna to know. So she said to me, "Virginia, I haven't heard from you for months. Harry used to write all the time. Why doesn't he write anymore?"

"What are you talking about, Verna?" I said.

"You don't think he fooled me with those letters, do you? That handwriting was masculine. I knew that Harry must be writing those letters."

"You devil," I said. "You let us go on thinking all that time . . ."

And never said a word. How's that for a class fan?

In some cases, I think there must be a relationship between the words "fan" and "fantasy." When I was doing *Barefoot in the Park* in Ohio with George Maharis, Jessica Walters, and Woody Romoff, women young and old used to steal George's underwear every night.

I've never in my life known what it was like to have a crush on someone. Even as a teenager, I never had a crush on a male star or anyone like that. I don't know whether it's a blessing or a curse. But the underwear manufacturers of America should have given George Maharis a permanent endowment, or a gift certificate, or a plaque, or something. I was hanging out all my old clothes, hoping that someone would steal them, just for status, but in vain. I guess George made a large contribution to their erotic zones.

Family fans can be the most fantastic. I know that Mama was a fan of mine. She loved me deeply. She just couldn't understand me, try as she would. Surely I must have belonged to somebody else.

When *Girl Talk* first went on the air, Aunt Celia and Mama were absolutely mortified. We had never been a theatrical family. Also, Mama did not ever believe that anyone would pay me. She always believed that I worked for nothing. Who in the world would pay her daughter to talk, to perform?

It's a joke. Butchers, bakers, door-to-door salesmen, they get paid, because they sell a product you can see and touch. But actors, performers, comedians? Never. Artists, painters, writers, musicians? Never. It's a part of the American cultural pattern, and we are all prey to it. If Lynn, when she was courting, had brought home a struggling young actor as a prospective husband, Harry would have entered intensive care. We would have had to hold the wedding at the funeral parlor, because Harry would have been in mourning. Everybody knows that actors do not, cannot, earn a living.

So when Aunt Celia saw *Girl Talk* in Chicago, she called up Mama and said: "Bessie, it's the most terrible thing that ever happened to us. You live in a hotel where you're respected, don't go downstairs. Stay in your room. It'll be off in a week. Why, the things they talk about, you never heard! You should see Virginia, she looks dreadful."

For a week Mama wouldn't leave her room. Finally, when she must have been desperate for oxygen, she decided to brave it. She figured to go down to the lobby late at night when the people were all napping in their rooms. Well, they must have napped early that night, because when Mama stepped off the elevator, she was greeted by applause. Mama looked around to see who was behind her, but she was alone. "Bessie," they said, "you must be thrilled about Virginia. It's a marvelous show. We can't wait for it to come on."

But poor Mama was in shock. To think that such a thing should happen to her daughter. But I know Mama loved me. To the end of her life she told the whole world, she absolutely insisted, that I was a natural blonde.

The Price of Love

Age—growing up—is often the most difficult thing of all to adjust to, both in ourselves and in other people. Each new decade becomes a treacherous milestone, heralded with feelings of fear and trauma. As we enter our twenties, our thirties, our forties, we think, Well, I made it through the last one but look at the one ahead. Each ten years adds to our mounting anxiety that youth, indeed life, is passing us by. And by the time we reach fifty, we have to be brutally honest: Youth has departed forever. Middle age has us firmly by the hand and our own September song is about to begin.

At this point, the worst thing you could possibly do would be to go to your high school or college reunion. When I went back, I thought they were all my teachers. My classmates had changed so much they didn't recognize me.

We mark the passage of the years in various ways—graduations, marriages, sickness, anniversaries, deaths. Recollecting afterward, we say, "Oh yes, that was just before Aunt Julie's divorce, remember?" And that's the way we measure time. That's the way the generations come and go.

One morning at ten o'clock, the phone rang in my apartment. It was Houston. My nephew David, whom I adore and who's named after Papa, said, "Hi, Aunt Ginny, this is David."

I said, "Hi, darling." At ten o'clock in the morning?

He said, "Aunt Ginny, I have bad news for you."

"Mama?" I said. Because Mama was eighty-four years old.

141

"No," said David. "Daddy. I think Daddy's dead."

"What do you mean, David?"

"He had a heart attack," said David. He didn't know how to tell me that his daddy was dead.

"Hannah," I called into the kitchen, "my brother Juddy died. Call Harry. Get Harry to come home."

I couldn't cry. Sometimes I cannot cry when I'm shocked. The world stands still and I can't react. I want to scream and I want to cry. Why can't I feel? Juddy was dead, and I didn't feel anything. God help me, I thought, I'm dying and I can't feel.

Finally, I said, "David, where is your mother?"

"Aunt Ginny, you won't believe it, but it's the first time Mother's left Daddy in all the thirty years they've been married. Patty is having a baby, and Mama went to Peoria." Patty was David's twin sister.

"Does she know? How can I get her?" I asked.

"She knows," said David. "Daddy's being buried in Chicago. I'm taking care of everything."

"I will meet you all in Chicago," I said, and hung up.

Now I have to tell you about Juddy and me. The only evidence of extrasensory perception I've ever had in my life came when Juddy had his first coronary. I'm not psychic but I'm enormously intuitive. I get vibrations from other people, not from former lives, including my own, or I'd probably cut my throat. But I'm a vibrating machine about other people. I get them so quickly it frightens me.

When Juddy had his heart attack, Harry and I were in Boston. I learned later that at the moment he had his coronary, I had said, "Oh, my God," and grabbed my chest.

Then I said, "Harry, a knife went through me here. What did I eat?" A half-hour later, my sister-in-law called to tell us that Juddy had had a heart attack.

Now I have to pay tribute to one of the most wonderful women I've ever known in my life, and that's my sister-in-law Joanie. After he recovered from that heart attack, Juddy wanted to move to Houston, Texas, and Joanie said all right. She said okay. "Whither thou goest . . ." (Was it Naomi or Ruth who said that in the Bible?) They only knew one couple down there, but the doctor said the climate was good for Juddy's health, so they picked up and moved to a simple little house in Houston, leaving their relatives behind.

Papa did a love-of-life job with Juddy and me. Not Mama, because she loved life in a different way. Papa spoon-fed us the love of life, the joy of life.

Parents create children for many reasons: to prove the man's prowess, his macho masculinity, to give the woman someone to fondle and love, to create a fine new citizen for the world. And although they were both wonderful men, I think if Papa was trying to create in Juddy a son in his own image, he was not one-hundred-percent successful.

I don't think Papa really wanted Juddy to go into his business, but it seemed a shame for him not to. Juddy was not in love with Papa's business. All his life Juddy loved mechanics and aviation. Now Papa couldn't put a light bulb into a socket. He was totally cerebral. Juddy could construct a miniature train set with his hands. He was a master builder with his hands.

Papa had a tremendous compassion, and Juddy had it too. But Juddy inherited Mama's fears. Fear was his constant bedfellow. Yet he wanted to be an aviator and loved to fly. (Isn't that ironic? While many people who live without fear on the ground are scared to death in airplanes.) And when they got to Houston, where the country is flat enough to land an airplane anywhere, Juddy still couldn't be an aviator because of his heart condition.

After Papa died, Mama followed Joanie and Juddy to Houston, where she lived in a senior citizen's home. We decided not to tell her right away about Juddy's death. I had wanted Mama to live with me, but I was away so much, she decided it was better to go to Houston. She always got along well with Joanie, and Joanie adored Mama. Joanie was as fine a daughter as any mother could have. She knew how to handle Mama, whereas I was terribly sensitive and needed a lot of handling myself. You sometimes had to sort of put a slipcover over the truth when you were telling me things.

Papa would say, "Ginny, darling, don't you think it might have been wiser to have thought about this a little bit before you did it?" Mama said, "What'd you do that for?" You know? She got directly to the point.

I was thinking about all these things on the plane to Juddy's funeral. When I arrived in Chicago, there was Joanie, who had been Juddy's constant companion since their marriage, who had left him for one day to attend the birth of their grandchild, and during the course of it had become a widow. Could she have saved him? Of course not. It happened in a second. The doctor had said, "You're fifty-seven years old. You're in perfect condition, but when you drive, don't drive over two hundred miles a day."

That day, for some reason, Juddy wanted to get home quicker. He had dinner with Mama. He got up the next morning. The cleaning woman greeted him, heard him say to his partner on the phone, "Be at the corner, I'll pick you up in twenty minutes." When she came by a few minutes later, he was on the floor, dead. Like that.

There's nothing anyone could have done. And God must have loved Juddy. He spared him the anguish of a long suffering. Ever since he had been locked in a dark closet as a little boy, Juddy had feared death. All his life, he was afraid of that moment, and when it came . . .

Thank God he went the way he did. Though at the time, it was no comfort to Joanie, to his children, or to me. I was destroyed. I love too deeply. This is my problem.

I will never get over him. He was so full of fun. Everybody loved him. At his funeral I was shocked because everyone laughed. They were laughing because Juddy had brought laughter to them. All his fraternity brothers were there, and they were talking about the crazy, wonderful things he did. He was loyal. He never had a bad word to say about anybody.

I sat all by myself. I couldn't talk to my friends. I didn't want to be near anybody. I couldn't look at him. I had to remember Juddy the way he was, and I was afraid I would see something that wasn't Juddy.

I want to tell you what I heard recently, and I wonder how true it is. In our profession, the childlike quality of the actor makes him want to look for the magical, the metaphysical. Actors are often the first to believe in cults, the first to believe in an afterlife. And this one actor was telling me—I don't know where he read it—that a group of scientists had measured the body before and after death. They measured excretion, they measured water content, air, all the component elements of the body. And guess what they found! There were a certain number of ounces that couldn't be accounted for, that left the body at the time of death.

Could that be the soul? Could that be the moment when a body is no longer the home of the person you loved?

After the funeral, we faced a dilemma: How do we tell Mama? Mama was still in Houston. She didn't come to the funeral. How do you tell an eighty-four-year-old woman that her only son has passed away? We decided to do it in stages. So I called Mama and said, "Mama, dear, Juddy has had another heart attack. We don't know what's going to happen, darling, but we've got very good doctors and we're doing the best we can." And every few days I called her in Houston and I told her, "Well, today he didn't look so well. The doctors weren't pleased today. It really was a more severe attack than we thought."

And then, about ten days after the funeral, I flew down to Houston with Joanie and we went over to the nursing home. We called the doctor in charge and said, "Please give my mother sedation." He had been told immediately the day that Juddy left us.

Well, what we didn't count on was age. The deterioration of a certain kind of sensitivity, not really of deep feeling, but just living and getting used to gradually seeing everyone around you die. A numbness sets in, a kind of necessary stoicism—not the raw nerve of youth that feels with such intensity.

They gave her a tranquilizer and I walked into the room and she said, "What are you doing here, Ginny?"

"I had to come out here, on business, Mama," I said. "You know, I represent Clairol, and they have a beauty show."

"Why didn't you call me and say you were coming?"

"I wanted to talk to you about something, Mama. Juddy didn't make it."

"Oh, my God," she said. That's the only thing she ever said about Juddy.

"It was a couple of weeks ago, Mama," I said. She thanked us by her silence for not bringing her to Chicago.

Then she said, "Now what's going to happen to me?"

"Well, Mama dear," I said, "I've come to take you to New York. Joanie's going back to Chicago to live. And while I'm on the road, we'll make provisions for you at a home. There is a perfectly beautiful nursing home in White Plains where you will have the greatest care in the world."

"I'm not going," she said. "I'm not going."

This woman who had lived in hospitals all her life was now refusing the care a nursing home could provide. It took us three days to get Mama to agree to come back east with me.

So that was the way we lost Juddy. I couldn't have his picture up anymore. I couldn't bear to look at it.

I can hardly bear to believe that all that life was mortal. You see, I think we're born with a belief in immortality. We always think it will happen to everybody else, but not to us, not to our loved ones. And some people can never accept the fact that we are common clay. It's very hard for me to accept.

I think it was Sigmund Freud who said that the purpose of life is to prepare us for death. I believe that with all my heart. I think that's what all of us are doing, whether we know it, whether we admit it or not.

I don't cry for Joanie or their children. I cry for Juddy. Joanie was the best wife a man ever had in the world. I adore her. No one was ever kinder to my parents or loved my brother as much as she did.

When grief comes to us, it seems unendurable. It seems that life is making inhuman demands on a body not equipped to withstand such shock and pain and emptiness. We feel inconsolable, because we realize what we've lost and what we must live without. If you really love, you never get over it. You learn to live with the pain, the rejection, but you never get over it. And death appears to be the ultimate rejection, both for the one who dies and for those who love and mourn him. Nothing else is so final. But for most of us, life has to go on.

I don't know if people who never love are better or worse off. At the end of the world, maybe I'll be able to tell you, but I don't know now. Because it costs so much to love. And most of us, sooner or later, have to pay the price.

The Two Faces of Virginia

I don't know exactly when it occurred to me that before I went back on the airwaves again, I would have to present a new face to the world.

Several years earlier, a friend of mine who was a very heavy drinker had her face done. Drinking is something the doctors warn you against if you're contemplating a face lift, because the skin tissue holds the liquid and they can't do the sculpting properly. It really is sculpting. And this girl was a catastrophe, because the skin around her eye was tightened up too high, and when she blinked, all of a sudden in the middle of the movement her eyelid would stall. You wouldn't believe it. We'd be talking and her eyelid would just come to a complete standstill on its downward or upward course, like a malfunctioning garage door.

I'd noticed for many years that so many people on television had allowed their surgeons to give nature a little boost. It didn't necessarily have anything to do with chronological age. And some people seemed to cultivate puffs under the eyes, maybe as a form of therapy. Facing the facts, it's sometimes called. At the airport, I used to say, "I'm going to have to pay excess weight on seven bags. Five on the floor and two under my eyes."

But now, I felt, the time had come. The television camera is unmerciful. It picks up details a microscope would miss. I believe this was after I had left *Girl Talk*, and I believe I had just made a tour for Cancer, and there was interest in the new Virginia Graham show in California. And if I'm going to conquer new worlds, I thought, I'd better get this surgery done prónto. I certainly needed uplifting. My spirits were soaring to the depths.

I was told of a very fine doctor, Dr. Tom Reese, who had done several lady stars. One prominent actress I knew of had undergone the operation every five years since she was thirty-five, and she was absolutely girlish when I met her on *Girl Talk*. So I decided to go see Dr. Reese.

When I told her, my sister-in-law said, "Ginny, do you think you should have the flesh cut into?" Well, I had totally divorced myself from the idea of the actuality of cancer, and I suddenly realized I had been giving it lip service. One part of me had been able to deny the anguish, to deny I ever felt it; and the other had been able to talk in public about cancer problems. Somehow, I guess, Virginia the Survivor had been able to talk about cancer without becoming sick. The survival part, perhaps tucked away in some little recess, has enabled me to do the work I've done.

The doctor must have conferred with the powers-that-be. When I asked him the question, he said, "Absolutely not. There's no danger of metastasizing." They gave me all kinds of tests.

I had always thought that plastic surgery was like having a tooth pulled. Because of course I was not going to Have My Face Done. I was only going to have them do a little work under the eyes. There was a little venetian-blind effect around my upper eye, which we had always considered a family characteristic. Nothing serious.

There was, too, a certain amount of fudge sauce below the chin that had to go. Because the most damaging thing for a woman, you see, is what we might call the second-string chin line. And when that sags, right under the first-string chin, you're in big trouble.

That was it, the eyes and the chin. Nothing done with the cheeks or the forehead. I don't have serious frown lines yet.

They took me to a photographer. I think he had specialized in taking underwater pictures of sharks. He must have used a specially developed camera with little magnifying areas on the lens that focus themselves like leeches on every single problem your face presents. I looked like a subversive prison warden. Or a sniper. There were definitely criminal tendencies in my face. Any traces of softness or humanity were obliterated by this camera. I think it's manufactured for plastic surgeons only. There is no other way you could use this camera except to convict someone of a federal crime on the basis of facial expression alone. (After you get to the operating room, they give you a mirror put out by the same people.)

When I saw that picture, I was tempted to call the whole thing off. Then I started laughing. You've got to do it, I told myself. Can you doubt that? There's nowhere to go but up. If you're ever on the brink, just get that picture taken.

Next, said the doctor, we're going to a hospital. That hadn't occurred to me. I don't remember where I thought it was going to be done. I'd heard of some people having it done in the doctor's office, then you go out and have a Chinese dinner. But this doctor said no, he did it in the hospital.

Well, I said, that's fine. That's okay. I'll go to the hairdresser and have my hair done, because after all, what's it going to be? Nothing. I'll get my hair done first, the way I would for anything.

When I finally enter the hospital, the first thing they do is give me a hair shampoo with a soap made to get rid of three-inch-deep vermin on sheep that were lost in the woods for a long time. They say to me, now you will wash your hair.

"I will *what?*" I say.

"You will wash your hair."

"I just came from the hairdresser." I am aghast. "Why should I wash my hair?"

"Now, Miss Graham," I am admonished. "We've heard about your sense of humor."

Miss Graham?

I had entered the hospital, I had embarked on this treacherous journey, under the name of Mrs. Harry Guttenberg, because the secret of my deformities, if any, are going to be kept from the world at large forevermore. At any cost. So:

"Miss Graham," I am told, "you will wash your hair." I begin washing. I am appalled. This is not only ten dollars down the drain, but the hair color I use to preserve my natural color is now running freely in the sink. I am now an exquisite tangerine color. As I wash, the blond ends become this beautiful orange hue.

When I have finished, my attendant says, "You will now take off your makeup because we want to do some tests."

I am standing there minus any of the other apparatus that keeps your body in the right shape. I am standing there in this depressing muslin gown. This muslin gown is what you would give your worst enemy for her trousseau. I have never seen such fashion brilliance, and I'm standing there, twinkle toes, barefoot in the dark, having a wonderful time. This is a marvelous dividend of an experience to go through just to have my chin and eyes fixed.

Now they start coming for blood, and I think, Ah, Dracula. At last my nightmares of Transylvania are coming true. The infinite charm and wealth and variety of human experience. Then they say, "Now we are going to X-ray and we would like a specimen."

At that point, I'm about to . . . Oh, here comes the cardiogram, which is definitely the best thing that ever happened to me. And I'm standing there in all my naked splendor when a young nurse pops her head in the door and says, "Excuse me, I heard someone say she heard Virginia Graham in here. Oh . . . oh . . . I didn't mean to disturb you."

She *heard*. I went in as Mrs. Guttenberg and when I opened my mouth and said hello, that was the end of my secret.

I'm getting a little panicky now. They've taken the cardiogram, they've taken blood, they've taken a specimen, they've taken my blood pressure, and we're going down to X-ray. I put on my little woolly slippers and bravely follow my attendant in all my muslin glory.

There are a number of people in X-ray already, waiting their turn. No one recognizes me. It could be

Asia. It could be Ponce de León was the first person there and I'm the second. No one knows me. Then the technician calls my name.

"Mrs. Guttenberg."

"Here I am!"

"Who was that? Who said that?"

"I did," I said.

"Miss Graham! You've been here all the time?"

I broke into a cold sweat. What is happening? I wondered. Who am I? What crazy business am I here for? If Rapunzel had let down her hair for me to climb out of that window, X-ray would never have seen me again.

I was terrified. What was I doing to myself? This is the procedure I went through for appendicitis, for an ovary taken out when I was eighteen years old, for cancer. Every time I left the hospital I thanked God for the fact that I'd never have to go back in. And here I'm doing just that of my own free will. Not because I have to. I've *chosen* to do this. This is elective. . . .

These unremitting thoughts attend me through X-ray, back up to my room, and into bed. I am close to panic.

In comes the anesthetist. His face is unmistakably Middle Eastern. I realize immediately that there is no way to look at him and think he came from Florida after a good winter. He tells me his name.

"Oh," I say, "how do you do, Doctor? Are you from Puerto Rico?" Which is terrible, because you never ask a person his nationality. But I had this awful foreboding in my heart, this premonition.

"No."

I wasn't content with that. "South America?" I ask hopefully.

"No, Mrs. Guttenberg, I'm from Cairo."

"Oh, I love the pyramids," I say. "King Farouk was my favorite pin-up man." What I want to tell him is that Guttenberg is my *married* name. I want to say that my real name is Graham. At the same time, I'm trying desperately to figure out what my real name is.

I want to warn the doctor that I once had a very unfortunate allergic reaction to anaesthesia, which is not uncommon, so I say, "Now, Doctor, the only thing I ask of you, my one fear is seeing the operating room."

On television and in movies, they prepare the patient. They lean over the patient and say, "Now we're going in, John, and . . ." This is not my idea of helpful preparation. I want to escape from any knowledge of the existence of the operating room.

At one time, they gave sodium pentothal to the patient in the room, which immediately put the patient to sleep. You would wake up back in your room after the operation was over, eliminating the horrible sights of the operating room. But in recent years, this practice has been discontinued by some doctors, who feel that it is a dangerous procedure. So now they have all this marvelous therapeutic information. It's the funereal approach to surgery: This may be your last day on earth. Prepare to meet your . . .

I'm hemmed in by a human wall, barricaded, a prisoner of my vanity. I can't escape. I want to run, to get out, to vamoose. Right this minute. That's all in the world I want.

"We don't take any unnecessary risks," he tells me. Well, I try to figure that one out. If I've learned the English language, he's telling me that the only risks they take are the necessary ones.

What is this I'm doing? I look at myself in the mirror and it all comes back to me.

"Please knock me out," I said.

Kindly understand that I have blood that is almost always free from medication. If there is a crisis where I may have suffered a compound fracture, I may take a Bufferin. But I don't take pills, don't ask me why. My stoicism is ridiculous, but I'm just not pill-oriented.

"We'll give you a Demerol," he says.

"Give me a double dose." That's me, telling the doctor what to do.

So I get a double dose. It has a total reverse effect

on me, and soon I am ready to represent the U.S. of A. in the first all-girl Olympic marathon. I have all the energy in the world.

Now we are in the hall. My eyes are closed. They think I am asleep but I'm desperately trying to communicate with someone, anyone, because I have the horrible feeling that this is what it may be like after, you know, you leave this world and are standing by to enter another one . . . you hope.

I wait. And wait. It's like being in the checkout line at the supermarket. All the carts are lined up. Nurses are standing by. Suddenly I decide that I'm choking, and I try to make this clear to all present. Demonstrating . . . explaining . . .

That's all I remember before The Surgery. It seems I wake up slightly on the operating table before it is finished, but they put me back under. I don't remember any of this.

When I wake up for good, I'm in the recovery room, got up like a football player, covered with bandages and plaster of Paris. The doctor has told me it will take a few days for the swelling to go down, and the black and blue to disappear. "And don't look at yourself in the mirror. That's one thing we advise all our patients not to do."

"How am I am going to keep from doing this?" I ask.

"By wearing dark glasses," he tells me. "We'll get you some."

I had thought I'd be out dancing.

"You'll be up and walking around, of course, and we keep you in your room overnight. Just don't look at yourself in the mirror. That's all I have to tell you."

I didn't need to look in the mirror. All I had to do was look at the expression on the face of my nurse when she saw my face. That expression was more brutal than any mirror. That expression was a perfect translation of: "I've seen head-on collisions that looked better than you do, kiddo."

How can I live with myself this way? I ask that question over and over again in my head.

But there's no pain whatsoever. None.

Twelve o'clock midnight, and the doctors come in. They woke me up. One of the assistants to the doctor said, "I think there may be a little blood clot forming under here, but there'll be no hematoma." He says to me, "You gave us a bad time, didn't you? Why were you fighting us in the recovery room?"

I remembered nothing, but apparently it took several people to hold me down. I fought and flailed around like Moby Dick. I don't know why he told me about it. I was not in good shape before, but I was absolutely a wreck after he told me that.

I have decided to teach a course in how to suture the lips of anyone about to give you useless information, and then I think: How ridiculous! I'm criticizing this doctor who came in at midnight to see how I was, to see if there might be a problem.

And we wonder about the mortality rate for doctors.

At some point, another nurse came in and said, "Oh, Miss Graham, you've had a face lift."

"A what?" I was insulted.

"You've had your face lifted."

"Oh, no, no, no!" I hastened to enlighten this misinformed girl. "That's what happens in hospitals. They sometimes give out the wrong information. I just had my eyes and chin done."

"Well, what do you think that is?"

"It's having my eyes and chin done."

"Oh, no," she said. "That's what we call a face lift."

"What's it called if I have my cheeks and everything?"

"That's more extensive," she said. "Grade two or grade three."

I just had a simple face lift. A mini-lift. The doctor had told me my chin might have to be done in two parts, because of the fullness. "If we don't get it all up behind the ears," he said, "we do a little cross under the chin." And now I'm very religious, because I have a beautiful cross under my chin, which you can't see.

So then I am ready to leave. Hospitals are very

kind. They let you leave in a wheelchair. The reason for this is not so much the humanity as the fact that you might faint from dizziness, fall, fracture your skull, and sue the hospital.

Lynn has sent me a great big elephant with candy kisses taped on it. She has a thing for animals. And other people have provided me with a few toys. I had sent Harry to buy a wig for my head. My first wig. It belonged by rights to Mary Poppins after she stuck her finger in a light-bulb socket. Or Little Orphan Annie scared out of her wits. Either one.

Out of the elevator and into the lobby I roll in my wheelchair, my dark glasses, and my wig. Don't ask me what I look like. All I have to do now is say my good-byes.

In the lobby I see a woman waiting for someone. This woman is looking at me thoughtfully. She's staring, to tell you the truth, and beginning to give voice to the eloquence of her thoughts:

"Is it . . . no, I don't think so . . . Yes . . . but no, it couldn't be . . . Are you? . . . You *must* be . . . No . . ."

I wave at her.

Now she is ready for therapy. She decides she has recognized me. This is a triumph for her.

"What in the world are you doing here," she asks, "with all those baby things?"

I give her a smile. "I just had the first fetal transplant."

At which point I was wheeled away to the outside world. And with all due modesty, Ethel Barrymore never made a finer exit.

That was Wednesday. I had gone in on Monday and the operation was on Tuesday. On Friday I had fifteen people to dinner. There was not a single mark on my neck, only a little bit of swelling. The eyes were what took longest, for me, to heal. So I wore dark glasses. I was able to do my own hair, and on Saturday night Harry and I went to Voisin for dinner.

The next time I was on Merv Griffin, he said, "Gee, you look fine."

"Oh, I just had my face done," I said.

"You *what?* What do you mean, you just had your face done?"

"I had my eyes fixed," I said. "They were charging me on airplanes for excess baggage. And while they were at it, they did my chinny-chin-chin."

Merv said, "I don't believe you. You're sitting here, Virginia, and telling the world you've had your face done?"

At which time I think they were giving mouth-to-mouth resuscitation to Harry, who had collapsed in the green room. He had always pleaded with me not to divulge my age to everybody I knew, how many years I've been married, how many wrinkles. He said no matter what you tell them, they're going to add five or ten years. Harry said, "I'd much rather have them say, 'My God, doesn't she look terrific' than, 'Who does she think she's kidding?'"

I told Merv the whole story. He couldn't get over it. I had joined the ranks of the thousands of men and women who went in and had their faces lifted.

We go for any number of reasons. I once did a show with a magnificent young girl in her twenties, and the first thing I said to her was, "You are the most beautiful girl, but you've got big bags under your eyes. You ought to get more rest."

"I slept ten hours last night," she said.

I pleaded with her to have her eyes fixed. She said, "I've wanted to. It's bad enough now. What will it be like when I'm older?"

Chronological age has nothing to do with it. Some people have what they call the "elk-dog look." Have you ever seen an elk dog? They've got a big swelling under the eyes and they always look like they're crying. It's a pleat of flesh that hangs all the way down the chin. One woman told me she had such a sense of deformity about herself that she might just as well wear a Halloween mask. Two weeks after she had it done, she was absolutely beautiful.

Why should men and women not know secrets like that? These days, men may outnumber women. I've been told that one hospital in New Jersey only takes care of men. I'm glad they've still got one place where they can privately go besides the men's room. When is the john going to become the john and joanna? Coed johns, now there's a terrifying thought.

One thing I cautioned the doctor about: "Please don't change the expression on my face, because I like it." I think there's a certain softness you need for maturity. So he kept that softness, and people tell me today that I've never looked better.

There has to be a rapport between you and the surgeon. You're buying his skill, but you're also buying his sympathy and understanding. Examine your motives. Do you feel that just by getting rid of a few wrinkles and a bag or two that you're going to be a happy person, if you were not a happy person before? Find out what your needs are. Are they plastic? Or are they spiritual?

To wonderful Dr. Reese, I say, "Thank you for giving me a new Reese on life."

Color me two-faced.

The Eleventh Commandment

When *Girl Talk* went on the air, I began getting mail from all over the country. Even in New York City, people are lonely. And even in New York City, you have to try to stay in contact with the rest of the world. Otherwise you go crazy, or die of loneliness, or both. You can't just relate to the people in your own community, no matter how small or large. It's too restricting, and the whole outside world is too big and alive and wonderful.

I used to get letters, you know, from Portland, Maine and Fresno, California. "If you were only my neighbor!" And I would feel so good, because that meant they liked me. And I would feel the same way, right back. One lady wrote that she thought I must be the best listener in the world. I made a point of showing that letter to friends who claim they can never get a word in edgewise.

When I was a little girl, Papa gave me a wonderful basic course in neighborliness. Papa used to say, "Darling, if Moses had waited a little longer, the eleventh commandment would have been, 'Thou shalt feel thy neighbor's pain.'"

I'd tuck what Papa said away in my head, and more or less forget about it, but sooner or later he'd remind me by saying it again.

One day, when I was old enough to do some thinking of my own, I said, "What about the Golden Rule, Papa? Do unto others . . . ?"

"That's a barter system," said Papa. "You're asking for an even deal. You're saying, 'If you do for me, I'll do for you,' and that's not the same thing at all."

Eventually, I began to understand. With the eleventh commandment, what you do is identify with the other person. You pretend that exactly what has caused that person's pain has happened to you instead, in order to find out what it feels like. This is a way of understanding the people around you, but it is also something else: It is a way of making friends. When he cited the eleventh commandment, Papa was giving me a magic ingredient in the recipe for friendship.

Can you imagine a life without friends? Can you imagine the dreariness of living out your days without the comfort and joy of friendship?

When I was a little girl, I had fantasies about friends. Like most children, I was sometimes very lonely and it was then that I loved my dolls the most. Loneliness stimulates the imagination, and for a long time I was able to believe that my dolls were real little girls like me. And of course they were perfect friends. They always minded me; they were agreeable to everything I chose to do; and I could pretend that they never grew tired of the sound of my voice, or bored with listening to all the fascinating things that I had to say. I used to creep up on them unawares, certain each time that I would actually catch them in real-life motion.

Later, I discovered that friendship was not so simple. Other little girls and boys were not carbon copies of me. They had inner feelings and needs, too, equally as demanding as mine, and not at all the same. What's more, I liked them, differences and all, and wanted to be friends.

But my real education in friendship began after I received my first rejection. That was when I got my first awareness of my own imperfection in the world outside Papa, Mama, Juddy, and me. There's nothing like a good, healthy rejection to make us take stock of ourselves. There's nothing more instructive, if you choose to be instructed. It's the best basis for self-education there is.

Our earliest experiences in friendship—the same as in life—are trial and error. That's the way we discover what's going to work for us and what is not. If a certain strategy works okay, we figure we're on the right track. If it doesn't, if we're rejected, we know that something must be wrong.

It is hard to change ourselves. But it's a whole lot harder to change another person. I'm willing to go even farther. I'm willing to say that it's next to impossible.

"No" is the second most important word in the English language. Mama taught us that lesson very young. It was marvelous training for Juddy and me. Would you like to know the most important word? "Yes." Papa said yes to everything, and Mama said no. And they were both telling the truth.

Actually, it was Mama who gave me my character. Whatever strength is in me she called forth, because she taught me the value of "no." I always said that Mama never needed plastic surgery because saying no never creates a wrinkle. If you smile too much, your face ages. And Mama said no to everything, but that no was life. Life *is* no. Life is not yes. Am I right? Otherwise, yes has no value.

Mama totally took away my conceit. Ego she couldn't take away. My ego she probably strengthened. But every time I thought I was some smart kid, the way you often do when you're ten and eleven, she put this question to me: "Who are you to think you are better?"

As time went by, I discovered that if I wanted to make friends—and I did—I had to do something besides fantasize. I had to do something besides shake hands and say hello and smile. Being grown-up is a lot more complicated than being a child. Papa's words came back to me time and time again, as they do to this day: Thou shalt feel thy neighbor's pain.

It helps me every time.

When I had the cancer, the first thing I called out to God was, "Why, God, why of all people does this have to happen to me?" I started to make a list of fabulous people who had died young. Then I tried to think what their anguish was when they knew they were dying. Who in God's name was I to think I was better and more deserving?

Somehow, wrestling with my own fear and pain, I was able to perceive that others had been there earlier. I was not the first person on earth to suffer from cancer, nor the first to ask why. And in thinking of others, my own burden was eased.

Recently, after speaking to the Junior League in Toledo, this woman came up to me with a friend and put her head on my chest and started to weep. I didn't know what had happened. I looked at her friend and her friend looked at me. Then I said, "Cry if it's going to make you feel better, but please tell me why you're crying."

"I have cancer all through my body," she said. "Every lymph gland is involved. I knew that you were operable and they took the cancer out, but how am I going to get through these days? How am I going to live?"

"I'll tell you how," I said. "You're going to live by thinking of the fact that every medical textbook is full of miracles. When I had occasion to pray for a miracle in behalf of a friend, I called the American Cancer Society. Lane Adams, to whom I was speaking, said, 'Virginia, there are cases of remission, there are cases of cures through chemotherapy that are unbelievable.'"

The tears were still streaming down her face.

"But nothing is going to help you if you don't help yourself. If I could only tell you how important it is to think positively. Because you have to help the chemotherapy and help the radiation and help everything they're doing, because this crying is a terribly deteriorating thing. It's important for you to be able to say, 'Well, let's get on with it and do the best we can.'

"From what you are telling me, you can't cry in front of your husband and children, because then the whole family will cave in, so you're trying to be a pillar of strength. And thank God you can cry with your friend here."

I said, "Anytime, day or night, that you are really and truly desperate, you call me collect. Because it's a small payment from me to the world, who helped keep me alive."

You know something? That woman and I talked about twenty minutes and she grew three inches in height before she left. She threw her shoulders back and walked away straight and tall. *She was able to share my pain because I was able to share hers.* And I couldn't have done that if she hadn't let me.

I have the most fabulous friends in the world. One of them is my wonderful Nan Goddard. She is a person of infinite tact and understanding, one of the finest women I've ever known in my life. Her husband Jack was my lawyer. When Jack died, an enormous part of Nan's life disappeared. Her daily life with him was gone, of course, but much of her social life vanished, too. Not her visits with tried and true friends, but with people she had met at island resorts, say, where all that mattered was who gives the biggest parties, and how do you keep dancing and drinking and swinging so you don't have time to think? Just forever, if necessary, and if anybody got sick or died, you dropped them and went on to a younger crowd because their youth was going to make you young, too.

So Nan became a widow, and there was one couple she was very fond of. For a while afterward, she didn't see them, so she finally phoned the woman and said, "I'm afraid I'm not seeing you because when I'm around at night I'm a reminder to your husband of how much he thought of Jack. Can you and I have lunch instead? Because I don't want to lose your friendship. You see," said Nan, "lunch is a widows' thing."

Nan was trying to think of their feelings, not hers. When she told me, I cried, because I knew what she said was the truth. Now I want to tell you that Harry admires my girl friends as much as I do. At our forty-first wedding anniversary dinner, there were a number of widows, including Nan. Halfway through dinner, a guest said, "This is one of the most marvelous evenings we've ever had." Nan said, "Virginia, no one would do this but you," and I said, "But why? Why should a live husband make you a more desirable woman? That is wrong. A charming woman is not a threat, whether her husband is living or not."

We plead with Nan to let us drive her home. She won't let us. She won't do it. She refuses to be picked up. She says, "I'll meet you at the restaurant." She takes people out to dinner. The widow cannot accept five invitations and not have somebody back. If she is of moderate circumstances, she gets cold cuts, but she has people to her home. She does not become a conscious dependent. You cannot command friendship and love through guilt. Don't make people feel guilty over you. And, of course, thank God, a lone woman can now go into a restaurant and get a table.

But the point about being single, or being a widow, or a person who lives alone for any reason is, you can't close yourself up, shut yourself off, whether it's going to a restaurant alone, or telling your closest friend how miserable you feel. You should be able to cry with a friend, but don't cry in a group.

Friendship requires concern and responsibility, just as marriage does. Friendship is not a one-way street. It needs care, it needs nourishing. And speaking for myself, I always enjoy giving a little bit more than the standard—like the extra measure of coffee for the pot. I don't always succeed, but that's my goal. Where friends are concerned, I think the worst mistake I can make is not giving enough.

Television has provided us with friends we sometimes never see in person. Our incredible means of communication today enable us to be closer to one another than ever before in human history, since the early days of Adam and Eve, when population was first discovered, or should I say invented, or should I say conceived?

A neighbor lives close by, usually next door. But a friend can be anyone you feel close to. All friends have the same basic curiosity. And when I'm on the road, meeting a lot of people, they often ask, "What is

Merv like?" "What is Dinah really like?" And I try to tell them in five easy words, which is frequently all we have time for, and finally they come up with the clincher: "What's Virginia Graham really like?"

This book is I. This book is what I'm really like. Virginia Komiss Guttenberg Graham of New York City by way of Chicago, Great Neck, and Hollywood, at home in spirit, I'm grateful to say, in all of them. In Chicago, still, are many of the members of my family, and many friends. I never return there but what I marvel at the wonders of that city and say, "Thank you, God, for letting me call Chicago my birthplace." The friendliness and warmth of its people, their zest and energy, the extraordinary grandeur of its buildings, the zip and excitement of its climate. And Chicago food! It's second to none. In Chicago, they ask, "What's Irv Kupcinet like? What's Lee Phillips really like?"

There are many landmarks in Chicago, and many brave people. One of the bravest is my friend Margaret Daly. Widowed, with a lovely daughter to raise, Maggie became a columnist for the *Chicago Tribune*. When her leg was injured some ten years ago, she had the first of nine operations before the leg finally had to be removed. She never sought sympathy, she never complained.

Once, at a fashion show she usually does the commentary for she was in a walker, so I got up to do a little kidding around for her. She was ashen from pain, but she never complained.

After the last operation, I was a little hesitant to call her, because I thought she might consider such an early call an intrusion, but I did. I got through to her right away and said, "How are you, darling?"

"Oh, Ginny," she said, "do you know what it's like to be without pain? For nine years I've suffered, but now I am without pain."

And I thought to myself, My God, she can walk taller than Mount Everest. What an incredible woman. She has all the humor and fortitude of the Irish.

All the Daly sisters are distinguished. Maureen

Daly wrote the classic *Seventeenth Summer,* and Kay Daly was responsible for helping to launch the Fire and Ice program for Charles Revson and Revlon.

And now I want to tell you about another special friend, Miss Totie Fields.

One day, on my way to a speaking engagement at Grosse Point, Michigan, Tony Martin came up to me at the airport and told me that Totie's leg had been amputated. Then Tony said, "on the brighter side of the news," that Shecky Green. who had undergone throat surgery at the risk of losing his voice, had been able to speak, even sing, that same day.

I verified the news about Totie when I got home, because I feel very close to her. For one thing, her jokes were on herself. She made other people laugh at her own expense, which is something I try to do, too. Also, she was in love with her husband, George Johnson. As a matter of fact, once Totie told us that George was considering becoming Jewish, and they were going to marry again at an Orthodox ceremony. Phyllis Diller and Eydie Gorme and I were going to be bridesmaids. We were planning to throw matzo meal instead of rice.

Totie was in Mt. Sinai Hospital in Beverly Hills, and when I got to Beverly Hills again not long afterward, I asked Eydie and her husband Steve Lawrence, who were very close to Totie, and loyal to everybody they know and like, if they thought it would be all right if I went to see her. Yes, they thought so, but call and see.

"Please, please, I want you to come," said Totie on the phone.

Well, I walked in. Now Totie used to backhand an Oreo cookie like a magician. Nobody saw it. Many heavyset people, you never see eat. They're secret eaters. They ate when no one's looking. But there is Totie, thin as a champion Weight Watcher, without a touch of makeup and looking absolutely beautiful. The only signs of vanity were her nails. They were long enough to write with and impeccably manicured. Totie was still in pain, and every once in a while her face would contract with a spasm and I knew her agony was excruciating. But there were her nails, as always, and I thought, Her vanity is going to help keep her alive.

"I cannot tell you what it's like to see you walk through that door," said Totie, "always smiling, always up. And I know so much about you. Tell me something, Ginny. Do you think I'm going to make it?"

My eyes filled with tears. Could there be any doubt. "Totie, I said, "if I made it, so can you."

Sometime later, in January 1977, to be exact, I was coming out of a building in Los Angeles when I heard a few comments about my being born out of wedlock, shouted loud and clear. When I turned around, there was Totie, getting out of a car with a fur coat and her prosthesis on, big as life but three times as thin.

"Look, Ginny," she said, "I lost two people." And she opened her coat to show me.

Before we leave her, I want to share you one more story. Totie always thought thin. One day in Chicago, we were passing Marshall Fields and she saw this dress in the window. She had to go in and inquire. Totie went up to the proper department and said to the saleswoman, "I'd like that dress in the window."

"I'm sorry, madam," said the woman, "it's a size seven."

"That's perfect," said Totie. "That's just my size."

"I beg your pardon," said the woman.

"I said *that's just my size*," said Totie. "I'll take that dress."

They removed the dress from the window and Totie took it with her. Probably, I thought, someone else will be wearing that dress. But now I like to think that Totie saved it, for many later occasions.

Totie exemplifies the eleventh commandment.

It isn't a foolproof prescription for friendship, however. (If a foolproof system has ever been worked out, they've kept it a secret from me.) But it's a step we can take ourselves. It's an initiative we can assume and direct.

If you want to be the very best kind of friend, you can do even better than feeling your neighbor's pain: You can feel your neighbor's joy. That is, surely, the final proof of friendship. So often, I think, in the modern competitive world, we feel that we have to outshine our friends, to achieve more than they. As a result, we sometimes have a tendency to put their achievements down, to patronize what they do.

This is another kind of game altogether. It may be a fun game to play. It may be gratifying, for whatever reason, but it's not a sign of real friendship. If people want to put me down, to suggest to me that my taste in clothes, or my earning ability, or my life-style is not on a par with theirs, they have every right to do so. But not as candidates for friendship. Surely we have a right to expect more than that from friendship. I'm not talking about honest criticism. I'm talking about trying to undermine the value of what you have done, the value of who and what you are.

Now I am not a Pollyanna, you know that. My friend Cindy Adams says that my tongue should be declared a lethal weapon. And if something really and truly upsets me, I have a very hard time keeping my thoughts to myself. Sometimes, I know, my judgment is bad.

A friend of mine bought an extravagant dress the other day and called me up to ask if she could stop by and show it to me.

I said yes. When she got here and put the dress on, I thought it was probably the most unbecoming expensive thing I had ever seen on a human being. She was in absolute raptures over her dress, but I really never saw anything more totally disfiguring. However, I didn't tell her so.

After she left, I said, "Harry, should I call her up and tell her the truth?"

"If you do, you're crazy," said Harry. "She has members of her family who can tell her."

So I didn't. But as I'm writing this down, I'm tempted to pick up the phone and give her my honest opinion. She must have been blind. Or she must have purchased it during a blackout.

The thing is, people want one of two things when they ask for your opinion. They really want to know; or they don't really want to know—because they want us to support a new image of themselves in its tryout stage, or maybe they just simply need approval, with no rationale at all. God knows, that's the way I sometimes feel. Just say yes, I don't care whether you mean it or not.

That's another way of feeling for our friends—pain or joy or something in between. Maybe just simply a need to share something old, something new, something borrowed, something blue. Without questioning. There are times, I think, when it doesn't even matter.

We can't be a hundred percent honest all the time. There has to be some actor in each of us, at one point or another. Acting is identifying with your character, as best you can. And friendship sometimes requires that we do a little acting, instead of being brutally honest.

So I won't call my friend. She wanted the dress. She bought it. Good.

Some people say you only make real friends when you're very young. But I met one of my dear friends, Goldie Glassman, only seven years ago in California. She lost her wonderful husband too young, too soon, and in sharing her grief, our friendship grew. Goldie is like a sister to me, and proves that our need to love and be loved is forever.

Yes is my favorite word. "Do it" my favorite advice. I'm definitely of the "Do it" persuasion. I believe in nudging opportunity before it gets a chance to strike.

Do you have a secret yearning to take piano lessons?

Do it.

Do you want a challenging new job but fear you may not be qualified?

Find out. Do it.

Do you have a hidden, private ambition, but hesitate to pursue it because you fear you may be rejected? I'll let you in on a secret. Just about everyone I know has been rejected a hundred million times. Every day of my life is fraught with failures and rejections, both little and big.

Sometimes—not always, but sometimes—I'm grateful for them. They keep me on my toes. They toughen my resolution. I like to consider them growing pains.

Banish your fears. Don't give in to them. Banish, overcome, surmount your worthless fears, whatever it takes. They are killers. Do it. Because otherwise you'll never know what you can achieve, what life is all about.

Yes is easy, no is tough. I really and truly do not have a tough bone in my body. I have a suit of protective armor to put on when I need it, but that's to cover up how close people are to the raw wound. For me, being sensitive is the easy part. The hard part is putting sensitive and tough together, being both.

Tender-tough Virginia, that's what I'm really like. That's my combination. How nice it would be, we could talk face to face, if you were only my neighbor.

The Hidden Scars

How much should we confide; how much should we hold within ourselves?

This always pertinent question was brought home to me afresh in California recently as I was lunching with a friend. I'll call her Sarah.

I've known Sarah many years. She's a bright, attractive, vivacious person in early middle age, married to a marvelous man, and has an active life, both social and religious. She devotes a large part of her time to community service, and she and her husband are blessed with financial security.

As a child, I used to think that privileged people were immune to ordinary suffering, that freedom from financial stress carried with it an exemption from the common physical and emotional ailments that beset us workaday mortals. Now I know different.

When I joined her at the table, I knew from the unfamiliar worry lines on her forehead and the slump of her shoulders that Sarah was upset about something.

Still, I wondered how serious her problem could be, and if she would want to confide in me. To a lot of people, I'm affectionately known as the road-show Abby, which comes, I think, from what I call my "listening eye." The listening eye hears as much as the listening ear—and sometimes more. Because people usually don't say what they mean. Their words are often a camouflage, a disguise for what they are really thinking and feeling.

But the listening eye sees—and hears—the body language, whose message can be quite different from spoken language. Sarah's body language today was full of new and unfamiliar tension.

"Ginny," she said, as soon as I was settled, "if I have to pretend with the rest of the world, I don't have to pretend with you. I have two wonderful children, I have a beautiful home in a lovely community, I thought I had a rich and productive life. But my husband is divorcing me next month."

I gasped. "What happened?"

"From the day of my hysterectomy, Hal has been impotent with me."

"Oh, Sarah, I'm so sorry."

"He won't touch me," Sarah said, her voice barely audible.

Suddenly, I was having that strange *déjà vu* experience, when some trick of memory makes it appear that we have lived this moment sometime before, in a different life. And then I was brought back to Sarah's problem and I thought: How many times this must have happened to people all over the world! Everybody talks about breast cancer, about the mastectomy, about the visible mutilation and changes that have disrupted marriages and made both men and women suicidal. But what has been said about the other, more hidden scars, the scars that people can't see?

We have these rigid classifications to pinpoint our sexual preferences. Women say they prefer a blond or a brunet, an athletic man or a scholar. Men, more famous for talking about sex for a much longer period of time, are even more to the point: "I'm a leg man," says John. Or a breast man. Or, "My husband is a fanny man," volunteers Marilyn. "That's what he likes."

One thing that all these people are saying is that a sensual man or woman wants a perfect creature to make love to, a perfect—and an *everlastingly* perfect —mate.

To a man, a woman is a mirror. He sees in her a pure reflection of himself in the form of his taste. When the woman ages, she is an unavoidable reminder to the man that he is aging too. If her body is vulnerable to time, if her flesh is mortal, so too is his.

"Can you understand?" Sarah was asking me.

"Of course, I understand," I said. "Don't forget, I had a radical hysterectomy too." Then, watching Sarah's face, I wondered: Should I confide? Would my experience benefit her? I didn't know, but it was worth a try. I decided to tell Sarah something I had never discussed with anyone except the people directly involved.

"Harry and I went through a very difficult period after my operation," I said. "For one thing, I mistakenly felt that abstinence was necessary, that it would save me from a recurrence. As a result, Harry and I lived through a very traumatic six months, but fortunately we were able to receive help."

I went to my doctor, talked to him, and he told me my fears were groundless. Harry and I were able to get help at the time we needed it. I suggested to Sarah that psychotherapy might help her.

"Not if Hal won't cooperate," she said. "I am beside myself. I know he loves me. Yet he's only impotent with me. He's marrying again in six weeks—a young woman he's known for several years. I don't know what to do."

"Don't divorce him," I said.

Well, it seems that in a number of states now there is what is known as no-contest divorce. It works on the same general principle as no-fault insurance.

Impotence is only an extreme example of a general repugnance to cancer. I've seen people who wouldn't drink from a washed glass which has been used by somebody they knew had undergone cancer surgery. I've noticed that some people flinch when shaking hands with a cancer victim. And I've witnessed the repugnance in show business toward people who've had it.

I decided to take a new tack with Sarah. "You know something, my dear," I said. "You're going to eat lettuce salad with lemon-juice dressing, and wheat thins instead of bread. You're going to stay slim and gorgeous and meet some other man and have a whole new life. Your husband is going to get his divorce and marry this girl, but he may not find what he's looking for in her, and then he might come back to you."

"I'm going to wait," said Sarah.

"Just don't wait too long."

Tears were glistening in Sarah's eyes, and she took out her handkerchief to blot them before they fell. Her hands were trembling. I'd never seen her so upset.

"You've always been such a paragon of strength," said Sarah. "Your life is successful, your marriage is ideal. Please tell me, what am I going to say to people when they ask me what happened to mine?"

"What do you want to say to them?"

"I don't know. The truth is so humiliating. I thought we had a perfect marriage."

"There's no such thing," I said, "as a perfect marriage. No marriage is perfect."

"But at least you've survived."

"And so will you," I said, "no matter what happens to your marriage. Listen, Sarah, any so-called perfect marriage is the result of propaganda and image-making. I know. I've devoted my whole life to image-making."

"Why did you do it?"

In order to answer her, I had to stop and think. It had been a long time since I'd been asked that question.

"Because I believe in decent standards of behavior. I believe in the family as a unit, whatever the hazards it's put through. I believe in the security and sanctity of the home, in the moral values the healthy home represents. I believe in decency, because decency is *logical*. It's decency that makes us civilized."

"But you're such a public person, Ginny. Doesn't it bother you that everyone knows so much about Harry and Lynn and you? Even on the air, you've revealed some very personal things. Are you sorry that you've shared so much of your life with other people?"

"You know, it's a peculiar thing, Sarah," I said.

"We've known each other for so many years. But I am a very private person. The real things that have gone on in my life, nobody knows about, not even you, who are so close to me. There are things that have happened, things I've covered up, and thoughts I've had, which are nobody's business. Even if they were somebody's business, I couldn't have survived without keeping them quiet."

"Yet you're always smiling," said Sarah, "always 'up.'"

"I'm living with the results of my image-making. I've had many, many unhappy moments in my life, personal problems, relationship problems. But I've always felt it would only hurt people to know I have problems like they have. Only last week a woman came up to me at a country club and said, 'Do you have any idea of the number of marriages you've saved?'

" 'No,' I said, as I always do. 'Tell me.'

" 'You're the model of the perfect wife and mother,' this woman went on. And I must have heard that thought expressed a million other times, in different ways."

"I wish I knew what to do," said Sarah. "I feel so ugly."

Self-pity drives me up the wall.

"Look at you," I said. "Take a mirror and look at yourself. Go ahead."

Sarah removed the compact from her bag, opened it, and looked at her face in the mirror.

"See? You look terrific. You're even lovelier than you were before your operation."

It was true. There is a certain radiant look about the survivor, a certain clarity and depth in the eyes, a certain lift of the chin, a *vibrancy*.

Even Sarah was smiling now, at the truth of my statement.

"But that doesn't change anything," she said. "I'm too young to live a celibate life, Ginny. What am I going to do?"

"That's entirely up to you," I said, "and you know it. We're no longer living in the Victorian age. Why, you can do just about anything you want to do. Most honeymoons today take place before the marriage."

"Doesn't that shock you?"

"Well, I used to be known as the squarest person on television. But, since this is a self-honesty lunch, I guess maybe I wasn't so shocked at what people were doing. I think I was shocked that they would admit it publicly. But inhibitions are no longer in fashion. Neither yours, nor mine, nor anyone's."

"Hal's the only man I've ever loved," said Sarah.

"Then consider yourself lucky to have shared so many happy years with him," I said.

"I do. But no one ever wants happiness to end. To tell you the truth," said Sarah, "the change itself is what scares me the most."

"How are the children taking it?"

"They don't yet know. We've got to tell them."

"They're going to need you," I said. "Speaking for myself, I think change is one of the hardest things in the world to get used to. But as we get older, nothing remains the same. Things just seem to get more so. I try to think of change as a challenge. I get along better if I say, okay, there you are, here I am, let's go."

Sarah nodded. "Oh, Ginny, I feel so much better." The worry lines, the nervous tension, were gone. They would return. But in the meantime Sarah was beginning to understand how to survive on her own.

"You may even want to go back to work," I said. "But one thing I know: You're going to be strong because you have to be, not only for yourself but for your children, and yes, even for Hal."

"You're right," she said. "I am. Thank you, Ginny. I must run."

We left the restaurant and said our good-byes. Then Sarah turned and was gone.

I stood on the sidewalk for a moment and watched her disappear into the crowd. No one would have guessed from watching her proud carriage, the elegance of her stride, her carefully made-up face, that inside, underneath, her heart was breaking, the victim of a scar no one could see.

Sarah, and how many untold others?

Late Love

My career as an actress provides me with searchlights, footlights, spotlights and limelights. And I must never forget the highlights and lowlights. They are sometimes the most illuminating lights of all.

Late loves are often the best loves, and after *Late Love* I went on to do more plays. There are a limited number of stage roles for women over forty, but I have a modest repertory that I'm especially fond of.

One of my most thrilling acting experiences was at the Drury Lane Theatre in Chicago in Leonard Spigelgass' play *Dear Me, the Sky Is Falling*. Gertrude Berg had done my role on Broadway with great success. At first I was doubtful about trying an ethnic role, because I wasn't sure I could handle it. But a number of people convinced me I could, and I'm nothing if not adventurous, so I agreed.

Vernon Schwartz gave us first-rate direction and allowed me to interpret the role the way I thought I should. The author himself flew in from California to see us, and when I took my curtain call that night, he got up from his seat, came to the stage, and embraced me. Then he told me in front of all those people that I'd done his play the way he'd prayed it would be done, and was afraid it never could be after Gertrude Berg passed away.

That's extremely gratifying, because when a dramatist writes a role, he usually has a very definite picture in his mind of how it should be played. It's thrilling just to have the playwright in the audience. He brings a special intelligence to the experience. He makes you hope that you're flowing directly with the grace of his pen. I had that opportunity one other time in

Northland, Massachusetts, when I was doing James Elward's *Best of Friends.*

Most theatrical people are dedicated. Make believe, of one kind or another, is "in our blood," as the saying goes. From Sophocles to Neil Simon, from the first actor who ever donned makeup to Laurence Olivier, the playwright and the actor—and all the artists and technicians who aid and abet them—have had a common goal: to alter the face of reality, to affect the nature of man.

One of the strongest actors I ever worked with was Fred Clark. Now I'll tell you about the dedication of an actor. Fred and I appeared in *The Crocodile and the Cockeyed Moose,* the last show he ever did before he passed away, at the Mill Run Theater in Niles, Illinois.

He was already dying. He was hemorrhaging internally while we rehearsed. For a Broadway play, you have a few weeks to rehearse, and you sometimes have out-of-town tryouts and previews. But with many other shows, including dinner theaters, you're lucky if you have five or six days, so you have to come in prepared, knowing your lines.

On the day of the opening, the director told us that Fred had been rushed to the hospital and was hemorrhaging. The day of the opening! There were no understudies. We went through all the motions, all our duties, heartbroken, not knowing what would happen. The producers might cancel the show, or they might call in another actor and have him go on book (he would use a book onstage for his lines until he memorized them).

Well, you all know about that herculean strength inside us, that ability to pop our heads back up, when we feel someone pushing them down, like a popping-up apple in dunking for apples? The man who went to the hospital in an ambulance and was strapped into bed and given strict instructions not to get out, escaped from the hospital and appeared that night and gave one of the best performances I've ever seen.

We had a fantastic run, and two months later Fred was gone. When he was hemorrhaging onstage, we all covered up. There is a camaraderie amongst theater people especially. That's one reason I love the business so much.

I came to the realization at Mill Run that when people love you, and love to see you in a play, they also like to see you as you are. So I began to ask my producers, "May I come out after the play is over and talk to the audience, sort of as though we were neighbors?" I think Buddy Hackett was one of the first to do it, when he was on Broadway in *I Had a Ball*. And my producers said yes, and I've been doing it ever since. It's the most incredible experience, to be someone else and then be yourself so suddenly and so close to the same audience.

That's part of the magic and part of the charm. I think there are very few among us who haven't longed to trade places with someone else at one time or another. This often begins when we're children and continues as long as we live. Actors take this longing a step further. Learning how to bring another person to life, how to make him (or her) come true, is the main concern of the actor's craft.

When you're lucky enough to create a great role in a great play for the first time, you join the ranks of theater immortals. My greatest sense of this, and one of my first, came when I watched the late Laurette Taylor in *The Glass Menagerie* by Tennessee Williams, when it was first produced on Broadway. It is a play about memory, and Miss Taylor brought a lifetime of memories to bear on the character of Amanda Wingfield, the anxious, distracted mother who longs to see her lame waif of a daughter happily married and settled down.

The second time I saw it, I went backstage with a friend who knew one of the actors in the cast. On our way to his dressing room, we passed Miss Taylor, still in her costume—an impossibly affecting wraith of a dress. She was standing in the shadows with the stage manager, looking at us while we passed as though she was not yet ready to return to the world she had lived in before the play began.

I'll never forget that actress. It's a great loss to the

world that she never had the opportunity to recreate her role in the film.

We all have our favorites. Judy Holliday in _Born Yesterday_. Richard Burton in _Camelot_. Anne Bancroft in _The Miracle Worker_. I feel richer for having known all these people. They are our models, the great ones. They are our aspirations.

Drama follows me everywhere. The Muses are my constant companions—the tragic, the comic, often walking hand in hand, creating some crazy, in-between brand of mayhem.

When I did _Barefoot in the Park_ in Buffalo with Marsha Mason (who later married Neil Simon, the author of the play), we performed in a theater-in-the round. It was summer theater, with young apprentices studying the various theatrical crafts. My experience with drugs up to that time was nonexistent —apart from the drugs you purchase at the drugstore. I had never even smelled the scent of marijuana. If someone told me he'd smoked a joint, I thought he had burned his elbow.

There we were in this enormous round theater, in the middle of the play. Every seat was filled, which is to say that there were between two and a half to three thousand people surrounding us and watching our every movement. There are no walls on the stage in this kind of theater. To get backstage, you must go down one of several aisles, which run between sections of the audience.

This was in the middle of the play, as I said. Suddenly we heard this terrible commotion that seemed to have no source. At first it was just distracting, but soon we knew that something was dreadfully wrong, because we could no longer hear ourselves speaking.

Then we saw it! This enormous automobile was crashing down the aisle, tires screeching, horn blowing, headlights glaring straight at us like the eyes of a monster in the darkness. It was headed straight in our direction and coming closer every second.

All thought of the play was forgotten. I ran like I'd never run before. I think the other actors ran too, but

I couldn't vouch for what they did. I was in too much of a hurry.

Somehow, somebody managed to overpower the driver and bring the automobile to a standstill. I don't know how. I wasn't around to see that either. The driver was one of the young apprentices, taking a trip on LSD. What a trip he gave us!

Regional theaters and stock companies serve a valuable purpose. If you live in New York, an abundance of theater is always just outside your doorstep. But most people don't live in New York. Most people don't live within walking range of professional theater companies. And regional theater helps bring us closer together—the audiences, the plays, the actors, the whole invigorating experience of theater.

Among the best of these theaters are the Chateaux de Ville, in Framingham, Saugus, and Randolph, Massachusetts, and Windsor, Connecticut, operated by Mario Saroli and Bunny and Jerry Roberts. Each beautiful theater is part of a larger complex serving both social and business functions. Four companies of actors are playing at any given time, first in one theater, and then the three others. When I was doing *Butterflies Are Free, I* remember that Jane Russell was in *Catch Me If You Can,* and Barry Nelson was also starring in a play.

The Kenley Players is the Tiffany of dinner theaters. John Kenley, one of the most interesting men I've ever met in my life, has these huge auditoriums, seating 3,500 and 4,000 people. A young man from Ohio, he was trained by the Shuberts, worked with them, and came back to Ohio to build these marvelous theaters. Paul Lynde has astronomical success there, because he's such a clever actor and he's also an Ohioan. A lot of people can live through the achievement and success of a neighbor.

These theaters also provide a fine training ground for young actors, and I never know what future stars I'll be playing with. Recently I did Muriel Resnik's *Any Wednesday* for Harry Lee Rogers in Glenview, Illinois, stage-managed by an incredible singer named Jim Linduska, and with a very promising young actor named George Tountas. George has two degrees: one in journalism and one in engineering. But he doesn't want to enter either of those fields. All he wants is to be an actor.

Late love it may be, my love for acting, but no less strong and fulfilling for that.

We Laugh, Sometimes,
to Keep from Crying

Mama had more friends than anyone else I know, but to the end of her life she and I were virtual strangers. She lived with this in her way, and I live with it in mine. She must have tried countless times to bridge the distance between us, just as I did, and been filled with despair at failing each time. This is sometimes the nature of mothers and daughters, fathers and sons. Each of us needs a certain kind of love and attention. And the others of us are either blind to what is needed, or unable to provide it in any case. Or both. We can take a lifetime to acknowledge how much we ache, how much we grieve, how much we feel, how much we need.

Close as I was to Papa, I knew very little about his family. He, like Mama, was one of eleven children, but Mama's family was nearby, whereas Papa's was mostly distant. Mama was the last of her mother's children. My maternal grandfather was often referred to as a great thinker. Some people might have spelled it with an "s". Some people said, in fact, that all Grandpapa thought about was enlarging his family. That's one way of putting it.

By the time Mama arrived, Grandmama had to support the family by running a millinery shop. Poor Mama was shuttled from one older sibling to another for care and safekeeping. It's possible, therefore, that Mama felt somewhat like an orphan, being sent as she was from Aunt Mary to Uncle Herman to Aunt Tillie to Uncle Max and back again. Apart from Grandpapa himself, it was not a physically demonstrative family. I don't recall ever seeing any display of affection, although Aunt Mary was certainly warm and loving toward all of us, however she chose to express her feelings to Mama.

Childless herself, Aunt Mary had the smile of a madonna and the soul of an angel. To err, she believed, was human; to forgive, divine. She always had an excuse for anything anybody did wrong, and she forgave them. She forgave everybody everything. She wasn't a sugar substitute. She was the real thing —the kindest woman in the world.

It was Aunt Mary who fed me sugarless bonbons when I had typhoid and had to swallow creosote. She invented them. That was the only way I could get it down. It was always Aunt Mary who volunteered to minister to us. I've never been able to understand why nature often seems to make the most maternal women childless. Is it only coincidence? Do maternal feelings, in being deprived, grow stronger in compensation? But Aunt Mary adopted a baby named Julius and loved him with a passion beyond anything else. He had a magnificent voice and brought her great joy.

Birthdays were never "remembered." With eleven children, who could afford it? Who could *remember*, for that matter, at the rate of almost one a month?

The voice of authority passed directly from Grandpapa to Aunt Celia. She was also childless, but she was able nonetheless to tell all her nieces whether or not their labor pains were real. Three of my cousins were born in taxis because Aunt Celia didn't feel the labor pains in time.

She fell in love with her husband because he spoke English. Uncle Al was a charming but henpecked man who worked at the stamp window in the post office. He would sometimes venture to sneak candy to Juddy and me, whereupon Aunt Celia would go after him with a broom.

I don't know where the family hatred for sweets derived from. That strain died out, however, with Juddy and me. Our appetites for sugar—mine especially— were insatiable. After Mama had a party, she had to put the leftover candy in a safe that was built into the wall, and lock it up.

Aunt Celia was absolutely devoted to Mama all her life. But Papa was not overly fond of Aunt Celia, though he gave her a job in his store. Maybe that was one of the reasons why. But there must have been others, too. For example, Aunt Celia was fond of saying one thing out of one side of her mouth, and another thing out of the other. This was probably an attempt to ingratiate herself with both sides in advance of any dispute.

To tell you the truth, Papa couldn't stand her. Mama consulted Aunt Celia so much that Papa developed a ritual. On certain nights, when he'd come home full of urgent need for Mama, he'd take a precautionary look under the bed first and shout in his loudest voice: *"Celia!* Is it all right with you?" If Aunt Celia had a headache, the whole thing was off.

She was a walking encyclopedia of misinformation on every subject. Her medical knowledge alone was mind-bending. She never met anyone who wasn't dying of an incurable disease. If the disease didn't already exist, Aunt Celia never hesitated to invent it. Death was her favorite prognosis. She was a milestone in the oral history of medicine.

Mama was a hypochondriac. She was always insecure about her physical well-being (and other things as well). Aunt Celia's prescription for Mama's condition was constant doses of herself. She fed Mama's hypochondria by appearing to do the opposite.

But she also had her good points. She was very loyal, and she was devoted to Juddy and me, and to the family as a whole. She took many trips with us. And it was always instructive to observe Mama and Aunt Celia at the table. Neither woman ever truly believed that Papa could pay for both of them to eat. If the food didn't come with the room, they would order just one dinner. One would take the soup, the other would take the fish, they'd split the meat and negotiate the dessert.

"I had the soup and most of the meat. You take the dessert." This was Mama.

"No indeed, Bessie. I've never in my life eaten dessert on Palm Sunday." On Shrove Tuesday, or Thanksgiving Eve. Or the last Saturday in October. This from Aunt Celia.

But if the food came with the room, they were like bears storing up for the winter. Both of them were always conscious of their weight. But Mama, I think, did all her dieting when Papa had to pay extra for her food.

Mama was extremely thrifty and tried with all her might to teach me the value of saving money. Alas, her instructions were in vain. "If you save a hundred pennies," Mama would say, "you'll have a dollar."

I never believed her for a minute. I am still not convinced that what she said is true. A penny is a penny. A dollar is a dollar. They are both money, but there is no other relationship between them whatsoever, in any way, shape, or form. One will never become the other—without the help of inflation, that is. Or deflation. If, when I die, there turns out to be money still left in my savings account, it will be through no fault of mine.

Mama once gave a dinner party at the Standard Club in Chicago for Harry and me. My cousin Gladys was invited, and Joanie and Juddy, Aunt Celia, Harry and me—seven altogether. After we were seated, we looked at our menus and discussed what we were going to have, the way you sometimes do when you're eating out.

"What are you going to have, Ginny?" This from Joanie.

"The veal, I think," said I. "Mama, what are you having?"

"Celia and I have already eaten," she informed us. Mama and Aunt Celia ate before they got to the club. They went to a counter and had a sandwich. That way, Mama only had to pay for five.

Gladys and I were so intimidated we only had a peach salad. Harry and Joanie made up for us, though, not to mention Juddy. They ate like famished wolves. No martyrdom for them.

Papa used to warn Aunt Celia that if she continued to talk from both sides of her mouth, she'd have a stroke. Well, she did and she did. Bell's palsy struck

Aunt Celia and her mouth was stretched out of shape, but it was only a temporary paralysis. After her illness, Aunt Celia picked up where she'd left off:

"Don't do that, Bessie! You know that's not right," out of one side of her mouth, followed by:

"Go ahead, Bessie. Do it if that's what you want," out of the other.

You never had to worry about which side she was on. Aunt Celia was safely ensconced on both sides of any debatable question. You couldn't prove a thing by her.

Mama was the opposite. She had only one answer for each question, and what she said was what she meant. Furthermore, Mama never talked about people behind their backs. She never really gossiped at all. I've always felt that the reason was she didn't feel secure enough.

Aunt Celia was the person we always called in an emergency, because she could be depended upon to come. And her greatest joy in the world was a funeral. One day there were two, one at eleven and another at one. You would have thought Aunt Celia had won *The Price Is Right.* Papa said, "Stick around. Maybe there's another one at twelve. You don't have to know the person." She was a foul-weather friend.

The amazing thing about these two close sisters was that later they never lived together. After Papa died, I said to Mama, "Maybe you and Aunt Celia could take an apartment together. That way, if you don't feel well, she's always there." But no. For some inexplicable reason, they never wanted to share their living quarters.

It often seemed to me that Mama was interested in everyone except her immediate family. She knew the names of the elevator operator's grandchildren, but not her own. It was a kind of determined modesty and self-effacement, I think, a wish not to attract attention. Mama liked to think of herself as being an ordinary sort of woman. She was not exactly an introvert, but she was an innately quiet person. No one was more beautiful. She had great imagination and artistic talent, and the natural elegance of a cameo.

Three years after Aunt Celia died, Mother passed away. Lynn, who was living in White Plains, where Mama was in a nursing home, called to tell me. Lynn was grief-stricken. She had always been so proud of her grandmother.

Mama's personality had changed in White Plains. She had feared for her health all her life, but in the nusing home she seemed reconciled to the penalties that time exacts from the strongest of us.

I wish I could reassure guilt-ridden families who have to make the decision whether or not to place a parent in a nursing home what a feeling of peace it gave me to know that Mama was being well taken care of. Her hours were filled with activities and many, many friends. But, of course, we carefully selected a wonderful home.

The night before she passed away, Mama had a presentiment. She went through the home, talking to all the people and thanking them for helping to make her life there so pleasant. The next morning at seven, a nurse came by, looked at Mama, and said, "You seem a little tired." There were no unusual physical symptoms. One hour later, Mama was dead.

Her body was taken to Chicago for burial. Joanie met me at the airport and we drove to the funeral home.

"Miss Graham," said the funeral director, "we're honored to have you here."

I did a double take, recovered, and made a mental note to remind Joanie to help me settle on a moderately priced casket, not the most expensive one.

"Bessie came in last night," continued the director.

"Oh, she did?" I said. Bessie? Another double take.

"Yes," he said. "And before we discuss anything, Miss Graham, there is something on my mind that's bothering me quite a bit. You do know that Celia's here?"

"What?" Three double takes in a row. I was running out of them.

"Celia is here."

"Wait," I said. "Are you by any chance talking about Celia Copeland, my aunt?"

"Yes," he said, "your aunt."

"What is she doing here?"

"Didn't you know?" He was genuinely puzzled. "In her will, she stipulated that her ashes were to be kept here until Bessie died. She expressly stated that she wanted to be buried with Bessie, in the same casket."

I felt like I was going to faint. Joanie appeared to be in the same condition.

"Are you telling me that they're going to be—"

"Miss Graham," he interrupted, "I know you're a fine woman. I know your charitable work and all the good things you've done, but we just cannot do this. It's totally against union regulations. If they ever found out we'd done this, we'd be in terrible trouble."

Joanie and I looked at each other. We no longer felt faint. We were on the verge of convulsions. We went to work on this poor man with all the powers of persuasion at our command.

"Who is going to notice?" I said. "No one's going to lift up the lid to see what's in there. The two girls must be together. That's the way they wanted it, and that's the way it should be. There's no doubt about it."

Reluctantly, but somewhat proudly too, the funeral director agreed.

Mama and Aunt Celia. Just imagine. They had it all figured out. Whoever died first would wait for the other. That way, they were getting two funerals for the price of one!

"Joanie," I said, "I'd give anything to have a tape of the conversation when they made these arrangements."

One of the undying wonders of funeral parlors, of course, is the practice of taking you to the most expensive casket right off the bat. At the height of your bereavement.

"You are not to get emotional," I warned Joanie. "You know how saving Mama was. How thrifty."

We saw quite a number of caskets before making our selection. We got Mama a beautiful casket. We even went so far as to hope that she might have chosen it herself. She and/or Aunt Celia.

At first I thought I didn't want to see Mama's body.

She had once been so vain about her figure. But I changed my mind. And Mama, in death, was beautiful again. She had rarely used makeup, but we had them apply a little makeup to her face. She wore a lovely dress, pinned with an orchid. And we put pearls around her neck and gave her earrings.

"I'm going to ask you to do me a favor," I told the funeral director, to whom we were already very grateful for agreeing to accommodate Aunt Celia so sensibly. "I want you to let the casket stay open. I want people to remember my mother at the height of her beauty."

And she looked wonderful. She was so beautiful that I sat by that coffin. I wouldn't look at Papa and I wouldn't look at Juddy, but I had to be close to this exquisite woman.

So we had the funeral and Aunt Celia must have enjoyed it. Afterward, we went to the Drake Hotel and sat around and talked. Mama's age was in dispute because she never would admit how old she was. Joanie gave a party on Mama's seventieth birthday. She invited forty people, but only thirty-nine showed up. The absent guest was Mama. She wouldn't admit she was seventy.

We talked about that, our laughter flavored with sadness. Mama had a good life, and she didn't suffer at the end. Then suddenly I remembered.

"Oh, my God," I said. "Papa's got her again."

"Who?" said Joanie.

"Aunt Celia," I said. "Can you imagine! He couldn't get away from her in life and now she's next to him again."

"In years to come," said my nephew David, "no one will know what happened to her. No one will know where she's buried."

That was true. Maybe, I thought, we can place an asterisk beside Mama's name on the tombstone and have it refer to Aunt Celia's name at the bottom. She'll be a footnote to Mama—the two of them finally together, sharing their dying, if not their living, quarters at last.

When I'm in Chicago, I go out to the cemetery and

visit. There are Papa and Juddy and Mama. And, of course, Aunt Celia. They are my legacy, or I am theirs. There are times when I can't separate our lives, our destinies, and other times when I have to.

I'm tied to my memories with the bonds of life itself. Mama and Papa and Juddy are with me every hour of the day. And at night, sometimes, I awake from a dream like a child and cry out to myself:

"Oh, Mama, Mama! Why couldn't you realize that all I ever wanted was your approval? Why did I have to wait until almost the end of your life for you to tell me you loved me?"

And try to fall asleep again, the pain of *Mutterschermz* still in the tears on my pillow.

Listen with Your Eyes

I love television. When I wake up in the morning, I open one eye and turn on the television set with the other.

I like all kinds of shows. I like the news. I like sports, I like game shows. I'm absolutely crazy about soap operas. And by now you surely know how fond I am of talk shows—from both sides of the television camera.

In my *Food for Thought* days, I did a game show called *Where Was I?* Bill Cullen was one of the panelists, and Orson Bean, and a lovely girl named Nancy Guild. The contestant would tell us a number of things he or she had done, and we had to guess where the person had been at the time.

The reason that show is still so vivid in my mind is the memory of the marquee in front of the theater. There, in giant letters for all the world to see, were the names of Bill and Orson and Nancy and Virginia.

Oh, I was so excited. My friend Bea Citron and I walked up and down the street, observing that marquee—and those lucky people who might happen to be walking by and see my name—from every angle. It was a breathtaking episode in theatrical history.

Soap operas are therapeutic. Because no matter how bad your problems are, the average soap opera makes your own life look like a playground. Frustration, depression, illness, and just plain bad news— there is no end to the miseries of the people who live in Soap-operaland. From Stella Dallas to Mary Hartman, the name of the game is suffering.

There's only one thing that bothers me about soap operas. Nobody ever calls first. They always drop in.

They always knock on the door. "Oh, maybe I should have called," the person says. Well, the only reason this person didn't call was because he or she might be told not to come. That would automatically put an end to all soap operas forevermore, if people called first. The plot would grind to a standstill.

Television, like life, is perpetual motion. It's a devourer of time and energy and talent. It has to be. There is so much time to fill.

Game shows, like soap operas, are habit-forming. We have a tendency to identify with the contestants and choose our favorite to root for. I would like to take you backstage with me to a game show now, and show you what happens.

First, you're met by a very nice person who tells you how delighted they are that you're there. You've had the foresight to bring five changes, if it's a daily half-hour show—which many game shows are—because all the shows are taped in one day, though of course your clothes and everything else are not supposed to indicate this. Some shows even have a fashion coordinator, who guards against clashing colors.

Your greeter takes you to your room or your suite. "Wardrobe would like to know if you need to have anything pressed." So you curse yourself, because you've been spot-cleaning and pressing for two days in order to be immaculate, forgetting that someone else will do it for you.

Then you go to the makeup room, where there are one, two, or three hairdressers. Blithely, you say, "I really don't need much. I did my hair at home." One half-hour later, you rise from the makeup table, your face thoroughly redone, and notice something awry in the rear of your hairdo. "Would you mind just looking at the back?" you ask a hairdresser, and that usually takes another half-hour.

You return to your room. There, on a table, is a thoughtful gift from the producers—a plant or flowers, a split of champagne with a little glass, perhaps, and peanuts or something edible. There's also a telephone, in case the compulsion to talk to somebody in the outside world proves irresistible.

When the proper time comes, you go onstage and the show is taped. Between each show, you have ten minutes in which to change your clothes. Between two of the shows, there is an hour break for refreshments, and everyone goes to the Green Room.

The Green Room is never green. It is yellow or beige or white or brown, but never green. The panelists are now able to relax and be sociable. The status of the show is immediately apparent in the quality of the victuals. If there's a buffet with guacamole dip and cashew nuts and a big fruit basket and wines and lots of booze for those who choose, then you know you're at a big-budget, top-flight show. The low-budget shows have roasted peanuts and Diet Pepsi. There are also shows where you have to gnaw on the wooden tables, if a craving for something to eat hits you.

Then back onstage for the remaining shows, after which you take your leave and go home. In certain isolated cases, a limousine takes you back and forth.

On talk shows, the Green Room serves a somewhat different function. The Green Room there is where you wait your turn to go on—and it's the closest thing to the family room at a murder inquest I've ever seen in my life. One by one, your predecessors depart for the stage, and you watch them on the monitor trying to outshine each other. Finally, if you're the last to go on, you're all alone. Sometimes, if you're last, you don't go on at all, because they run out of time.

I'm not a nervous performer, but I like to talk while I'm waiting. Some people don't; I do. If you're a singer, your manager or someone from the record company comes with you. I'm usually alone. I have no representative with me. I'm all by myself, or Goldie or one of my other girl friends comes along. That's very chic, a girl friend.

And nobody talks to anybody—with an occasional exception. Everybody's waiting for their act to go on. There is an absolute minimum of camaraderie. I once had a conversation on the topic of face lifts with a charming actress and personality who was the soul of demure curiosity backstage. "How long does it take?" "How much does it cost?" "Does it hurt?" "Is there any guarantee?" In front of the camera, she was so thrilled with our intimate discussion that she couldn't wait to share her knowledge of my firsthand information with everyone tuning in. She was too late. They'd been told about my face lift long before she reached them with the news. But they were ignorant of hers until I spilled the beans.

Entre nous, just between us friends, there's a whole school of elocutionist performers who make every syllable count: act-*tress,* re-*cord,* et-cet-er-*a.*

That's typical Green Room behavior. Once in a while, someone is friendly and nice. Recently, for example, a fine young actor named Sam Elliot came up to me in the Green Room, introduced himself, and said, "I've wanted to meet you for so long." That made me very happy. I'm a veteran. He was a relative newcomer, and he was paying tribute to my experience.

An interviewer once asked me if women are different on a talk show when men are present. I thought about this question for some time and replied that today some women may act the same with both sexes. But in the days of *Girl Talk* we were different away from the presence of men. That was the charm of the show. It was tables for ladies, it was under the dryer.

When we women are having a facial at the beauty parlor, all our makeup is off, we're wearing smocks, and you can't tell what our social and sexual pretensions are. We're able to talk then about anything in the world, with very few inhibitions. But once our new makeup is applied, and our hair combed out, and our dresses and coats put on, suddenly we're our old public selves again, sizing each other up, competing. We're Pavlov's dog. The change is a highly conditioned reflex.

It's the same thing at a party. When the first guests are all girls, our voices are naturally raised, our body movements casual, our conversation easy and straightforward. But the minute the first man arrives, we're transformed into different creatures altogether, playing up to the opposite sex. We're ever so dainty and feminine, we're ever so alluring.

I've often wondered why there's never been a man-talk show. It could be called *Locker Room* and concentrate on the way men talk when women aren't around. When I suggested this to a man, he said, "It would never get on the air. Every other word would be censorable. Half the dialogue would have to be bleeped. Take away the four-letter words and cuss-words, and man talk loses much of its zest and flavor."

It's much more complicated being a man today than being a woman. The myths that have upheld and soothed men for centuries are collapsing on every side. Male power. Male superiority. Male *right*—the right to dominate. So the man is wearing jewelry, he's going to the hairdresser to have his hair styled, he's wearing gorgeous clothes. Today's men are better dressed than women by far.

I look at an average couple coming into a restaurant, and the man looks much more interesting. We women all look alike. We're in uniform—pantsuits and all. It's the men who are showing their personalities in new ways.

I think it's wonderful that men are learning to express their emotions more honestly toward women and toward each other. Why should a man have to feel that he must come on macho all the time? Why shouldn't a man allow people to see that he's vulnerable too? I think the greatest test of strength in a man or a woman is the ability to deal with emotion—to feel it, first, and then deal with it well, which sometimes means to express it directly.

I think there is more truthfulness in soap operas today than in talk shows. There are virtually no restrictions on what a soap opera character can do. Murder, bigamy, incest—just name it and someone is doing it. They may suffer the torments of the damned in consequence, of course, but the soap operas pull no punches about what is going on. The misdeeds are up front.

On some talk shows—my own and others—I've seen people get up and flagrantly lie. L-i-e, with a perfectly straight face. I've been lucky enough to have great directors, who enjoyed the follow-up expressions on my face as much as I did. I've had them train the camera on me when I absolutely could not believe my ears.

These people remind me of the joke about the man who came home and found his wife in bed with his business partner. Whereupon she looked up at him coolly and said, "Who are you going to believe—me or your eyes?"

Anyone who goes on a talk show and lies, deserves to be castigated. They're asking for it. They're setting themselves up for a put-down. I don't see why they should go unchallenged. But there's a certain hosty and hostessy courtesy or indifference toward any relationship to the truth, which drives me up the wall. Everything is coming up pablum. And one reason the conversation is so bland is because a twenty-year-old kid is writing all the questions, if not the answers.

I love spontaneous face-to-face confrontations, where the mettle of both parties is put to the test. But nowadays you know it's not likely to happen, because the whole world is edited. Truth is edited at the moment.

What is the purpose of a talk show, after all? To inform? Or to entertain? Both, I think, each in its turn and sometimes together at the same time. Information can be presented in an entertaining way, and an entertainer, at least the very best kind of entertainer, can also inform you with the very nature of his material and talent. His or hers. (We have to invent a new pronoun. Either that, or become one sex. No more "His" and "Her" towels. Just neuter: "Ours.")

When Lynn began her talk show in California, she asked me for advice. "What," she said, "are some of the things I should remember?"

"Listen with your eyes," I said. "That's first. Let

your eyes be the channel through which your interest is focused. The rest of your face can be completely deadpan, but your eyes must be expressive. And they will be, they have to be, if you concentrate their attention on your guest. Our eyes are the most revealing instruments God gave us. The camera may not show the direction of your gaze, but your guests will know at once if your attention is not on them. Your guests enjoy talking with *you*, not with the camera.

"Second, ask pertinent questions, not impertinent ones. That way, your guest learns to trust you. And the greater the trust of your guests, the better your show will be."

I might add that Lynn has become a terrific hostess.

From time to time, people ask me if I think one can train to become a talk-show host. Absolutely not. Well, maybe not abso*lute*ly not. Maybe maybe. You need so many skills. You need intelligence and diplomacy and wit and awareness. You need presence. You need daring. And you need the world's largest supply of curiosity. Curiosity must be the basic ingredient.

Johnny Carson has tremendous skills. So has Merv.

You also need discipline. That's one of my worst faults. I admit it. I'm very well disciplined in some ways, terrible in others. For one thing, I don't like to be told what to do in a certain tone of voice. I think I'm still rebelling, the way I did as a child being told when I should blow my nose, and when I could eat an olive. I think my biggest weakness was not being able to accept the strength of the discipline that Mama was trying to teach me. It's a childish rebellion, and I get furious with myself. After I do certain things, I ask, "Now why did I do that?" I'm my own therapist. I'm very honest with myself.

Unfortunately, I think many talk-show impresarios and guests have the philosophy that a talk show is a toilet, a public outhouse. For the first time in modern history, the bathroom is in the living room. And to think of the furor when Jack Paar mentioned a water closet on the air coast to coast.

The modern sexual vocabulary appals me—the license with which it is used in public. I'm opposed to all forms of censorship, but can't we exercise a little restraint, a little respect for the sensibilities of others?

A good talk-show host is like a good cook. I've had very elaborate meals without any zip or excitement. On the other hand, I recently had an inspired potato casserole, with big Idaho potatoes, sliced, and a caramel crust and a million flavors. There may be a basic recipe for this casserole, but a good cook will make it even better, because she won't prepare it by rote. She'll flavor and blend that casserole as much by instinct as directions.

There is no true, exact recipe for the dishes she makes, because there's always a secret ingredient. It's the same secret ingredient that the best of the talk shows have—that old mysterious elixir called magic.

Reminiscing with Monty

Monty Morgan is a handsome, debonair, and witty man who is also one of the best television directors in New York and a marvelous raconteur. Every once in a while we take time out from our busy schedules to have lunch and catch up on what we've each been doing since last we met.

Invariably, when we do, the conversation turns to *Girl Talk* and the years we worked together to make it the kind of good show we wanted it to be—informative, thought-provoking, entertaining, funny, perhaps sometimes even more than that.

Recently, Steve O'Connor, the son of an old friend who is studying television in college and wants to become a producer, was in town and I thought, What a perfect opportunity. I'll have Steve and Monty come for lunch together.

So I did, one cold and blustery December day. And no sooner had Monty, Steve and I sat down to the table than I was at it, starting with one of my favorites. "Do you remember Bibi Osterwald, Monty?" I began, and we were off. Here are a few of our memories of those extraordinary *Girl Talk* days, recollected in tranquility and pieced together these many years later as best we could.

"Yeah," said Monty. "Bibi Osterwald is an actress and singer and a wonderful woman. She said she had always had a desire to play the banjo. The other guests laughed and Bibi said, 'I knew you'd laugh.' But the next time she came on *Girl Talk*, she brought a banjo. An elderly man who'd heard her remark had written and sent her a banjo. And as she talked about it, she was so moved and touched her voice got trembly. She struck a couple of chords and started to play and then she really broke down and cried."

"A banjo from a man she'd never seen," I said. "We receive so much love and support from strangers. People who come to our house for the first time for dinner send the largest bouquets of flowers."

"Really," said Monty.

"Oh, yes. Other people send chocolate-covered orange slices, which I happen to love."

"And inside it says, 'To Jane from Barbara,'" said Monty, "because somebody else sent that candy to Jane."

"Hush, Monty," I said. "Remember Ruby Dee?"

"She was very strong, very articulate," said Monty. "She married Ossie Davis. She was talking about the height of the civil rights movement and how some of the problems were very hard for adults to deal with. But if they're hard for adults, think of the children. Then she began to talk about the church that was bombed one Sunday morning and four children were killed. And as she told it, her voice began to quiver and she broke down and really sobbed. I came down from the control room and looked out and the audience was in tears. Virginia was in tears. Everybody was in tears. We went into a commercial."

"Ruby Dee is a great actress," I said. "Actors have to be totally disciplined during a performance, but they are so vulnerable in real life."

"I think actors watch the emotions of others more carefully," said Monty, "because they never know when they're going to have to play that part themselves." Monty used to be an actor.

"You know what I think is a marvelous story?" I said. "Glenda Jackson and the clothes."

"Glenda Jackson was on Broadway in *Marat/Sade*," Monty said, buttering a roll. "She's so articulate. She doesn't smile very much because she is a serious kind of person. But when she got to the *Girl Talk* studio, she was all smiles. I looked at her and said, 'Something good must have happened.'

"'Yes,' she said, 'my husband is coming to America for the first time and I'm so excited because I'm going to be able to show him New York, which I love. Besides which, he's bringing me some smashing new clothes.'

" 'Why should he do that?' I said. 'We have such good shops here.'

" 'Well,' she said, 'he knows what I want.'

" 'How can he possibly buy clothes to fit you?'"

" 'That's easy,' said Glenda. 'We wear the same size.' "

"She's my favorite," said Steve, "Glenda Jackson."

"Remember Dr. Virginia Apgar, Monty?" I said. "This fabulous woman who developed the great test for discovering mental defects at birth? I was so in awe of her. There are few people I would genuflect to, and she is one of them. I remember asking her what she was currently seeing that impressed her the most, and this studious, noble woman said, 'I was just in Denver, and there in the shopping district I saw maternity wedding dresses.'

"I said, 'What!'

" 'There are so many pregnant brides nowadays,' she said, 'they decided to get right to the point.' "

"Her hobby was wood-carving," said Monty.

"How would you describe her?" I asked.

"She had white hair," said Monty, "and she looked like a polar bear you wanted to hug."

"A benign, a very benign polar bear," I said.

By now, Steve was as rapt in our memories as we were. What a nice lunch, I thought.

"I remember the letters," said Monty. "You can get four thousand letters that are glowing and wonderful, and the letter that will stand out is the bad one. I used to open all the letters to the stars because if they were awful, there was no point in sending them. A lot of them were terrible. One letter to a great European beauty went on and on: 'Every time I see you on television, I get sick. You're disgusting, you're a slut, you're cheap. You're a rotten whore and you shouldn't be allowed on television.' Then under her name and address, she wrote a postscript: 'P.S. I wish I was you.' "

"That's a wonderful story," I said. "The privileges of beauty are enormous."

"Do you say that from personal experience?" Monty asked.

"Yes," I said. "It's a line from a French novel I once read."

"Let me tell the Arlene Dahl story," said Monty, "while we're on the subject of letters. Arlene came on *Girl Talk* and talked about a new liquid face lift soon to come on the market. You just applied it and you looked fifteen years younger. After the show, the calls and letters started coming in. Hundreds of letters—all of which I sent to Arlene. Well, not a word from her until she came on the show again. Then she asked me if I would please stop sending her that mail. She didn't know what to do with it.

"'I don't know either,' I said. 'What am I going to do with it?'

"'Why don't you send it to Rhonda Fleming?' said Arlene."

Letters are one of the best ways of gauging response to a show and *Girl Talk* got hundreds of thousands.

"Can you remember, Monty, the biggest mail response we ever got to any show?" I said.

"Yes," said Monty. "It was to Dr. Claire Weeks and her book, *Hope and Help for Your Nerves*. She's an Australian psychologist and I visited her last summer."

"You did?" I said.

"Yes."

"Did she remember you?"

"Oh, yeah. She lives in Sydney and she was a remarkable guest. When we had her on the air, people would call during commercials crying, 'Where can I reach that doctor?' Her topic was not so much about the nervous breakdown as how careful you have to be during recovery, because the setback can be worse than the breakdown. She was such a gentle, soothing woman."

"Isn't that surprising?" I said. "I always thought cosmetics were the most popular subject."

"Well, cosmetics were always popular," said Monty. "And anything to do with face lifts."

"When did you first meet Virginia, Monty?" asked Steve, my friend from North Carolina. "What were your first impressions?"

"When we first met," said Monty, "it was on a kine-scope. I was in film programming at NBC. I was screening a whole bunch of kinescopes and one of them was Virginia doing a cooking pilot. She was making a salad, or something, and of course she was talking while she worked. I trust Virginia wasn't as dazzling then as she is now, because the kinescope was in black-and-white. But Virginia was using her hands as she told you how to make the salad, and her bracelets, two bracelets, fell into the salad. She went right on mixing the salad. She saw her bracelets going in, but she never referred in any way to the bracelets."

"Just like Julia Child," said Steve.

"Yes," said Monty. "Julia Child. That's why we're having cold cuts today."

"But," I said, "they told me the salad was just as good with the bracelets."

"Virginia hated the title, *Girl Talk*," said Monty. "She cried for three days. I said, 'Virginia, don't be ridiculous. You get used to a title. *Open End,* for example. What kind of a title is that? And all those others they joked about then. 'Are you going to see the *Tonight* show tomorrow night?' 'Did you see the *Today* show yesterday?' But people get used to a title. They don't do those jokes anymore."

"Do you remember the silent screen star," I said, "who arrived with the two magnificent wig boxes? I thought, How wonderful to have that vanity, to be well-groomed and prepared for any emergency. And one was ice and the other was vodka."

"Oh yes, drinking," said Monty. "Because our shows took place late in the afternoon, women some-times brought their problems into the studio. They may have just had a fight with their lovers or husbands."

"Or both," I said. "Listen. I have to interrupt with

two stories. I heard them yesterday at Eva of New York."

"What's Eva of New York?" asked Steve.

"My favorite hairdresser, where they perform magic on me every week I'm in town. Yesterday I happened to overhear two young widows. They were under the dryer, certain their conversation couldn't be heard beyond them. But the way today's dryers are constructed, every word was audible throughout the room.

"'I'm dating two men,' said one, examining her nails, 'and it's absolutely impossible to have two love affairs going at once.'

"'Yes,' said the other, sympathetically. 'The only time you can do that is when you're married.'"

Steve thought this was the funniest story he had ever heard.

"The other one is just as good," I said. "I was talking on the telephone with a friend who's been married eight years, and she was telling me all about her new mink coat and the big trip to Europe they're going to take. She said her husband had won the sweepstakes, so I told her to put him on.

'It's true, it's true,' he said. 'I got six hundred dollars a month for life. I can't believe it. I'm absolutely thrilled.'

'That's wonderful,' I told him. 'What did you have to do?'

"'Nothing,' he said. 'My first wife just remarried.'"

"Sometimes a guest arrived a little bit high." said Monty. "One day, one very big star was downright drunk."

That was true. I was terrified.

"'How can you do this to me?' I said to Monty. And Monty said, 'Who would dare tell —— —— she couldn't go on.'"

"We got a great, great many letters," said Monty, "and I answered every single of them. I wrote: 'How could you? Do you realize that that woman was under the care of a physician? She was desperately ill and we had an ambulance standing by.'"

"Did you ever have Phyllis Diller?" said Steve. "I'm crazy about her."

"Oh yes," said Monty. "I'd booked her first for the Jack Paar show. She used to live at the Hotel Earle in Greenwich Village and eat at the delicatessen on Tenth Street. She said they had the best potato salad in the world. She had asked for the recipe but they wouldn't give it to her. At last, she discovered that the secret ingredient was sugar. She even figured out what the mysterious little black dots were. It dawned on her that they were potato peelings. She loved potato salad. She had it three times a day. She thought it was a meal in itself.

"So when she got to the studio, she told me she'd just had a party in California and made potato salad and brought some with her, would I like to try it? I sent my secretary to Phyllis' hotel, the Waldorf, to bring back potato salad. And when she returned we gave it to Totie on the air. Totie was on the same show."

That was my wonderful friend, Totie Fields.

"Totie tasted it. This great big bowl of potato salad, and Totie used a fork to make the trip from the bowl to her mouth and that was the end of the potato salad and the end of Totie Fields. She never said another word. The show ended with the camera on Totie, chewing away."

"Speaking of funny ladies," I said, "tell Steve the Hermione Gingold story."

"Which one?" said Monty. "There are so many. Hermione in a fabulous creature, in the great tradition of English comic actresses. Over there, she and Hermione Baddeley are known as 'the two Hermiones.' She's had a splendid and glamorous career going back to the early Noël Coward days. Her voice is as taut and expressive as music from a violin. No one else has a voice quite like Hermione's."

"Yes, I know," said Steve. "She's wonderful. Everything she says is funny."

"Well," said Monty, "one day she was on *Girl Talk* with Betty Friedan and Eve Merriam, who has a new hit play called *The Club*. Now remember, this was during the most impassioned days of Women's Lib, and Betty was a zealous advocate of the overdue rights of women.

"She went on and on on the subject of women's high-heeled shoes, and how in ten years the women who wore them were going to be on crutches. She looked at Hermione's feet and said, 'Those are the shoes I'm talking about, the ones you're wearing.'

" 'Let me see *your* shoes,' said Hermione to Betty.

"Betty was wearing penny loafers. She took off a shoe and gave it to Hermione to examine. Hermione took it gingerly in her hand, held it up in a supremely ladylike way, and said, 'Imagine drinking champagne out of *that!* ' "

We all laughed.

"Tell the Gloria Swanson story," I said. We were having coffee now. Everyone except Steve refused dessert, including me.

"I had booked Gloria Swanson, a great star of the silent screen, with Paula Prentiss, a new young star," said Monty. "Everybody was appalled, even Virginia. I thought it was an intelligent contrast because we were going to talk about the old Hollywood and the new. But I must have gotten a little uptight, because after a while I went up to Gloria and said, 'Everybody seems to be taken aback. They say I've done something awful to you by putting you on with a young girl. Now you can't be worried about that, I'm sure.'

" 'No,' said Gloria, 'it doesn't bother me. How old is she?'

"I told Gloria my guess.

" 'Well,' said Gloria, 'I'm seventy. If she's lucky, she'll survive. But that doesn't bother me at all, because it's raining for all of us.' "

Steve had to leave at two o'clock. He was already on his second cup of coffee.

"Tell Steve about *The Sea Gull*," I said, "before he has to go."

"That was something," said Monty. "We took *Girl Talk* abroad that year and went to Stockholm to visit the *Sea Gull* set. Except it wasn't a set. It was a real old house on a lake, and it was October and dreary and dismal and cloudy and cold. Right out of a Gothic novel. And we did a show with Vanessa Redgrave and James Mason and Simone Signoret. Simone and Virginia took one look at each other and it was instant—"

"Dislike," I said.

"To say the least," Monty continued. "Which was very nice. Because when it happens on both sides, it's usually very stimulating. If it happens on only one side, it can be a bit difficult. Of course, Simone is French. She isn't really at home in English. They got on the topic of religion, and Simone said that she believed in nothing. She is half Jewish, and she said if God could take away six million Jews, how could she believe in anything? 'I believe in nothing, I have no faith, I have no God, I'm a total nonbeliever, I am an atheist, I only believe in my fellow man, and I don't believe in anything else.' That's the gist of what she said.

"Well, of course, Virginia is very religious. And she listened to this really lovely lady with the sad, sad eyes. Then she asked Simone what she did in times of great problems and personal stress, when something bleak and overpowering happens, something tragic. 'What do you say then, Simone?'

" 'Oh, *mon dieu!*' said Simone.

" '*Mon dieu!*' repeated Virginia, and that's the way we went off the air."

"That's a marvelous story," said Steve.

Big drops of rain suddenly hit the windowpane. I went to the closet to get Steve's coat and umbrella.

"It's raining for all of us," said Steve, as I helped him put his coat on. "I love that line. Thank you so much, Virginia. What incredible lives you lead, always at fever pitch. Maybe I should change my major, I'm not used to so much drama. How do you manage to live through it all and come up smiling?"

"That's the story of our lives and the whole theme of my book," I said. "We do it. We survive, that's all. Don't worry, you'll learn . . . in time."

The Language of Mothers

It's hard to be a parent.

Because there's a terrible language barrier between the generations. The vocabulary of each one is different. By that, I don't mean the catch-phrases. I mean the difference in point of view.

Parents are never farther from their children than when they become teenagers. The onset of puberty can create an appalling chasm between them.

This leads to the "battered parent" syndrome. Sooner or later, most parents are prey to this. Each son or daughter is absolutely convinced that each mother and/or father is ruining his or her life. Overnight, the teenager becomes a complete stranger to the parent, and vice versa.

Being a grandparent is easier, partly because less is traceable directly to you. Being a grandparent means you've been through it all and survived, never mind the battle scars.

These somewhat gloomy reflections are by way of introduction to one of the most marvelous experiences that Harry and I have ever had together, in January of this year. Now I have to state categorically that each of our two grandchildren is a genius, beyond any question. Of course, you know what the definition of a genius is? The typical grandchild of typical grandparents. I'll tell you something, Virginia and Harry are no different.

Sye, our wonderful son-in-law, wanted very much to have his daughter Jan mark her passage from child- to adulthood by undergoing the Jewish ritual called the Bas Mitzvah. I was familiar with the Bar Mitzvah for boys, but not with the ceremony for girls. Basically, the meaning is the same: the end of innocence; the beginning of adult responsibility.

This had been a dream of Sye's mother, Rose, since the day that Jan was born. There were few things in the world that would mean more to her than being present at Jan's Bas Mitzvah. She was of the Orthodox Jewish persuasion, and a woman totally devoted to the temple.

On the telephone, she'd say, "Oh, I want to go, Virginia. I want it so much." We even discussed what she was going to wear. And I kidded her. I said, "Rosie Bohrer, if I have to carry you on my back, you're going." Then, late in December, she complained of pains in her chest. Eight days before the service was to take place, Rose passed away in the hospital. This would have been heartbreaking at any time. Eight days before such an occasion, it was tragic.

I had tried to teach Jan and Steve about death when they were growing up in New York. We went to Central Park in the middle of winter and looked at a tree.

"Take a good look," I said. "Pat the bark and look at the little squirrels that are nesting in the tree. Inside of what looks like a very dead, frozen tree is life, but it's waiting for its turn to come back. We'll make a mark on this tree, and in the spring, we'll come back and see how much beauty has been there all the time. If a miracle like that can happen, how can we say that when someone leaves this world they're gone forever."

And I went on to explain how the birds in spring teach their young to fly.

Death can be a very frightening thing. When I was a child, we had this terrible experience at my grandmother's funeral. The tombstone caved in and they insisted on opening the casket to see whether Grandma's body was damaged. When the lid was up, my cousin screamed, "The body moved. She's alive!" and fainted and fell in the casket. That was a scene to be remembered all through our growing-up years, Juddy and me. It would make *Jaws* look like a musical comedy.

One of the prerequisites for the Bas Mitzvah is that the girl undergo a period of several years' preparation. Jan had never had this formal religious training. But through the special dispensation of Rabbi Edgar Magnin of the Wilshire Temple in Los Angeles, she was able to complete the training in a very concentrated three months, during which she studied very hard.

I love churches and temples. God is everywhere. You can find him in a modest little frame church or in St. Peter's in Rome. He can be equally majestic in both places. But a majestic building can give you a better sense of the glory of man. Together, they are awe-inspiring.

The Wilshire Temple, which is over a hundred years old, is majestic. It has a magnificent dome and beautiful wood, which shines and glows with the patina of time and worship and the mystery of life. And there on the platform, that special January day, was our own Jan. Slim as a reed, her beautiful hair falling back, dressed in a black cap and gown. Her father and mother sat behind her.

Jan and her mother, Lynn, lighted the candles, their faces absolutely radiant in the candlelight. There's nothing more flattering in the world. There were these two lovely women—two generations of love. And Lynn was learning from Jan, the mother from the child.

Then Jan read the opening prayer in Hebrew, and translated it into English. And then she gave a little talk. She spoke of our symbol for life, the tree in winter, and I was so moved, because I thought, we're coming full circle, three generations of love and tradition now.

She repeated my own instructions: "If you are looking for God, listen quietly and you will hear God say, 'Here am I.'" It was as though Papa and Mama and Juddy were with us, too. Jan went through a whole list of problems that have no answer in life.

Jan thanked her mother and father, spoke of how

happy she was that Harry and I were there, and said, "My Grandmother Bohrer wasn't able to be here, but I'm sure if I listen very quietly, I'll hear her say, 'Here am I.'"

Well, there was a silence in the temple and it was as if an angel of God had spoken. I will never feel more fulfilled than I did at that moment. My little Jan was growing up. She was ready to fly.

Stevie has a monopoly on the biggest, most gorgeous boy-eyes in the world. He's cornered the market. "Nana," he whispered, sitting next to me, "I have such terrible cramps, such pains in my stomach."

"What's the matter, sweetheart?" I said. "Are you nervous for Jan?"

"I'm so scared for Jan," he said. And I thought, How wonderful. What a tribute to Lynn and Sye. In spite of all the screaming and yelling, he loves his sister.

If I call Stevie Little Boy Beautiful, would that be terrible?

I thought that everything to follow would be an anticlimax. But no. From the service in the temple, we proceeded to one of the assembly rooms for the cutting of the bread. The loaf of challah, a ceremonial egg bread, was four feet long. And surrounding the center of the enormous table was a display of hors d'oeuvres to do credit to King Henry VIII. Even he would have been impressed.

In the center of the table there was a huge round of every fresh California fruit you've ever tasted in your life. Strawberries the size of plums, pears, pineapples, oranges, apricots, mangoes, and a marvelous thing for which I'll take time out at this point to give you the recipe.

Peel as many bananas as you need. Sprinkle them with a little bit of lemon juice so they don't discolor. Then roll them in a sweetened whipped cream. Roll them again in shredded fresh coconut. Cut them on the round in slices two inches wide. Refrigerate until time to serve, when all your guests will exclaim, "Heaven!" It is the most divine dessert, and looks as gorgeous as it tastes.

Jan had taken off the black cap and gown and sat

at the table for young people, who had come to welcome a new member to the temple family. And we grown-ups sat at tables in the balcony.

And I want to tell you something. Sye's face when he looked at Jan was alight with radiance. When joy comes to someone who tends to withhold a display of emotion, who is not a gusher, it is a moving experience. Joy radiates from the whole body, but what you see is the face. Sye's natural reticence and austerity were not sufficient to keep his love and joy and happiness from shining through, even with his heartbreak at losing his mother. His eyes were wet with unshed tears.

Virginia Graham faded into the background. That's what I had wanted to do and I was able to do it. Virginia Graham had a walk-on part that day. She was content to be a bit player.

I don't want you to feel that I'm being humble or modest. But I have this kind of explosive personality. Just this once in my life, however, I was thoroughly restrained.

Earlier, one of the rabbis had said to Jan, "Now listen. I know you have a theatrical mother and grandmother, but don't ham it up." The same rabbi later told me a story about a young producer's son. This youngster had been rather difficult during his training period, not nearly so devout and attentive as he should have been. So at his ceremony, after his speech, he looked solemnly out at the "house" and said, "I want to thank my producer and my director and my stage hands, who made all of this possible." It was just terrible. They had to pull the kid off.

Hollywood children! Or maybe it isn't just Hollywood kids. I guess maybe you find them anywhere.

I asked the rabbi how he thought Jan behaved. "I have never seen a young woman more beautiful," he said. And Rabbi Magnin, who is eighty-six years old and has been with the Wilshire Temple for sixty-one years, said to me, "An angel stood on the pulpit today."

Well, when somebody so esteemed confirms what

you know to be true . . . We were aglow with happiness. Not much in our lives could compare with that moment.

The next day Lynn had a luncheon at the Beverly Hills Hotel for her California friends and those who had come from New York. Forty people had made the trip.

The theme of the luncheon was Jan's rainbow. Flowers were everywhere. Against the back wall in this beautiful room was a sweeping rainbow of flowers. It would have won a prize in the Rose Bowl parade. There were flowers of every color, every shade in the rainbow. And at the end of the rainbow was a bowl of yellow chrysanthemums—the pot of gold.

There was one big table for Jan and her friends with a rainbow of flowers on it, and smaller tables for grown-ups, a rainbow on each with the number of the table in the rainbow. The ceilings and walls were covered with balloons. There was a little orchestra and the bandstand, too, was decked with flowers. Everywhere you looked, there was a rainbow.

After this marvelous luncheon, there was the candlelight service. First, Jan lighted one candle. She used this as a taper to light seventeen others. Then, in her own words, she called up the people who had meant the most to her, the people who had played the most important parts as she was growing up. She lighted a candle for her other grandmother, the absent one, and said, "This is for my Grandmother Rose. I'm sure she knows how much we miss her today."

Then Virginia Graham went completely to pieces. I had already been crying, but now I was out of control. I don't know why. Rose and I were never intimate friends. In many ways we were totally different, and yet there was such a strong bond between us. We shared the language of all mothers. It is the same language, the world over. A mother in China and a mother in Spain know the very same things. Whatever their native tongues, they speak the language of mother love and *Mutterschmerz*, mother pain.

After this magnificent luncheon, everyone met that night at Lynn and Sye's home where there was a cold buffet. Many of the flowers had been brought from the hotel and tables were set up. It's an amazing thing about eating. The more you eat, the more you can eat. The stomach is most accommodating. It can stretch to a degree beyond belief. And even after all that food at lunch, we were starved.

Then we sat around on pillows on the floor. And we talked and laughed and had the kind of fun you can only have with people you've known a long time, when you can completely relax.

Lynn didn't want us to leave. She had not even been to bed the night before. She hadn't closed her eyes. And at one o'clock in the morning, she couldn't bear to see us go.

After lunch the next day at the Hillcrest Country Club, everybody kissed and said good-bye. Then Harry and I flew back to New York and home.

Before we left, I asked a question of Jan. I said, "Pussycat, were you scared?" She said, "No, Nana, no. I really wasn't." Just like her Grandmother Virginia. So now, I thought, it's Jan's time. It's her destiny that will be unfolding in the coming years, hers and Stevie's. And it's ours to try to help them in any way we can.

I've often distrusted ritual, and felt that it was empty of meaning. Not always. There are times when it reverberates with the rhythm and force of life itself. There are times when it shows us how human we are.

It's difficult being a parent. There are times when we feel that it's downright impossible. But, oh my God, how thrilling to be a grandparent! How wonderful to see the new generations coming, the glowing eyes, the shine of the fresh young faces, the intelligence in the minds, the potential in the bodies. They are our hope, our future.

We try to learn from experience, to profit from the mistakes we make. Experience is like a mountainside where the only way is up. As you climb, you can look back and see the terrible pitfalls you just barely avoided. Then you look at the youngsters following behind (you *think* they're behind; maybe they're ahead of you on a different trip) and you see a certain pitfall and you scream, "Be careful! Watch out for that!" But to a child, the voice of experience is no more than an echo, often delayed at best. It goes off into space and sometimes doesn't bounce back until many years later. So all we mountain climbers have to hope that, sure-footed as we think we are, our echoes ring true when the right time comes.

The interesting thing about climbing a mountain, and I've thought of this so many times, is all the crests and valleys, all the ups and downs. Oftentimes we don't know exactly where we are, because of the vastness of the mountain, and the fog and rain and snow and various other weather conditions. Sometimes we wonder if a precipice lies one foot ahead. But sooner or later, the weather clears up, if only temporarily, and we're able to see a certain distance ahead and behind us.

That's what I was thinking, on the airplane coming home.

Let me close this chapter as I close Act IV, the curtain speech I make at the end of each performance when I'm appearing in a play: "Thank you, God, for giving Harry and me a beautiful child. Thank you, too, for giving us a son-in-law before the gift of our two wonderful grandchildren. But above all, thank you for allowing me to live long enough to hear my grandchildren talk back to my daughter."

We salute you, mothers and fathers of the world, sons and daughters all. We are but two in a hopefully endless parade of parents, and we, too, began this journey as children.

Colored us battered but proud.

On the Technicolor Screen

Can I tell you about my movies? It won't take long. This will be an extra short chapter, because there are only three of my movies, and one of them is yet to be released.

I made my first movie appearance in *A Face in the Crowd*. Remember that one? It was written by Budd Schulberg and starred Andy Griffith.

I only had a bit part. I was at Sardi's sitting with Faye Emerson when Andy Griffith walked in. I was not supposed to have any dialogue. The waiter was going to come up and ask what we'd like to drink, and that would be the end of our parts in the scene.

But when the waiter reached our table, something happened. My mouth just sort of opened involuntarily, and I said, "Water on the rocks, please."

I just don't like nonspeaking roles. It's very difficult for me to be part of a tableau. My tongue feels left out.

So if you belched, you missed me in *A Face in the Crowd*. My payment was a dozen American Beauty roses, thorns attached.

After a seven-year rest, I bowed to popular demand and agreed to accept a role in *The Carpetbaggers*. This was a speaking part. Paramount flew me out to Hollywood, sent a limousine to meet me at the airport, and stocked my hotel room with fruit and flowers. Wardrobe and Public Relations were in constant attendance.

Then I was told the bad news. I could have my choice of two roles: a newspaper reporter, who would be onscreen for half a minute; or a madame, who would be on for three minutes.

My legions of fans would never accept me as a madame, so I knew that role was verboten. I accepted the part of the reporter.

The next day I went to the studio to report for work. My scene was shot between twelve and one. As Jonas Cord strode into the hospital to the side of his dead stepmother, I yelled out, "Mr. Cord, may I have a word with you?"

Now I had two film credits.

Following an even longer hiatus, I received a call one day from Roberta Hodes at City College in New York about a big role in a movie she was producing for Public Television called *The Secret Place*. Of course, I said yes.

The pay was "scale." That means it's the absolute union minimum. So I knew the role was for me. I've had more experience with scales than a fish.

The Secret Place is about a little boy and a Jewish temple. The temple has been abandoned. Then a group of religious youngsters decides to rebuild it with their faith and their labor.

One day, the little boy passes the temple and is invited in. His parents are of the Jewish heritage, but they have cut their ties with the temple and with Judaism. They are neither atheists nor agnostics. I play the grandmother, madly in love with my French lessons, my karate, my Yoga, and my grandson. I am what is called type-cast for the part.

My grandson falls in love with the life of the temple and the whole spirit of Judaism. His parents are very upset and think a terrible thing has happened. This is not the way of life they chose for their son.

Grandmama is called upon to redirect his energies. So I introduce him to Chinatown and the Chinese arts, and take him away to a Yoga farm for Yoga exercises.

But nothing works. The boy is constant in his new religiousness and, what is more, he converts me when I attend his Bar Mitzvah. Jon Mathews, the child who played the little boy, was so wonderfully appealing that I lost my heart to him. Each day, I couldn't wait to get to work.

Those are my three movies. Now I'm resting once

more. But who knows? One day soon, John Schlesinger, or Robert Altman, or Francis Ford Coppola, or Ingmar Bergman, or George Roy Hill, or Sidney Lumet, or Francois Truffaut or Martin Scorcese or Dino di Laurentiis may beckon. And there I'll be, in front of the movie cameras again.

It's nice to be enshrined in movie history. It's nice to know that somewhere in the world, there may always be a theater that will be showing my movies from time to time. Somewhere on earth, it may be my face up there on the silver, or Technicolor, screen.

It's destiny, only destiny, once more. That's all it is.

Irene

You've already met me as an actress. Now I want to introduce you to Virginia Graham, the Queen of Musical Comedy. Yes, musical comedy has given me yet another role and another field to conquer. Singing. Dancing. Maestro, are you ready? Strike up the overture, please!

On December 17, 1975, the telephone rang. How would I like to appear in *Irene*?

Irene? Debbie Reynolds had scored a great success on Broadway in *Irene* a few seasons before, and I thought, My God, I'm already a June Allyson look-alike, are they asking me to be a Debbie Reynolds look-alike too?

"I may be a little overage for the part," I said, hoping desperately for a contradiction.

"No," said the caller, "not the lead. You'll play the mother of Irene, the Patsy Kelly role."

Only a Patsy Kelly look-alike. "How much do I get?"

He offered a generous sum.

"I accept," I said. "What do I have to do?"

He told me. After rehearsing, I would join the cast in Miami and open there on December 29. Then, by bus and truck, we would tour forty cities in sixty days.

December 29? It was already the seventeenth, and Christmas was closing in.

"Only fifteen days before I open?" I said. "Only two weeks for rehearsal?"

"Well," he said, "not quite that much."

"How much rehearsal?" I said, my heart in my mouth.

220

"Three days," he said. Two in New York, alone with coaches, and one with the rest of the cast in Miami.

How on earth could I possibly do it? Well, I thought, another challenge. The worst I can do is fail. It isn't as though my life is on the line.

On the appointed day, I went to the rehearsal hall. In this hall, there were three people besides me: the director, the dance instructor, and a pianist.

Irene is the story of Irene O'Dare, a young Irish lass who helps her mother, Mrs. O'Dare, run a music shop in New York City in 1919. Irene tunes pianos on the side, and it is while she is tuning a piano at the swanky Marshall estate on Long Island that she meets and bewitches the young heir, Donald S. Marshall, III.

Irene is persuaded by Marshall and Ozzie, his scatterbrained cousin, to join the staff of a dress salon to be run by "Madame Lucy," who introduces himself with a song: "They Go Wild, Simply Wild Over Me." For social purposes, Irene is asked to impersonate a countess at a ball. This leads to complications, all of which are happily resolved when Irene and Marshall realize they are meant for each other, and Mrs. O'Dare meets "Madame Lucy," who turns out to be her only long-lost, true love.

The score includes "I'm Always Chasing Rainbows," "Alice Blue Gown," and "You Made Me Love You." And the cast includes a singing and dancing chorus of young men and women.

"Have you had dancing experience?" asked the dancing teacher.

"Yes," I said. This wasn't quite true. I was in a ballet once, as a child. But I was cast as a tree—the single stationary body on the stage, which I think was an indication of my problem. But I did move. I got a muscle cramp in my leg that caused me to do a little dancing.

"Is your rhythm okay?" she said.

"Oh yes," I said. "I got rhythm."

She began to instruct me in the finer points of the Irish jig. After a few minutes, she called a halt.

"Can you count?" she asked.

"Oh yes," I said, with absolute conviction. "I can certainly count . . . unless I'm under duress."

"If you can count to eight, you're fine."

"I'm fine?" Counting? This is what has made stars of Margot Fonteyn, Gwen Verdon, and Donna Mac-Kechnie? This is their secret?

It was true that at the count of eight I had to take my first step. But never until that moment had I realized that I have a problem with right and left. When I'm driving a car, I can make a left turn and a right turn, but somehow my feet never received this education. Meanwhile, I discovered muscles in my body I had never known were there.

"Isn't it wonderful how quickly she's catching on?" said the director, hopefully, trying to catch the eye of my dancing instructor.

Then it was his turn, the director's. He took all the roles but mine. He was Irene, he was Marshall, he was Madame Lucy, he was everybody but Mrs. O'Dare. He was not Mrs. O'Dare because I was Mrs. O'Dare. I knew that. I clung to that knowledge, that fact, with all the powers of rational persuasion I could summon.

Then I ran through my song, my solo, "Daughter, Sweetheart, Darling" (doesn't that sound like me?). This presented a slight problem which we were never able to resolve. I have a pleasant, if modest, contralto voice (we *think* it's a contralto), but I need the right pitch, the right key. There are certain people who will claim that I need a different pitch and key each time I sing, but I will not lower myself to answer their base accusations. I will not stoop so low. My problem is simple. Gertrude Lawrence had the same difficulty.

After these exercises in mutual frustration, I went for my costume fittings. To say that Mrs. O'Dare is not a fashion plate is to understate the case. Mrs. O'Dare clothes herself in various grades of burlap bags. That's for dress-up occasions. For everyday, she weaves her own cloth from materials at hand and moulds it to the proper shape with cornstarch. That's the way she fits her dresses to her body. This is my complete wardrobe. How can anyone believe in my character? From the neck up, I'm Virginia What's Her Name. From the neck down, I'm trying to be Mrs. O'Dare of Ninth Avenue, circa 1919. I have to be honest. I have to tell you that this was not an ideal role for me.

On to Miami and the dress rehearsal—my first encounter with the other members of the cast.

The billboards outside Dade Auditorium all said: "Virginia Graham in *Irene*." I was supposed to be the star. But when I saw the rest of the cast performing, I realized beyond any shadow of a doubt that I was only a supporting player. Meg Bussart as Irene was the star. She and the chorus. I want to tell you about the chorus.

I don't know how many of you have been privileged to see *A Chorus Line*. There are many companies in many cities, and there will continue to be for a long time to come. It's an absolutely wonderful show. After you see it, the chorus line never looks quite the same again.

The chorus in *Irene* was fantastic. They were totally dedicated dancers. Chorus members are young people who, in many cases, will never go beyond the chorus. They want to learn every new step. They have exercise classes. They want to keep agile. They're often the first people to begin rehearsing and the last to finish. I take off my hat to them.

I also made them take a certain call, the least I could do for the spirit they gave *Irene*.

And if you think I took my curtain call and did my Act IV (Act III in this case) in Mrs. O'Dare's getup, well . . . I had about thirty-five seconds between the final curtain and my curtain call to transform myself back into me, and all I can say is thank God for clothes. I couldn't have survived without them. I put on the most ravishing gown I could find. No one can do that better than I can.

We played three nights in Miami and then took to the road. Harry deserted me soon thereafter. He couldn't stand the pace. A bus-and-truck tour means that the whole show travels from city to city—the scenery, the orchestra, the costumes, the lights, the cast. There were many one-night stands, but the most we were allowed to travel in any one day was eight hours.

"Good-bye. Good luck," said Harry, and returned to New York.

So I became acquainted with the wonderful world of motels all by myself. And one thing I want to say right away. I have never walked into a hotel or motel, with one exception, where the toilet seat wasn't up. Don't they realize that women have to go to the john, too?

Don't they realize that women travel? I don't ask that the seat be down all the time, just half. At least give women a fifty-fifty chance. The only hotel I know that doesn't have the seat up always is the Beverly Hills Hotel in Los Angeles.

There was one motel that was a real humdinger. I arrived by way of a charmingly rustic cobblestone path and a sprained ankle. That was before I even registered. Afterward, I found my own way to my room, dropped my luggage, and took off my clothes to enjoy the incomparable, indescribable pleasure of a hot tub bath.

Then I discovered that my room was blessed with one of the new prefabricated bathtubs, patent pending. It resembled a small coffin set into the wall. There was not a handle on it. If you are the size of a midget —and I am not—you might be able to sit down in this tub doubled up. There was no place for the soap. There was nothing to grasp to help you get out of the tub, if you're lucky enough to finish your bath. You're supposed to get on your knees, turn on your knees, put your head forward, and somersault over the edge of the tub, hoping there will be a big mat underneath to ease your landing.

Did I forget to tell you that it was now two o'clock in the morning? Did I neglect to mention that? I looked at that tub, and I couldn't stand it. I summoned the manager.

"We are going to do a dry run with your bathtub," I said when he arrived at the door. "You are going to show me how to take a bath. You're going to get in with your clothes on and show me how to get out of that tub."

"I don't know what you're talking about," he said. His wife had been a fan of mine. Otherwise, he would probably have thrown me out.

So I led him into the "bathroom" and showed him the tub. I pointed out the faucet system, which was absolutely incomprehensible. There were no instructions for the faucet system, just a lot of knobs and buttons.

The manager got into the bathtub. It was a very tight fit. "I've got my clothes on," he said. "It will be easier—"

"*Easier?*" I said. "If you were naked and slipped, you'd break your neck. Just show me how to get out of that tub without bodily damage."

"I want to tell you something, Miss Graham," he said. "I want to thank you for calling this to my attention because it will cost eight million dollars to rip out all these tubs and put new ones in."

"You will admit they're awful?" I said.

"Yes," he said. "I'll tell you what I'm going to do. We have a special handle that goes on by suction. You should have asked for one of the special rooms."

"What?" I said.

"We have rooms with magnetic bars on the tub for the handicapped—"

"The next time I come," I said, "I'll say, please, may I have a room for the handicapped. I won't forget that."

At one motel, three couples checked out while I was signing in. I wouldn't swear that it was a hooker joint, but it was so transient that when I got to my room, the maid was still making it up.

"When can I get in?" I said.

"How many towels will you need?" she said.

"I beg your pardon," I said. "I'm not renting the room by the towel. I'm renting it by the night."

And the food! Why, in a land of such abundance, do so many of our restaurants serve terrible food? Not a fresh vegetable in sight. In one place that I will not name, I ordered a ham sandwich. A simple ham sandwich. The bread was stale, the ham was almost non-existent, and the lettuce was dirty. I didn't speak to the waiter. Instead, I wrote a letter to the owners. In return, I got a chit for the price of the sandwich. In case I'm ever passing through, right, I can use it?

We went to Georgia, Alabama, Kentucky, Mississippi, Tennessee. We played the Grand Ol' Opry in Nashville. We went to New Orleans. And there was one scene that I did pretty well—the scene where I meet Marshall's mother when I'm trying to put on airs. I'm dressed up in the most atrocious outfit, and they're teaching me how to use a trick fan.

There was no longer any pretense that I was the star. The real star, Meg Bussart, was a terrific girl. She made friends with Steve Cochran, one of the lighting technicians, and it was always a pleasure to see them together. They were so circumspect.

It turned out that I had met Meg before. In my Clairol years, I was a judge at a beauty contest in which Meg was a contestant. She didn't win, but I had gone up to her afterward to tell her I'd voted for her, and to encourage her theatrical ambitions.

I kept telling our audiences that I was just lucky if I helped bring them out to see the real talent in the show.

I had my own car. The CB radio is the most marvelous thing for the lonesome traveler. The other buffs don't know who you really are. All they know is your CB name. Mine was Den Mother.

Now I want to tell you about the power of the mind. I've noticed in the past that when I go from one climate to another, very often my ankles swell. Then, after a couple of days, they usually go down. But this didn't happen in Florida. They were swollen in Miami, and by the time we got to Sarasota, they were swollen even worse.

I arranged to see a doctor after the Sarasota show. He took my blood pressure. All my life I've had low blood pressure. It's been an enigma to doctors, because they don't know where I get my vitality from. But it was up.

"Your blood pressure is very high," said the doctor. "How long have you had high blood pressure?"

"I don't know. I haven't had a checkup. The last time it registered high, my husband was ill."

"It's not physiological," said the doctor, "it's emotional. Take a little Valium and it should go down. I'm also going to put you on a drug I want you to take every day."

It was Diocide.

"Every ten days on this tour, I want a doctor to take your blood pressure."

I proceeded with the tour. And wherever we happened to be, there was a doctor waiting to take my blood pressure. Meantime, my blood pressure went down and so did my ankles. But when we got to Arizona, my eyes were as yellow as daffodils. Also, a number of my body functions were somewhat irregular.

"I don't like it," the Arizona doctor told me. "I think you've got a little mononucleosis. And that requires rest."

"Rest?" I said. "I've got six weeks to go on this tour, and I haven't got a stand-in. How can I rest?"

"Okay," he said. "I'll give you an antibiotic. But I really think you ought to check into a hospital."

A hospital?

Sonia Uhlman, an old friend who lives in Phoenix, had heard I was coming and asked me if I would address the American Cancer Society on a Saturday.

"How can I do it, Sonia dear?" I said. "I have both a matinee and an evening performance." We were in Tempe, just outside of Phoenix.

But how could I say no to the American Cancer Society? I've never said no to them in my life. The subject of the talk was to be the psychological effects of breast cancer, which I hadn't had but which I'd worked closely with. I felt like I couldn't refuse this call for my help.

"All right," I said. "I'll do it." Somehow. And I did.

I also called Harry to arrange a doctor's appointment for me the minute I got back to New York at the end of the tour.

Now I want to show you what the mind can do. I had no choice but to work, not because "the show must go on," but because the livelihood of so many young people depended on me. I never missed a show. Gradually, my body functions returned to normal. My liver condition disappeared. The urinary infection was checked. My blood pressure was steadily down. By the time I got home, the yellow was gone from my eyes and my cardiogram was normal.

I'm compelled to believe that the mind is an enormous power. I couldn't have done what I did without those doctors. But I couldn't have done it, either, without my own corresponding will, my own determination to help my body heal by supporting it with all the resolution my mind could summon forth.

After the tour was over, I came back to New York with a whole trunkful of new memories. And just last week, when I was thinking of Meg and Steve, and a very promising young man in the company named Dick Fuchs, I got an announcement in the mail. It was from Meg and Steve. They had gotten married. We had all known that they liked each other, but Meg and Steve had behaved with such dignity, it was difficult to know how much. We couldn't really tell how serious their feelings were.

So *Irene* and Irene both had happy endings, which made me very happy. Because they are my favorite kind.

From Whence
Cometh Our Strength?

When I started to write this book a few years ago, Lynn and Sye had just decided to begin a new life for themselves and the children and put down new roots. New Yorkers both, they wanted to give Jan and Stevie the chance to grow up in natural surroundings, where they'd be able to roam the countryside with freedom and to experience the joy of learning about another part of America firsthand.

To begin with, they bought a pre-fab house in Montana. Lynn says to this day that it was the most beautiful place they ever had, and the children were crazy about it. In the summers they searched for fossils in the ground and learned about geology and archaeology from an Indian guide who became their friend. They went out to spend the Christmas holidays, planning to continue on to California, where they had decided to settle permanently.

On Christmas morning, Lynn called. "Mother," she said, "I don't want you to be frightened, but our house has burned to the ground." Late on Christmas Eve, Lynn had sat up in bed because she smelled smoke. She awakened Sye and when they went into the living room, they were met by a wall of flame. They were able to get the children out of the house, and within minutes everything was destroyed. I think one bag of clothing was saved. It was an isolated house, and by the time the nearest fire department responded, there was only a single pole rising above the ashes.

It was a fluke fire that apparently started in the chimney of the fireplace. Their dream house had vanished. Instead of going on to California, the family returned to New York. It wasn't until late June of 1974 that they moved to California, where Sye became the Peat Marwick Mitchell partner heading all their West Coast operations.

It was a terrible moment for me when they left, because I had just returned from California and *The Virginia Graham Show,* and I had been hoping to spend some time with them. Perhaps I should caution other grandparents here about the danger of becoming too close to your grandchildren, a danger I've forgotten many times in my life. It's easy to forget. Grandparents have certain rights—far more rights, I sometimes think, than they are given—but they must always remember that the youngsters belong to their parents, not to them.

So when I heard that the Bohrers were definitely going to California, you can imagine my heartache. Then, before they left, Sye had trouble with his gum, which was diagnosed as some kind of abcess, or infection. Two weeks after they moved to the Coast, Sye developed phlebitis and was confined to bed. His gum still gave him trouble, but his doctor advised him to treat first things first and get his phlebitis under control before tackling the other problem.

That September I was speaking in Las Vegas, and I decided to continue on to California afterward to see the family and the new house. One of the first things Lynn said was, "Mother, what do you think has happened? Sye went to the dentist and they're taking a biopsy of his gum."

"Well, darling," I said, "that doesn't mean a thing. Wherever there's inflammation today, I think it's almost mandatory. It's like taking your blood pressure. It's nothing."

One week later, she called me in New York. She was crying so hard I could hardly understand her.

"My God," I said. "What's happened?" Finally I was able to distinguish the words that were to haunt us for the next three years.

"Mother," she cried, "Sye has cancer of the jaw.

The biopsy showed osteogenic sarcoma of the upper jaw."

Well, I don't have to tell you the effect of this on Lynn, on Harry and me, and on Sye's family. Being associated with the American Cancer Society, I began calling everybody I knew. Soon there was a network of communication the like of which I had never seen before. If I live to be a hundred, I'll never be able to repay those dedicated doctors for their work.

Sye was operated on by a fine doctor and the prognosis was a good one. Twenty-two months passed, and just when everyone was about to breathe a sigh of relief, the cancer reoccurred. Sye never complained, he never questioned. His dedication to his clients and his work was greater than ever and he continued traveling all over the country, never missing an opportunity to serve his client to the utmost. One of his greatest attributes was the love and respect he gave to and received from all his business associates. But now Lynn felt that the children should be told. When she called to ask me what I thought, I said, "That's the most terrible thing I ever heard of. How can you do that to children? First of all, his chances for survival are good. His lifestyle is not going to change. He's going to continue to work. Why should young children be burdened with such fear?"

"I've spoken to a number of people, Mother," said Lynn, "and though what you say is true, I feel that telling them is the best thing to do, the right thing to do, and I'm going ahead."

I was heartbroken, and I'm here to tell you that I was absolutely, one hundred percent wrong. It was the wisest, most unselfish possible thing to do and I'll tell you why. Both children put a concentrated effort into making their father proud of them. Already good students, they became super students. Stevie was named president of his class three years in a row. Jan outdid herself working, undertaking projects, writing poetry. Equally important, they wanted to share in every possible moment of their father's life.

Sye and the children had always been close. He

had never been an overly demonstrative man. For the most part, his emotions were held in private and not advertised. But the bond between him and the children was vastly strengthened. Stevie was curled up in his father's arms all the time. They kissed and they hugged and they loved. And Jan, in addition to everything else, was able to make her father transcendently proud when she took on the responsibility of her Bas Mitzvah.

The end came for Sye on Saturday, October 1, 1977. I was at the Hayloft Theater in Manassas, Virginia, appearing in *Any Wednesday*, for Frank and Nina Mathews, two of the finest people I ever knew. Sye's body was flown to New York and on Monday, October 3, the funeral took place. Walter Hansen, a close friend and partner of Sye's, delivered a magnificent eulogy. And for everyone who loved Sye, the time of grieving began.

Recently, I received a letter from Muriel Humphrey in answer to a letter I had written to her when I heard of Hubert Humphrey's passing. I thought to myself that he and Sye might never have met personally but I likened Sye's behavior to the Senator's.

Grief starts early sometimes, and takes many forms. So often, we think that the burden we have to carry is too much, too heavy. Harry has taken a bad fall and is in a nursing home, where his hip is slowly mending. Now he has to undergo a very serious kidney operation. This was the year I haven't been able to talk about. Sometimes, I wake up in the small hours of the morning and think that I'm not going to be able to breathe.

But strength returns from its hiding places. Lynn is very busy now creating a memorial to Sye at Cedar Sinai Hospital, in Los Angeles, where he received his chemotherapy over the months. Instead of sending flowers, his friends contributed money to this fund. And I think to myself, there will be a wing named after Seymour Bohrer, who loved life so much, and I would compose the words on the plaque to read something like this: "A man is immortal as long as his name is respected and loved on this earth."

Father George, of St. Malachy's Church for indigent actors in New York, gave me perhaps my greatest comfort. He called upon me to participate in a service for his church. I said to him: "I'm not on very close terms with God these days, Father. I can't understand why old and sick people are still creeping through life when my young son-in-law didn't even live long enough to walk the rest of the way."

"Virginia," he said, "have you ever asked from where the strength has come which has helped you withstand the pain in your life, especially this last year? Two robberies, Sye's passing, and Harry's illness?"

"But why," I said, "do I always have to have the strength for tragedy? Why can't my strength lead me to joy and happiness?"

"Why?" he responded. "Because your strength in sorrow has given strength to everyone whose life you've touched. And perhaps that is God's greatest gift to you."

I sometimes doubt the source of the strength that keeps me going. I sometimes fear it will be unavailing. But my doubts and fears do not last. They pass, and are replaced by the certain knowledge that strength will come again—somehow, some way, from Somewhere.

What Is the Color of Love?

When I'm backstage at a play, in my mind's eye I am little Ginny Komiss at the Francis Parker School, where I played all the male leads. Standing there, feeling like a child dressed up in grown-up clothes and waiting to go onstage, I sometimes wonder: What are the colors of emotion? Could I color loneliness gray? Anger red? Happiness yellow? Sadness blue, serenity green? Pain . . . what is the color of pain? What is the color of childhood, no fair saying pink and blue? Motherhood? Fatherhood?

Think about it, and no snap judgments, please.

One of my biggest faults is making snap judgments. You probably know by now that I am not a kid. I have been around. I have had an experience or two. Yet when I saw the woman who was cast as Mrs. Colby when we took *Late Love* on the road, I made a lulu of a snap judgment. I walked in and there was this little woman, about five feet one or two. In my own voice, which has been known to cause Echo himself to run for cover, I said, "This is the mother? This is the mother-in-law? You have to be crazy. This is just a tiny little woman. Why, if I stand in front of her, we'll have to use subtitles. I'll dwarf her."

Afterward, she went to the director and said, "I wouldn't displease Miss Graham for the world, so please release me from this commitment."

And he said, "No, Miss Royton. I want you to do a reading."

God has been with me often, but never was he better to me than when he sent this dream of a woman, Velma Royton, into my life. She had been trained in the British theater, and when she came out on stage, she was elegant. She could wear hemp and make it look like silk. This five-foot-two woman became majestic. No one could look more regal than Velma. She had worked with the Lunts, who were probably the most disciplined stage actors this country has produced.

She and her husband had a drama school and she was a collector of wounded animals. Life is full of wounded animals. There are days when I think that just about everyone I know is a wounded animal of some kind. Many people shut their eyes to them.

But not Velma. There was a young girl with no family studying acting at the school, and Velma took her in. I have to tell you that the husband ran away with this girl and left Velma. Whatever bitterness she had, whatever scars she carried, she kept them all inside. She was a genuinely brave woman. When she asked you how you felt, she actually wanted to know. Most people you should never ask, because they tell you and that's the end of your day.

Velma had never known the love of a mother, never in her whole life. And if you look into the background of so many actors, I think you will find they're seeking the love that, at some time of life, they didn't get. Applause from an audience is to actors like sitting in a mother's lap and being fondled and kissed.

Who are we anyway, besides the characters we play? We go from one role to another, forever being someone else. And even with my limited experience, I find that everything one says, both myself and other people, turns out to be a line from a play. "All the world's a stage . . ." Shakespeare, I tell you, knew what he was talking about. How does an actor, especially, say, a Method actor, decide where the character stops and the person begins? That's what makes actors so fascinating. How much is real? How much is make-believe?

I never saw a woman with so many friends as Velma. They were all these great ladies of the theater, with the large Milan straw hats and parasols on the hot summer days in New York to keep out the sun. And they all had these wonderfully unmade-up faces with luminous eyes that seemed to hold the mysteries of the ages in their depths, acquired through their talent and beauty and manners. Oh my God, is there anything more gorgeous than good manners?

These women would call each other every night and every morning, checking to see if everyone was okay. If no one answered the phone, *zip*, they were over there to find out what was wrong. You sleep better when you know a loved one is tucked in bed safely.

I found in Velma the relationship I never had with Mama. She had been raised by governesses as a child and had never known a mother's kiss. Maybe that bound us together.

I dearly loved to drive, and we used to drive from theater to theater, Velma and I. Then, for some reason, Velma began traveling by bus. So I went to one of her friends and said, "Have we hurt Velma in any way? She's refusing to ride with me and I feel terrible."

"No," said her friend, "it isn't that. Velma's had a slight touch of pneumonia, and she was afraid she'd make you sick. She said anybody could replace her, but nobody could replace you." Velma was the perfect human being if I ever met one—always thinking of the other person.

Velma got an apartment on Park Avenue, a maid's room. A maid's room! She decorated it. People with talent can do anything. Velma could reupholster and she could paint. You walked into this tiny maid's room and it was heaven, the most beautiful blue and white heaven. And over her couch was a painting by Sargent. My home is filled with Velma's flowers, her tiny paintings. My home is filled with bouquets from Velma. When she passed away, I knew that the sadness of losing her would be with me forever.

I love color. I love good grooming both in a house and on a person. When I see some people with the nerve to walk around with no face on, I think they're the most conceited people in the whole world. How dare they think they look well without help? How dare they feel they're better than the rest of us?

Mustard complexions and sagging eyes, puffy bags, and no support from the chest down! It's the look of late pregnancy. I think you have to be well-groomed. I think it's important for your own morale to be well-groomed. I think your hair should be washed and brushed. You don't have to use artificial eyelashes. Whenever they write up my artificial eyelashes, they outdo themselves. "Palm fronds" was the latest. Someone wrote: "Miss Graham's black eyelashes are like palm fronds." Well, I went to look at some palm fronds and they're from three to eight feet long. Your average palm frond is not the size of a rose petal.

I do that because I love it. I'm play-acting. I'm a little girl wearing grown-up makeup and clothes. I don't care. I like it, and I like how I look. I enjoy playing with color. Also, I think we do a lot of hiding behind makeup. A friend of mine went to a psychiatrist. Her makeup makes mine look like the foundation layer. She was absolutely Fu Manchu. The psychiatrist said, "Madam, you will have to take that face off. I haven't the vaguest idea who I'm talking to." It was true. The same thing happened when I met her on the street. I kept walking, because I had no idea who I was looking at, either. No, actually I did. And actually, she did need the makeup. I love her, but she did need the makeup.

Shyness, and the feeling of inadequacy we all have within us, can be concealed and sometimes even conquered by making ourselves attractive. I know that when I wake up in the morning and look at myself I say, "Who invited you? What's your name?" And then I look closer and say, "Oh my God, is that you here again?" And then I might not feel so good.

But I put on my makeup and comb my hair and, you know what, by the time I get dressed to go out I feel terrific. I try not to let people see me on the street and say, "Oh, you've gained a little weight, I see. You ate too much! Are you feeling okay, Ginny?" Some women have such a lovely way of going straight to your Achilles heel.

I'm not doing it for them, though, or anyone else but me. I'm doing it for me.

There is no age limit on love. I was in St. Petersburg, Florida, recently, which is the living tribute to, and apprenticeship for, a visit to old St. Peter personally, because it is what is known as a Senior Citizens Community—a beautiful city with beautiful people. I was standing there talking to these two lovely people who looked like a Hallmark golden wedding anniversary card come to life, and guess what! They're shacking up. They're not even married. Who can afford to give up Social Security, when bedlock replaces wedlock?

Another couple told me they were married thirteen years, but they'd been going together for thirty-two. "You had parents, didn't you," I said, "whom you were supporting?" And the woman said yes. They had to wait nineteen years to make it legal.

How do you divide love? When my grandchildren were born, I was afraid that if I loved Stevie inordinately, Jan would suffer, much as I loved her. Now that may seem absolutely ridiculous in a person as full of love as I am. I used to think that only girls were special, that having a daughter was the most marvelous thing that could happen to a mother, and all my dreams were re-realized when Jan was born. I must admit that over the years I've learned that sons are the most marvelous things that can happen to a mother and father as well. I know how my son-in-law's mother felt about him, and rightly so. He was one of the finest men I've ever known. For he gave to his wife and children everything a son can give to his parents: the love and security he must have known in his growing-up years. He was never too busy to show his family how much he loved them. And Stevie taught me about little boys. They are sensitive, they are adorable, they are sweet, they are always in need of love. He is so special, and I thank God for both of my grandchildren.

It is a great misconception to consider a man weak if he cries. He may be weak. He may be strong. But crying is not what decides the one or the other. I never felt closer to my father than when I saw him respond to music one day by weeping. Music can bring back memories like nothing else in the world, and he had been reminded of his father.

Some of us like to think, at least some of the time, that boys are little men, and that men are little boys wearing their fathers' clothes at all stages of life, no matter how much they grow up. And thank God they are, because why else would they need a mother-wife combination?

I'm very suspicious of people who repress themselves, deny themselves. I'm not talking about discipline now. I'm talking about basic natures. People become very mean when they are dieting. I don't like to be around them. Nobody I have ever known behaved nicer while on a diet. Dieters are irritable and they are angry. And they always look at you with contempt.

I have a friend who only ate rolls from my plate. He would never take a roll at a dinner party when the bread was passed, and when I was ready to eat my roll, I'd look down and it was gone. Now there's a whole group that feels that if they eat it from your plate it's not as fattening. My mother used to push mashed potatoes off to the rim of the plate and then work them in with the peas. Then there are the apple pie eaters who say, "I just want the fruit." But unfortunately the crust has dissolved into the apples, irrevocably, attached itself, as it were.

Can I tell you something? I survive on faith. That's what keeps me going.

Here's one definition of who I am. One night at dinner, a new friend asked an old friend, "What's Virginia really like?" The same age-old question. But here is what my old friend replied: "If you put Judy Garland (for showbiz spunk), Vivian Vance (for breezy), Shirley Booth (for smarts), Tallulah Bankhead (for nerve), Gracie Allen (for dizzy, and one crazy non sequitur after another that end up making sense), Florence Nightingale (for bandages), Angela Lansbury (for class), and every other woman in the world (for plain female beautiful) together, you'd have the basic outline of Virginia Graham. You've heard of Everyman? Virginia is Everywoman."

That's a swell definition to have a person toss off just sitting around the dinner table. I admire all those women more than I can say. So I held up my water glass and gave my old friend a toast: "Here's looking atcha," I said.

And I'll tell you something uncanny. My new friend said, "Virginia, as I look at your face, I can see you at all ages at the same time. I can see a baby Virginia, a teenage Virginia, a newly married Virginia, a middle-aged Virginia . . ."

"Stop right there," I said, "Don't go any further. I can take it so far. You mean my face has a certain ageless quality?"

"Yes," he said. "I can see you at ninety-five right this minute. It's already in your face, the whole span of life. I believe it's some kind of magical projection you have, quite unconscious on your part. I mean, that's not what you're trying to do. It happens in spite of yourself. I see it on the face of only one other person, though oddly enough, he is an actor, too."

The thing is, my friend may be right. I think part of it is energy. But also—and this news is bound to fascinate, indeed galvanize, every gynecologist in the world—I am getting younger every day! Honest. So, you see, the cells of my body are traveling in both directions at once, from youth to—to maturity, and from maturity to youth. That way, there's no telling what interesing things may happen to my face at any given time, with the traffic of the years going opposite ways.

And there is also no telling what interesting things may happen in my life. There are a thousand new things I want to do, a hundred new emotions I want to feel. My memories are made of yesterdays, but my dreams are built in tomorrow. I want the Artist of My Destiny to help me fill my days with every subtle shading of the rainbow. Paint me, I pray, the way I really want to be. Draw me in constant motion, picture me in love with life, and color me alive.

We Deliver!
And So Do These Bestsellers.

Bantam Book Catalog

Here's your up-to-the-minute listing of over 1,400 titles by your favorite authors.

This illustrated, large format catalog gives a description of each title. For your convenience, it is divided into categories in fiction and non-fiction—gothics, science fiction, westerns, mysteries, cookbooks, mysticism and occult, biographies, history, family living, health, psychology, art.

So don't delay—take advantage of this special opportunity to increase your reading pleasure.

Just send us your name and address and 50¢ (to help defray postage and handling costs).

BANTAM BOOKS, INC.
Dept. FC, 414 East Golf Road, Des Plaines, Ill. 60016

Mr./Mrs./Miss_____
　　　　　　　　　(please print)

Address_____

City_____State_____Zip_____

Do you know someone who enjoys books? Just give us their names and addresses and we'll send them a catalog too!

Mr./Mrs./Miss_____

Address_____

City_____State_____Zip_____

Mr./Mrs./Miss_____

Address_____

City_____State_____Zip_____

FC—9/78